OUT OF THE SHADOWS

To Pastor Jack —
Thank you for your very warm &
Christian welcome to those of us in the
WCG who found the road back to the
Christian Church.

In Christ,
Tom

Out *of the* Shadows

Finding *God's* Truth in a World of Deception

J. Thomas Lapacka

CPH.
SAINT LOUIS

This work about my struggles to find the true God and peace with Him is dedicated to my wife, Linda. She has been my faithful companion and friend through these many years of searching and struggling. Never once has she wavered in her love and support for me. In those dark nights when I wrestled with life-changing theological questions, she always encouraged me to press on and not to rest until the truth was found. May our Lord richly bless her.

Quotations in chapters 3 and 8 from *The Subtle Power of Spiritual Abuse* by David Johnson and Jeff Vanvonderen, © 1991 and published by Bethany House, are used with permission.

Scripture quotations taken from the HOLY BIBLE, NEW INTERNATIONAL VERSION®. NIV®. Copyright © 1973, 1978, 1984 by International Bible Society. Used by permission of Zondervan Publishing House. All rights reserved.

Copyright © 2001 J. Thomas Lapacka
Published by Concordia Publishing House
3558 S. Jefferson Avenue, St. Louis, MO 63118-3968

Manufactured in the United States of America

Library of Congress Cataloging-in-Publication Data

Lapacka, J. Thomas, 1949–
    Out of the shadows : finding God's truth in a world of deception / J. Thomas Lapacka.
    p. cm.
    ISBN 0-570-05246-7
    1. Lapacka, J. Thomas, 1949–   . 2. Christian biography. I. Title.
BR1725.L24 A3 2001
248.2'4'092—dc21   2001002903

1 2 3 4 5 6 7 8 9 10   10 09 08 07 06 05 04 03 02 01

Contents

Acknowledgments

Few, if any, works are done in a vacuum, much less alone. So it is with this book. First, I must thank my dear friend Rev. George Mather, who encouraged me to write my story, telling me that many others would benefit from reading it. George became my pastor, praying for Linda and me, helping me to wrestle through theological issues, and always pointing us to Christ as our true rest. Rev. Larry Nichols has become a friend. He tirelessly edited my manuscript, ensuring clarity of thought. Larry and I have had many helpful exchanges on the phone that have contributed to my greater understanding of the Gospel. Finally, I want to thank Pastor General Joseph Tkach Jr., who graciously reviewed chapters 7 through 9, which pertain particularly to his father and himself. His comments were most helpful in giving a more balanced view of the events we both experienced.

Foreword

*O*ut of the Shadows is a true story about a man, his family, and their spiritual pilgrimage from active involvement in a cult to conversion to orthodox Christianity. Tom Lapacka was a well-known and respected member of the Worldwide Church of God (WCG), which was founded by Herbert W. Armstrong. As a young man, Tom became an avid follower of Armstrong and rose in rank in the organization to top executive positions at the church's international headquarters in Pasadena, California. Then things changed, slowly but surely. Tom is now an ordained minister in The Lutheran Church—Missouri Synod. In this narrative, Tom tells of his exodus from Pasadena, the struggles that brought it about, and his arrival in the Promised Land of grace.

After researching and writing about cults for more than 22 years, rarely, if ever, have I heard an account such as the one you are about to read. It demonstrates with clarity the faithfulness of God. Like all cults, legalism was the dominant motif of the WCG. Tom's story is a somber testimony of the effects of the Law, which bound his conscience and shackled his soul, finally driving him not toward God, but away. Nearly 500 years ago, a German monk named Martin Luther sat in the small confines of his quarters in an Augustinian monastery. Luther, too, had been driven by guilt to seek a holy life and to please God. But the more diligently he searched, the more alienation Luther felt. The more he tried to keep the Law, the more he failed. The more responsibility he knew he had before God, the more his inability to live responsibly became apparent. Driven almost to despair, Luther discovered the gracious words of the Gospel as St. Paul wrote: "For in the Gospel a righteousness from God is revealed, a righteousness that is by faith from first to last, just as it is written: 'The righteous will live by faith'" (Romans 1:17). This rallying cry of the Protestant Reformation would stretch itself through the centuries and touch millions of lives. One of those touched by the Gospel is Tom Lapacka. Once Tom started to read Scripture with unveiled eyes, he began to experience the wondrous and healing powers of grace. Tom discovered the heart of God as found in the life, death, and resurrection of Jesus Christ. Tom has discovered that Jesus is not his taskmaster, but his Savior. This narrative relates how this all came about in Tom's life. It is a story from God's heart to his and now from his heart to yours.

The Worldwide Church of God itself has undergone a vast transformation from cult to Christianity. After Armstrong's death in 1986, Joseph Tkach Sr., Armstrong's handpicked successor, almost immediately began to "deArmstrongize" the WCG. The past 15 years have wrought an incredible amount of change in the WCG. With Larry Nichols, I co-authored the book *Discovering the Plain Truth* (Intervarsity Press, 1998) in which we tell the story of the new Worldwide Church of God from the perspective of outside researchers. Tom, on the other hand, will relate the many changes in the WCG from his unique perspective as a top leader within the organization—a perspective we can never share. The names of Joseph Tkach Sr., as well as the new Pastor General, Joseph Tkach Jr., appear in *Out of the Shadows.*

As Lutheran ministers, Larry and I have been pleased to help Tom. He taught us much about the WCG. At the same time, we are honored to have been in a position to assist him on his faith journey. Today, Tom is director of communications for The Lutheran Church—Missouri Synod (LCMS). Before accepting this call, Tom was pastor of an LCMS congregation not far from where he had been caught in the deceptions of a cult that lived in the shadows and knew not God's grace in the person of the crucified and resurrected Christ. Now Tom cannot get enough of God's grace and wants to share it with you as he tells of his emergence from the darkness into the light.

—Rev. George Mather

Introduction

My Own Journey

Truth is incontrovertible. Panic may resent it; ignorance may deride it; malice may distort it; but there it is.—Sir Winston Churchill (Information)

I have a story to tell. It has been a struggle to decide whether to dig into this painful past, a past filled not only with my struggles and anguish, but also those of a whole host of other people whom I know well. This deep sense of hurt, betrayal, and disillusionment is not easily laid aside, as I wish it could be. My inner turmoil is not the result of a blinding moment of agony; rather, it is the result of a gradual and insidious buildup of many moments and agonies over the years. People experience physical pain when they are injured or deep emotional hurt when they lose a loved one. But this is a different kind of inner turmoil: a spiritual pain that has gnawed at my soul, driving me into moments of deep and almost comfortless anguish.

Fast approaching 50 years old, I awoke one morning to the realization that the previous 30 years of my life had been a tragic mistake. Imagine a 30-year dream almost instantly transformed into a nightmare. The last three decades of my life had been earnestly spent believing that I was a blessed participant in a spiritual revolution of epic proportions known as the Worldwide

Church of God (WCG). In what seemed to be the twinkling of an eye, this illusion was swept aside. Far from traveling in the light of truth—and much to my horror—I realized that I had been walking in spiritual darkness, immersed in shadows and illusions. It is part of my struggle and pain to relate how I have emerged from the shadows and into the light. As the light of a sun-filled and cloudless day dissipates the shadows of darkness and night, I will relate my story of how the glorious light of truth has displaced the shadows of 30 years. I feel a kinship with Dimitri Volkogonov, a three-star general and former head of the Soviet Army's Political Administration, who became director of the Institute of Military History in 1985. Volkogonov, once a devout Marxist, wrote in *Autopsy for an Empire:*

> For many years I was an orthodox Marxist, and it was only late in my life, after long and tortuous inner struggle, that I was able to free myself of the chimera of Bolshevik ideology. I felt enormous relief, and at the same time a sense of deep regret that I had wasted so many years in Utopian captivity.[1]

The utopia that Herbert W. Armstrong promised, and for which I had labored and sacrificed, crumbled just as did the Soviet Union. I feel the same deep regret for wasting 30 years of my life and that of my family chasing a hoax built on heresy and buoyed up by the sacrifices of hundreds of thousands of people like myself.

This is not a documentary or a dispassionate history; rather, it is a personal narrative of my experiences as a member, minister, and executive in the Worldwide Church of God. Many other WCG members—past and present—will identify with this account. Indeed, many have walked in the same shadows for the past decades. And, sadly, many continue to live under the shadows cast by Herbert Armstrong and his utopian dream.

Readers should note at the outset that the purpose of this book is not to tear down, but to edify. In the early 1990s, God performed a truly miraculous work in the Worldwide Church of God. Through the work of the Holy Spirit, what was once a cult has been transformed, and many WCG members are now evangelical

Christians. Dr. Ruth Tucker, visiting professor at Trinity Evangelical Divinity School and author of 12 books, wrote in the July 15, 1996, issue of *Christianity Today* that the historic changes in the WCG represented the first time such an "unorthodox fringe group" had made the move to Christianity.

Many who still count themselves members of the Worldwide Church of God or who find themselves ensnared in any one of the numerous offshoots of the Armstrong movement do not yet understand what those who have moved out of the shadows have grasped about our past misconceptions. We were called a "cult" for decades, but we denied it, of course. We were taught that the word *cult* was used to describe us by mainline Christian churches and denominations. Because they regarded us as a cult, we regarded them as wrought with paganism and false teachings inspired by the devil. Any opposition from other church bodies was considered "persecution," similar in our minds to what the Christians of the early church faced. We believed that we were God's true little flock.

I received a great shock when my predecessor, an executive of the Worldwide Church of God, told me in the early 1990s that we were, in fact, a cult. He said we were making progress in shedding our cultish practices. His words shocked me beyond measure, and I felt as though the wind had been knocked out of my sails.

As I continued to investigate on my own, his words proved true. In the books I read, I saw more clearly that some major characteristics that constitute a cult were very much part of our organization.[2] So many people are easily influenced and led into cults, yet defining a cult is no easy task. Various disciplines define the term differently, taking at least three main approaches. The theological approach, used mostly within Christianity, defines a cult as a group that teaches doctrines that are not orthodox. The psychological approach seeks to offer insights into the basis for a cult, that is, its psychological characteristics, such as mind control and manipulative techniques. The sociological approach, like the psychological, tries to define a cult based on a study of people and cultures.[3] In reviewing my years in the WCG, I will present not only the theological or doctrinal model, but also certain cultic sociological and psychological characteristics that were present in the Worldwide Church of God.

The following are some primary characteristics of cults.

1. *The deity of Jesus Christ is diminished or denied.* The WCG taught, for example, that there were two separate and distinct deities within the Godhead (we used the term "God family"). Jesus was ranked lower in the family than the Father. Further, we believed that Jesus could have sinned while in the flesh, which in effect denies His deity. We called this the "great gamble," teaching that the Father put everything on the line when He sent Jesus to earth as a man. If Jesus had sinned, He would immediately have been disqualified as Savior and Lord. Orthodox Christianity always has taught the union of the human and divine natures in Jesus Christ. Thus, Christ's deity would make it impossible for Him to sin. Many cults fail to understand or grasp that Jesus' human nature is not to be separated from His divine, as though Christ were some sort of a split personality. Jesus was and is fully divine as well as fully human; however, He is without the taint of original sin. Thus, we have a Savior who could not only represent us as man, but also stand before the Father as God.

2. *The doctrine of the Trinity is diminished or denied.* In cultic circles, the denial of Christ's deity goes hand in hand with the denial of the Trinity. In the WCG, we believed, taught, and published that God was a family comprised of two separate Gods and that the Holy Spirit was simply the "power of God," who was present to carry out God's will but not a full and distinct Person within a Triune Godhead. This mirrors an ancient heresy that dates to the fourth century and is attributed to Macedonis, who defined the Holy Spirit as a divine energy diffused throughout the universe. Modern Jehovah's Witnesses also teach that the Holy Spirit is God's "active force," not a Person of the Triune Godhead. So many heresies find their seedbed in the misunderstanding that God is one essence, yet three Persons (Father, Son, and Holy Spirit), distinct but not separate. This truly is a divine mystery; however, just because human minds cannot comprehend God does not give license to invent a god that we can understand. Any person who will deny the Trinity—as did Armstrong's Worldwide Church of God and as do many of today's splinter

14

groups from the WCG—is sadly outside the true Christian faith.

3. *God is humanized, and man is deified.* Although a certain aspect of this is true (the incarnation is God becoming human, and salvation is, in a sense, drawing believers to Christ-likeness), cults teach that God has somehow completely emptied Himself of divinity and has invested humanity with the marks of deity. In the WCG, we believed that it was within man's potential to become God as "God is God." This is a clear failure to separate creation from the Creator, which St. Paul says is the ultimate sin of false religion (Romans 1:18f).

4. *Cults claim divine revelation apart from the Bible as a source of authority.* On this point, Herbert W. Armstrong taught that God had given him 18 "revealed" truths to restore within the "one true church" on earth, which, of course, was the WCG. These truths included God's desire for a hierarchical form of church government; God had restored the true Gospel through Mr. Armstrong after more than 18 centuries of error; God is a family, not a Trinity; the Christian is now only "begotten" but will only be born again in the future time of the resurrection; and the modern identity of the 10 lost tribes of Israel. Since Mr. Armstrong's death, most of these "revealed" truths have been found wanting in the light of credible biblical scholarship. Amazingly, the utter poverty of the scholarship that supported his heretical teachings has not phased those still left among Mr. Armstrong's followers. Because he claimed to have been taught personally by Christ—"the living Word of God"—Mr. Armstrong's followers trembled at the thought of questioning even his most audacious claims.

5. *There is only one true church on earth, and we are it.* Every cult teaches this, and the WCG was no exception. This extreme sectarianism denies the orthodox teaching that the church is the universal body of Christ. The one exclusive community of faith known as the WCG was the sole recipient of God's grace on earth. We believed that all those who did not conform to our teachings were false churches. This infatuation with being "the only ones" or "the only true church" engendered a "we vs. they" attitude among WCG members. The WCG became a kind of bastion of "truth" that must be protected at all costs from the onslaughts of the heathen and "pagan Christianity."

6. *Salvation is achieved through a combination of grace and works.* This was a dominant theme in the WCG. Although we would often hear that one is saved by grace, this was often followed by a reminder to keep the Law so we could "make it" (attain salvation in the kingdom of God). Therefore, we never had the assurance of salvation in and through Christ Jesus alone. When we spoke of God's kingdom, we often would say, "I hope I make it." To ensure that we would "make it," we kept a long laundry list of Old Testament laws that had been selected rather capriciously. Our Herculean efforts at law-keeping only unsettled us all the more because we could never be certain that our obedience was good enough to be acceptable to God. So, we would strive all the more "to qualify" ourselves to be granted eternal life with God. When any degree of salvation is based on human merit, Christ's finished work on the cross is replaced by the need for additional human works. Therefore, sinners who have broken God's Law can never be certain of anything, but they continue to experience guilt, thinking there is always more required to appease God's wrath. All cults, as well as non-Christian world religions, teach this.

I hasten to add, however, that the current leadership of the WCG has rejected all these non-biblical positions and has come to embrace fully the Christian teaching that salvation is by grace through faith in Christ alone. These vast changes and shifts away from Armstrong's errors have not come without a severe price. In the wake of these transformations, turmoil has resulted in the WCG from losses in both membership and financial contributions.

Aside from the obvious doctrinal errors, certain sociological and psychological characteristics are also prevalent in cults and were evident in the WCG as well.

1. *The leader of the cult wields total power and absolute authority.* This has certainly been the case in the history of the WCG. Herbert W. Armstrong set up articles and bylaws that gave him absolute unchangeable authority. These articles and bylaws are still official, which has been a cause for concern among current WCG leadership. Greg Albrecht, spokesperson for the WCG, wrote:

> The WCG continues to address the substantial number
> of doctrinal and organizational issues that a transfor-

mation of this magnitude involves. Doctrine was our first priority, we believe both of necessity and divinely inspired . . . Following the sale of our headquarters campus [in Pasadena, California] and relocation, the WCG will then be able to address a number of other issues that need resolution, including structure and governance.

I look forward to this hope becoming reality for the membership of the WCG.

2. *Cult leaders are self-appointed, persuasive persons who claim to have a special mission in life or to have special knowledge.* I remember that Mr. Armstrong was often referred to and often referred to himself as "God's apostle." He compared his apostleship to that of the apostle Paul. Just as Paul had claimed that he was taught by no man but by Jesus Christ (Galatians 1:11–12), Armstrong audaciously made similar claims. As Paul had opposed Peter (Galatians 2), Armstrong had even dared to oppose Paul on at least one occasion. He faulted the latter for not collecting tithes from some of his Greek converts. (See 1 Corinthians 9:1–12.) Mr. Armstrong's special mission was often referred to as the "Work" (another oft-used term among the cults). By this Armstrong meant the "Work" of bringing God's end-time message of warning to the modern descendants of the 10 lost tribes of Israel. Part of the "Work" included building three college campuses, each of which would be called Ambassador College. Other parts of the "Work" included spending millions to boost the circulation of the church's magazine, *The Plain Truth,* and to purchase radio and television airtime. Millions more were spent to fund the Ambassador Foundation and its 20-year tradition of world-class concerts in the exquisite and lavish Ambassador Auditorium. Enormous sums of money were spent to whisk Armstrong around the world in his Gulfstream II jet to visit various heads of state. In the final analysis, his trips accomplished little besides providing photos for *The Plain Truth.*

I must reflect on the enormous sums of money that gushed into WCG coffers over the decades and the cost to the members who faithfully gave and gave and gave. The "Work" was all-important, much like the ideology of the now-defunct Soviet Union. The individual member became lost in the "Work," being used and spent and, sadly, often cast aside when he or she faltered

OUT OF THE SHADOWS

in allegiance or dedication. Now, years later, the "Work" is finished, lying in the ruins of history, a subject of research, debate, and memory. Having consumed millions of dollars and drained scores of thousands spiritually, it has been relegated to the infamy it so richly deserves.

Yet there are other groups—yes, even some Christian congregations—that are obsessed with their "work," clothing it carefully in biblical language while claiming to serve God. And God's people are used up and spiritually abused to feed the ego of some self-exalted "spiritual" leader. I have learned that people, not programs, are paramount. If people have to suffer to ensure a program's success, regardless of how it is "baptized," it is a tragic miscarriage of the pastoral commission Christ gave Peter: "Feed My sheep" (John 21:15–19).

3. *Cult leaders are often charismatic, determined, and controlling.* Again, Armstrong was no exception. He was a man with a mission, and nothing was going to prevent him from accomplishing it. His voice was authoritative and his manner extremely persuasive. Everyone thought that what Herbert W. Armstrong said was law. If he gave personal advice, the recipient thought he should follow it because he had received it from "God's very own apostle." To disagree with Armstrong or to veer away from his way of doing things was the same as disobeying God. Tragic consequences resulted from his pontifications. Families were split apart, jobs were lost, and careers were ended when he spoke his authority into peoples' lives. In the same *Christianity Today* article quoted previously, Dr. Tucker comments that Herbert W. Armstrong "was larger than life." He was able to attract millions through his radio programs and their combination of wisdom and prophecy— and more than 200,000 people joined the WCG.

4. *Cults tend to venerate their leader, and the leader allows it.* To Armstrong's credit, he did seem to try to prevent people from making too much of him. On one hand, he would claim that he had done nothing himself, only Christ through him. On the other hand, he often would thunder that God had raised him up for this special end-time mission. For the average WCG member, Herbert W. Armstrong was a VIP in God's eyes, thus he deserved service and support. And service and support were most "cheerfully" rendered by virtually everyone.

When delivering a sermon, we ministers in the WCG often would quote Mr. Armstrong along with the Bible, as though quoting Mr. Armstrong gave extra weight and authority to what we said.

5. *Cults harbor double standards.* One blatant example in the WCG was the elevated position enjoyed by the members of the clergy and the leadership. Those in the upper echelons of the WCG could afford the best material possessions and creature comforts (houses, clothes, cars, and food) while the laity lived with much less. Mr. Armstrong and his Pasadena-based executives lived in luxurious homes, but the ordinary folk struggled to pay monthly apartment rents and to make ends meet. Armstrong flew in a Gulfstream jet, dined on the finest china, and had his every need addressed by attentive staffers. At the same time, he encouraged financial sacrifice on the part of the membership so the "Work" would get done.

6. *A cult member's time is monopolized by church activities, daily routine, or ritual.* We had weekly spokesmen clubs for the men, weekly Bible studies, weekly two-hour church services, annual holy days that sometimes lasted eight days, regular church activities, and more. If you were a local leader, more work often was needed to help the minister, for example, accompanying him on visits or assisting with counseling. Added to this was the recommended minimum of 30 minutes of daily prayer, 30 minutes of daily Bible study, and fasting at least once a month. We were busy people. This left us little time to pursue higher education (which was frowned on) or personal hobbies. Those who gave themselves wholeheartedly to the church were indeed busy.

7. *Cults claim exclusivity.* We were taught that God directed His attention exclusively at His one true church—the Worldwide Church of God. Every other so-called Christian group was deceived. Sooner or later (later being either in the millennial reign of Christ or in a second resurrection to physical life) unconverted people would have to come to the same doctrinal understanding that we had so they could be saved. Mr. Armstrong believed that the history of the true church was taught in Revelation 2 and 3, where he saw the seven churches as seven "eras." He taught that the Worldwide Church of God was the prophesied "Philadelphia era." At the conclusion of the work of this era, the infidels would finally fall on their

knees to worship at the feet of those of us who would be born as gods into the God family. (See Revelation 3:7–13.)

Such exclusivity can be found in extreme forms of denominationalism, in which members of a denomination believe and claim that their denomination is the "one and only" true church. Where such beliefs are held, it is not a far leap to feel disdain and distrust for others, even in the Christian church. Even now as a Lutheran pastor I find the ugly head of sectarianism showing itself in the Christian community. I encourage all who claim Christ as their Lord and Savior to love those who claim the name of Christ, rejoice in the clarity of doctrine you may have, and engage in open discussion of differences with other Christians, but let us not disgrace our Lord by denigrating fellow believers in other Christian denominations.

8. *Cults discourage social contact with "unconverted" friends and relatives.* Conversion to the WCG meant association only with its members, lest we be "polluted" by the world. The sad result was that in many cases, including my own, we estranged ourselves from family and friends. Outsiders thought we were "religious fanatics." Such name calling did not bother us because we had one another, and we thought they were the ones who were deceived. We also believed that being laughed at and "persecuted" was further proof that we had the truth. After all, didn't Jesus say His followers would be persecuted for righteousness sake?

The Worldwide Church of God was a classic cult. Granted, it never achieved the notoriety of the Jonestown cult, nor did the federal authorities storm our buildings as was the tragic case of the Branch Davidians in Waco, Texas. Perhaps that is precisely what makes it so hard for many current and former WCG members to say, "I was in a cult." After all, we were not planning mass suicides, engaged in weird practices, nor operating as antigovernment gun-toting anarchists. Our leader was not a Jim Jones or a David Koresh. We were simple people who were zealous for God and His Word. We listened to a man who seemed to have it all together. We believed, but he deceived us, though I do not think he did so deliberately. Herbert W. Armstrong was simply misguided himself, influenced by his time and culture and swept along by what appears to have been a latent desire to be "successful." Armstrong's efforts flourished at a time when God's grace was being turned into license in the United States. It was a time when people seemed to care little for God's Law or for proper obedience to it. In his own understanding, Armstrong's ministry sought to address the concept of "cheap grace." Time showed, however, that he overreacted and emphasized works at the expense of grace. In so doing, Armstrong lost that grace altogether, leaving legalism in its place. Legalism is the deadly poison that always has haunted the church and is the one certain hallmark of all the world's cults and false religions.

I hope that by telling this story and pointing out some painful truths, I will praise our Lord for what He has done in my life and in the lives of thousands of those who, like me, were walking in the shadows. This story is an affirmation of God's mighty work through the Holy Spirit. It is a testimony to those men and women in the Worldwide Church of God who trust the saving grace of Jesus.

I hope this story is helpful to Worldwide Church of God members who are in need of assurance that what has taken place in the WCG is truly the Lord's work. I also hope that my story might prompt discussion among those in pseudo-Christian organizations who are still walking in the shadows and do not know it. Perhaps these words will enable members to stop and reflect on what they believe, who or what they are following, and whether it is the orthodox faith delivered to the church by our Lord, taught by the apostles, and preserved in the church for nearly 2,000 years. Finally, I trust that those who have been blessed with an orthodox Christian upbringing will have not only a deeper appreciation for God's truth, but will be reminded to remain vigilant so they will not be led astray by some "new wind of doctrine" championed by a charismatic leader who offers visions of great works that obscure the crucified Christ.

ENDNOTES

1 *Autopsy for an Empire: The Seven Leaders Who Built the Soviet Regime* by Dmitri Volkogonov, translated and edited by Harold Shukman.

OUT OF THE SHADOWS

2 Information on the characteristics of cults is available in several good reference works, including Ruth Tucker, *Another Gospel* (Grand Rapids: Zondervan, 1989); David Johnson and Jeff Vanvonderen, *The Subtle Power of Spiritual Abuse* (Minneapolis: Bethany House Publishers, 1977); Ronald Rhodes, *The Culting of America* (Eugene: Harvest House Publishers, 1994); and George Mather & Larry Nichols, *Dictionary of Cults, Sects, Religions, and the Occult* (Grand Rapids: Zondervan, 1993).

3 In his book *Unmasking the Cults* (Grand Rapids: Zondervan, 1995), Alan Gomes presents a serious and well-reasoned case for why the psychological and sociological approaches present serious deficiencies and why the theological approach to defining a cult is to be preferred.

Chapter 1

Stepping into the Shadows

Heresies perish not with their authors, but, like the river Arethusa, though they lose their currents in one place, they rise up again in another.—Clement of Alexandria (*Stromateis I*)

Some of my earliest recollections revolve around life in the church. My parents, however, were not particularly religious people. Dad, who grew up in a Polish ghetto in Springfield, Massachusetts, was a Roman Catholic by birth and remained so throughout his life. I never remember seeing him go to Mass, though, and the only way he was involved with the church was to give offerings fairly regularly. Whenever the census taker came around, however, he would invariably check the box indicating Catholic as his religion.

In contrast, my mom was a Southern Baptist. She had been raised on a tobacco farm in the North Carolina tidewater region. I recall that she went to church a couple times on Easter or Christmas, and Dad even went along once. Usually, Mom stayed away from church. But she did watch Oral Roberts on television in the early days of black-and-white TV evangelism. She would tune in to the tent meetings where Roberts would preach his fiery sermons and conduct his healing revivals.

I do not know why my parents felt as they did about the church. Dad always spoke positively about it and always insisted that I should go. He believed it would be a good influence. He never condemned any religious denomination or fellowship; he just did not participate in the life of the church. Mom was not as gracious toward the church as Dad. She regularly castigated many people as church-going "hypocrites." At the same time, however, she insisted with Dad that my sister and I attend regularly during our childhood years.

Sadly, my parents were like many professing Christians. They remained strangers to the church where Christ offers forgiveness, spiritual nurture, and assurance of salvation. But is the church merely a place where people gather, sing a few hymns, hear a sermon, drop a dollar in the plate, then head home with little or no benefit? Such a perspective demonstrates a woeful lack of understanding of how the church is portrayed in the Bible. In Scripture, church is spoken of as the "bride of Christ," "the mother of us all," the "congregation of the saints," the "anchor of faith." It is in the church that we meet Christ our Savior. It is in the church that we receive faith through the reading and preaching of God's Word. It is in the church that God washes away our sins and gives us to new life through Baptism. It is in the church that Christ strengthens our faith by giving us His very body and blood in the holy sacrament of Communion. God is present among His people. He has promised never to leave nor forsake us. If we believe the Scripture with its promises, wild horses could not keep us from attending church regularly. Consider the attitude of King David, who doubtless was a busy man, but he always made time for regular worship. He believed in the presence of God in His temple when he wrote: "I rejoiced with those who said to me, 'Let us go to the house of the LORD'" (Psalm 122:1).

We also should consider the impact our non-participation in regular worship has on our children. A recent study has disclosed that when both parents attend church regularly, 72 percent of their children remain faithful. When only the father attends, 55 percent remain faithful. If only the mother attends, 15 percent remain in the church. If neither parent attends regularly, only 6 percent remain faithful. The statistics speak for themselves—the example of parents and adults is more important than all the efforts of the church and Sunday school.[1] The question is quite simple. Do we want our children to remain in the faith as adults? If so, worshiping with them as a regular part of their weekly childhood experiences is essential.

As a child, the nearest church to me was a Southern Baptist church. It was about two-and-a-half blocks from my house in the small lower middle-class community of Oak Hill, which is just outside Richmond, Virginia. The stately Venerable Street Baptist Church was a colonial brick building adorned in white trim that sat on a gentle knoll. It took me several years to ask why the church was named "Venerable Street" when it was located first on Cedar Street, then on Hartman Street. I was told that the church used to be in the city but "the neighborhood changed," which is a euphemism that meant African Americans had settled in the city and the whites had moved to the suburbs. This shift in Richmond took place in the 1950s, and the members brought their church name with them. At the time of my childhood, segregation was the norm, and each race had its own churches, schools, and neighborhoods. I mention segregation because it would come to play a large role in shaping my beliefs about British Israelism and the superiority of the Anglo-Saxon race, which the Worldwide Church of God had embraced fully and which it taught until 1993 when this concept was rejected by WCG leadership.

My life as a youngster in the 1950s was good. We lived in a stable neighborhood. The men went to work, and the women stayed home with the children. Everyone seemed to have a nice house with a big yard, a car, and all the essentials, including a black-and-white television. Everyone knew everyone else in the immediate neighborhood. Neighbors would stand in the early evening at the back fence, talking and sometimes disagreeing.

All the children knew one another and played together. We roamed the neighborhood and surrounding forests with no fear of harm. Crime did not seem to threaten us in the same way it threatens young people today. Life was good, perfunctory, and predictable: going to school, coming home to play, doing chores, and going to church on Sunday. Church attendance was part of most of our lives, and many of my neighborhood friends were as regular in attendance as I was. Several of us went to Venerable Street Baptist Church because it was the closest church.

For me, going to church was not an ordeal. As a child I seldom went to the 11 A.M. worship service, nor did most of my peers. We went to the 10 A.M. Sunday school. Venerable Street Baptist conducted a strong ministry for its youth. The Sunday school was full every week. The church sent buses through the neighborhood to transport children to the church. The facility was new and modern, and they had a good staff. The focus was always on Christ—His birth, life, death, and resurrection.

As opposed to the church of my childhood, orthodox Christianity was not the focus of the teaching of the Worldwide Church of God. Instead, we spent most of our time on issues that had little to do with Jesus' atoning work of salvation. Under Armstrong's leadership, we were preoccupied with things such as the identity of nations, end-time prophecy, the millennial reign of Christ, Sabbath and holy days, clean and unclean meats, and "qualifying" for the kingdom of God by observing the "dos and don'ts" of the Law, which the church taught was essential for salvation. These "shadows" obscured the cross and the atoning work of Christ. It was as though a veil had been placed over my eyes, preventing me from seeing the glorious and liberating light of the Gospel. This legalism would lead me away from the Jesus I learned about at Venerable Street Baptist and into a world of religious hyperbole, judgmentalism, legalism, and, finally, personal despair. Paul speaks of a veil that is cast over the face of unbelieving Jews because of their focus on the Old Testament Law and their refusal to acknowledge Jesus as their Messiah and Lord:

> Therefore, since we have such a hope, we are very bold. We are not like Moses, who would put a veil over his face to keep the Israelites from gazing at it while the radiance was fading away. But their minds were made dull, for to this day the same veil remains when the old covenant is read. It has not been removed, because only in Christ is it

taken away. Even to this day when Moses is read, a veil covers their hearts. But whenever anyone turns to the Lord, the veil is taken away. (2 Corinthians 3:12–16)

It has been only in the last few years that I stepped out of the shadows and turned to Christ as the way, the truth, and the life, trusting in Him alone for salvation.

I remember our pastor at Venerable Street Baptist, Pastor Shaddock, as a kind and gentle man who faithfully preached God's Word every week. He always had a pleasant smile and a warm handshake, even for us young people, which made a lasting impression on me. I felt that he was truly a man of God, and I gladly listened to his sermons. As I grew older, I began to attend worship right after Sunday school class.

It has been a long time since I attended Venerable Street Baptist Church. Memories have faded, and many of those I do recall seem trivial today. However, several themes emerged from my childhood church experiences that I believe were essential to my journey from Calvary to Sinai, from grace to Law, from the light of the Gospel to the shadows of a misguided understanding of the Old Covenant.

One experience was developing a love for the church. I thank my parents for insisting, despite their own unfortunate lack of participation, that I attend worship. Church was a wonderful place to be. I felt God's presence and enjoyed a sense of awe, especially when I went into the sanctuary. At church, I learned many fundamental Christian truths. It was like meeting God on a weekly basis, and each week I would hear the call to repentance and the exhortation to trust in the Lord for salvation. Each week I was assured that Jesus was my friend, that He loved me, and that He had died for me so I could live forever with Him in heaven. It is of vital importance that parents take their children to church so they may hear this Gospel message. We dare not underestimate the power of God's Word to work faith and assurance in the hearts of all who hear—even our children. As Paul wrote: "Faith comes from hearing the message, and the message is heard through the word of Christ" (Romans 10:17).

The pastor's invitation to come forward followed the worship service. For me it was always a moving event to see someone go forward, confessing before all that he or she was a sinner who earnestly desired forgiveness and wished to trust in Jesus Christ's sacrifice for sin. I remember the special Sundays when new converts were baptized. They came out in their white baptismal robes with a wonderful look of peace and joy on their faces. Then, before the entire congregation, they stepped into the baptistery with the pastor and were immersed in the "waters of Jordan." I, too, looked forward to the day when I could make that public confession of faith and have my sins washed away. But that moment would come later rather than sooner. It would occur not in the baptistery of Venerable Street Baptist Church in front of the congregation, but alone in a galvanized water tank outside an old redwood building on the grounds of the WCG's Ambassador College in East Texas.

Christmas at Venerable Street Baptist was a favorite time. We were reminded of God's love for us and that He sent His Son, born as a baby, to live among us. As a child I could identify with the baby Jesus because knowing that He also had been a child meant He knew what it was like to be "a little guy." The Christmas story reminded me, too, of God's love for children, that they are close to His heart and receive His divine care.

In my teen years, I began to receive literature from the Radio Church of God, which was later renamed the Worldwide Church of God. I was shocked to learn through this literature that the celebration of Christmas Day was "pagan." Christ was not born on December 25 (which most Christians know), and Christmas was supposedly a continuation of the Roman feast of Saturnalia, which featured many evils that continued in the Christian church to the present. According to Jeremiah 10, my beloved Christmas tree with its inviting, warm multicolored lights was a pagan symbol. Herbert W. Armstrong claimed the Christmas tree was instituted by Nimrod's mother, Semiramus. She supposedly had married her son, and had, after his death, used the evergreen tree as a symbol of his rebirth. This was the first insidious intrusion into my simple faith. I found myself drawn to Armstrong's interpretation of Jeremiah 10 regarding Christmas and its pagan tree. The whole concept of Christmas started to become an abomination in my eyes.

The call from Mr. Armstrong was to be faithful to the Word of God regardless of the consequences in one's personal life. As a young child, I had learned in Sunday school and church that God had to be first in one's life, so what Mr. Armstrong said made sense to me. In retrospect, I now know that his fundamental premise was incorrect. Something once used or celebrated by pagans is not necessarily bad. Christmas, as celebrated by the Christian church, is not pagan. Instead, it is a time of rejoicing over God's great gift to humanity. But I was young and impressionable, and no one I talked to at church could refute my newfound knowledge about Christmas. When I brought up the pagan origins of Christmas, quoted Jeremiah 10 about the heathen cutting trees from the forest and decorating them, and denounced the commercialism of the Christmas season, I drew fairly weak responses. The best response anyone could muster was, "Well, it doesn't mean that anymore," or "You are just getting too fanatical." The "church team" was batting .000 in my eyes. Their answers convinced me that they did not know anything or did not seem to care about the "truth." For me, the number one priority was to obey God. If that meant personal difficulty, so be it. I was like the Jews that Paul talked about in Romans who had a zeal for God, but not according to knowledge (Romans 10:2).

How was I going to present all my newfound knowledge to my parents? (Tact was not one of my strong points, and this lack of diplomacy would cause me no end of grief until years later when I studied public speaking at Ambassador College.) At age 15, with a lump in my throat, I announced to my parents that I refused to participate in any further Christmas celebrations. This frontal assault went over like a lead balloon. What followed were some pretty heated discussions that consisted mostly of my parents doing the discussing (lecturing) to me. Their arguments, however, were the same ones I had heard at church, which failed to dissuade me from my conviction. My parents' scriptural knowledge was limited, and their arguments boiled down to a command: "Observe Christmas or else!"

This argument did not sit well in my 15-year-old mind. I remained more or less steadfast in my convictions. I thought at the time that I was completely "alone in the faith" in Richmond. (I later discovered that the Worldwide Church of God had a congregation of more than 200 members in the city.) I was not sure exactly what was permitted or banned on Christmas, so at first I did not have a "no compromise" attitude toward the holiday. Years later as a student at Ambassador College, however, I learned to be strict in total separation and avoidance of the Christmas season. Told it would not be right to accept Christmas cards or gifts, I was polite and thankful but firm in my refusal to participate. So with the zeal of a man with a cause, I resolved to refuse any gifts or cards during the Christmas season. "Christmas is pagan," I bluntly remarked. To participate in the festivities would be an affront to God . . . and that was that! What had been a wonderful time of family, friends, and worship became a battlefield littered with hurt feelings and deep misunderstandings.

This major decision was the first step in the process of alienation from those I loved most in my life. The hurt continues to some extent to this day. The wounds in my family have been healed, but some scars remain sensitive.

Easter was another wonderful time of year for me as a young boy. In Virginia, the dogwoods, tulips, and daffodils were in bloom; the grass was green from the spring rains and smelled so sweet when it was freshly cut. The warm spring sun shone brightly on the field behind Venerable Street Baptist Church, inviting us to break out the baseball bats and gloves for another season.

In the church, our attention turned to our crucified Savior. As a young boy and teenager, my understanding of the atoning sacrifice of Christ was limited, but the basic message got through. It was because of sin—my sin—that Jesus had to die. In His death was forgiveness of sin, and in His resurrection was new life for the repentant sinner. Venerable Street Baptist decorated the sanctuary with fresh lilies, everyone bought a new set of spring clothes to wear to church on Easter, and the kids went wild over Easter eggs and chocolate bunnies (which do not have much to do with the "reason for the season").

But I learned from the Worldwide Church of God that Easter, like Christmas, was a pagan celebration! In fact, Herbert Armstrong had written a convincing pamphlet titled *The Resurrection Was Not on Sunday!* Armstrong wrote that Jesus said He would be three days and three nights in the grave and then be resurrected to life. It was a simple matter, Armstrong wrote, to count from late afternoon on Friday to early Sunday morning and discover that this period of time is considerably less than 72 hours. Further, Mr. Armstrong claimed that Jesus wasn't even crucified on a cross, as commonly depicted in most churches, but on a stake. The cross, he maintained, was a pagan symbol of Tammuz, the son of the pagan Nimrod of Genesis 10. Even the first letter of Tammuz's name is a *T,* which is an *ankh* cross. These facts, coupled with some references to the use of the *ankh* cross as a common symbol among the Egyptians and Assyrians, made it an open-and-shut case for me. Then there were the hot cross buns that Mr. Armstrong found in Jeremiah 7:18, which mentions baking cakes to the queen of heaven, who was supposed to be Ishtar (where the word *Easter* was to have come). Was I shocked! Here again I was convinced that the Baptist church was deceiving me about Easter, just as it was about Christmas.

But the message of Easter had not been compromised at Venerable Street Baptist, despite the fact that Armstrong was writing and preaching on the radio that all the churches had it wrong and he alone was right. Of course, Armstrong put things in such a way that made it logical to conclude that only he had the truth. He would say, "Knock the dust off your Bibles and see for yourself. Don't believe me; believe your Bible." And sure enough, with his proof-text hermeneutic, those of us who were not grounded in orthodox Christianity were swept off our feet by his powerful and persuasive arguments. By my early teenage years, I was coming to the conviction that almost everything the churches taught was in error. The truth had been lost. Only in these last days had truth been revealed to Herbert Armstrong, a belief that is not far removed from the claims of the Mormons, another non-Christian cult.

Pastor Shaddock and the Sunday school staff at Venerable Street Baptist Church did strongly proclaim that Christ died on the cross for our sins. So when I was perhaps 12 years old, I stood among the pews one Sunday after church, talking to a man in his late 20s or early 30s. He had his Bible in hand and turned from one passage to another as he explained how I was a sinner and in need of Christ's forgiveness. This was the part of the Easter message that I remember most. "The wages of sin is death," he quoted, "but if you call on the name of the Lord, you will be saved." I wanted to do God's will more than anything else, but I was not sure what His will was.

It wasn't long after that conversation that our pastor gave his routine post-sermon invitation, and I was moved to go forward. Pastor Shaddock asked if I had repented of my sins and had accepted Jesus as my Savior. I said that I had. Then he turned to the members of the congregation and asked if they would accept me into fellowship. With one voice they said, "We do." The excitement and joy of that occasion is hard to put into words. It meant I was publicly taking a stand for Jesus. Easter reminded me of the Lord's willingness to publicly endure shame on my behalf. Now I had the privilege of professing before all my faith and belief in Jesus as my personal Savior.

After church I rushed home to share the good news with my mother. But to my utter dismay, she was not happy. "You're too young," she said. I reasoned, then argued, but nothing would move Mom from her position. The pastor dropped by a few days later, and she told him that I was too young to be baptized. Of course, his hands were tied, so my baptism was delayed six long years. Instead of the beautiful ceremony at Venerable Street Baptist, I was baptized under East Texas skies in a galvanized horse trough.

I think this disappointment was one of those fork-in-the-road experiences. Because I was not baptized at Venerable, and thereby lost the opportunity to become a member, I was not further anchored in that fellowship. It also further alienated me from my mother. I felt her position was unreasonable because she never made an effort to examine my faith to determine if there were grounds for my baptism. That, of course, was my understanding as a child. Now I understand that Scripture shows Baptism as a gift of God, something He does for us and to us, not something we do for Him. It is not a matter of working up the faith or becoming good enough to be baptized; rather, it is receiving the gift of faith given through the Word of God and the water. In Baptism, God truly washes away sin and gives us new birth through the Holy Spirit. The call to be baptized goes to all people, even children. Peter preached on Pentecost: "Repent and be baptized, every one of you, in the name of Jesus Christ for the forgiveness of your sins. And you will receive the gift of the Holy Spirit. The promise is for you and your children and for all who are far off—for all whom the Lord our God will call" (Acts 2:38). The Baptism of children, even infants, has been the teaching and practice of orthodox Christianity for nearly 2,000 years.

At Ambassador College, I learned that Mr. Armstrong taught that baptism was a decision the mature individual must make. This reflected the position of those who adhere to "decision theology," which is essentially the belief that a person can come to God by his or her own willpower, however weak, and "wrestle with God" until He grants repentance. But this position ignores Scripture, which states that "no one can come to Me unless the Father who sent Me draws him" (John 6:44). This passage shatters the idea that we are free to come to God when we choose. Further, it overlooks St. Paul's declaration that the carnal person is spiritually dead (Ephesians 2:2; Romans 8:7) and unable to come to Christ on his or her own.

Armstrong strongly recommended that baptism not be performed until one was mature enough to make this momentous decision. He taught that, as a rule of thumb, 18 years old was the youngest one should be to receive baptism. Only on rare occasions would baptism take place for those younger than 18 years old. Such baptisms were allowed only with special permission. Over the years, I turned away young people from baptism, counseling them to wait until they were 18 years old. I said that at that age they would make a more informed decision and could be more confident the baptism would be "genuine." By "genuine," I meant that upon repentance and the laying on of hands, they would receive the Holy Spirit. Undoubtedly, I succeeded in doing to them what my mother had done to me—pour cold water on their passion for Christ. I regret the legalistic approach I had adopted, and now as an ordained minister in The Lutheran Church—Missouri Synod, I readily and gladly baptize infants, following Christ's command to "let the little children come to Me . . . for the kingdom of God belongs to such as these" (Mark 10:14). Today the Worldwide Church of God no longer takes a hard and fast stance on the proper age for baptism. It is left to the minister—in concert with a child's parents—to determine when baptism is appropriate. The current practice of the WCG is not to baptize infants, though they would not declare such baptism invalid.

Another important aspect of my early Christian experience was learning about sanctification, or holy living. Of course, I did not have the slightest clue what *sanctification* was, but I did know that God expected me to live a good life. And a "good" life was defined by the cultural and religious tradition of the Southern Baptist church. What the Southern Baptist Convention teaches now, I am not certain, but in the American South of the 1950s and early 1960s, what comprised the "good" life was fairly clear: no smoking, no drinking, no cards, and no dancing; obey your parents; stay morally clean; love and serve your country; and go to church. Not all of these prohibitions and commands are necessarily bad; in fact, most of them are good. However, a problem arises when behavioral codes written by humans and enforced by religious institutions are considered to be the will of God. By placing ourselves under these legalistic codes of conduct, we deny ourselves the full freedom of the Gospel, which God intends us to have. We also set up standards to which neither we nor others are able to conform. Consequently, we judge ourselves harshly and perhaps judge others more harshly based on our success or failure to live up to these codes and standards.

The Protestant reformers of the 16th century rallied to the cries of "faith alone" (*sola fide*) and "grace alone" (*sola gratia*). Just as the Pharisees in Jesus' day had surrounded themselves with a host of man-made laws, rules, traditions, and human regulations that no one, including themselves, could observe, modern legalism continues to render grace null and void. Yet Paul clearly wrote: "For it is by grace you have been saved, through faith—and this not from yourselves, it is the gift of God" (Ephesians 2:8). Despite this clear reference to grace in the Christian life, many devout Christians receive Christ in the Spirit, then resort to laboring under the rigors of various systems of Law and good works in the hope that somehow this will help qualify them for heaven. This was the case in the Worldwide Church of God.

Several years ago, I was among a few top leaders of the Worldwide Church of God who accepted an invitation to visit with Dr. D. James Kennedy in Ft. Lauderdale, Florida. He was anxious and excited to hear with his own ears the story of our transformation. Toward the end of our visit, he asked if he might pose some questions. We agreed. Dr. Kennedy asked his famous question, "If you stood at heaven's gate and God asked you why He should let you in, what would you say?"

We responded, "Because of Your Son." Kennedy was visibly excited by the answer and explained that the reply demonstrated to him that we understood that salvation was by grace through faith alone, as St. Paul had written. He added that many people would have answered, "Well, God would have to let me in because I've been good and done many good things in life." Such an answer shows a "works" mentality, which we in the WCG had rigorously subscribed to for years. It saddens me that some of my former parishioners and colleagues still labor under the Law and believe that good works are *required* for salvation. The Bible clearly teaches that good works are important in the Christian life, but they cannot save us. Such reliance on works renders Christ's finished work on the cross inoperative. Good works flow out of faith and are a fruit of the Holy Spirit in a believer's life, but they are not the cause of salvation.

This penchant for "works righteousness" that I had absorbed at Venerable Street Baptist Church provided the perfect seedbed for life in the Worldwide Church of God. That we are "saved by grace" had been preached from WCG pulpits, but in reality we had a system of works that would have made the Pharisees proud to call us brethren. By the late 1960s, the WCG taught strict adherence to tithing. Although a tithe is giving 10 percent, WCG members had been called to render a triple tithe in some years. We scrupulously avoided unclean meats, circumcised our male babies on the eighth day (both of my sons underwent this ritual), cast out all leaven products during the Passover, gave of the first-fruits of the field and the firstlings of the herd, observed the weekly and annual Sabbaths, and, for those members who had farms or gardens, let the ground lie idle in the seventh year (the land Sabbath).

During a trip to Israel in 1985, I visited a Jerusalem *kibbutz*. I told an Israeli author and his archeologist friend how we observed our religion. I spoke of the exact degree to which we practiced the weekly and annual Sabbaths, how we fasted on the Day of Atonement, removed leaven before the Days of Unleavened Bread, and observed an intricate tithing system, among other things. They marveled, saying that we were more Jewish than they! One of them even exclaimed that we were the remnant of the first-century Christian church. Rather than alarm me, this statement only confirmed the absolute correctness of my chosen path. In fact, part of the WCG's past public statement about how the church should be categorized was to say that it was "Judeo-Christian." But no little warning light went on in my mind. By that time I had not only bought the farm lock, stock, and barrel, I was selling parcels to anyone who would listen.

In analyzing what prepared me for the message of Herbert W. Armstrong, I found those in leadership positions in my Baptist church unable to respond to my objections to Baptist doctrinal teaching. In retrospect, however, the questions were not all that difficult to address. What about Christmas and Easter? Is it wrong to eat pork and other unclean meats? Was Christ really in the grave three days and three nights? How much different would my life have been if I had encountered someone with enough scriptural understanding to help me see the error that was sucking me under.

As a teenager, the issue of clean and unclean meats became a major doctrinal issue for me. The biblical statements in Leviticus 11 and Deuteronomy 14 were crystal clear. For a Southerner, these passages meant no pork chops, no ham, no fatback, no Spam, no Vienna sausages, no hot dogs (I don't recall beef or turkey dogs being available at the local grocery in the early 1960s), no shrimp. That removed a fairly large slice of my daily meat intake. Again, I boldly faced Mom in the kitchen one afternoon after school as she was frying pork chops and told her pig was out of my diet. The sparks flew, and some rather "salty" language was used in assailing my proclamation of "truth." But I was unbending—at least until Dad got home and invoked the ever-so-effective "Eat what's on your plate or else." I knew that "or else" meant a leather belt across my posterior, so I caved in and choked down a chop. We had continual skirmishes over the issue of pork, so Mom finally sent me to the church to have the pastor straighten me out.

Pastor Shaddock was a stereotypical grandfather: warm, fuzzy, cheerful, and always glad to see you. I was warmly welcomed into his office and asked what was on my mind. The pork issue came up, and I pointed out to him the scriptural injunction against eating this dreadful meat. I believed the case to be shut and sealed. How could he possibly explain away such a clear prohibition in Scripture? I thought I had Pastor Shaddock backed into a corner, but he presented an argument that was totally unexpected. He explained with his warm and winning smile that because of the invention of modern refrigeration it was okay to eat pork. *Wow!* I thought. *That has to be the dumbest thing I have heard yet.*

After discussing the issue a little more and reaching a stalemate, I pressed on to another urgent issue. This issue appeared continually in the pages of *The Plain Truth*—the return of Christ. I certainly thought Herbert Armstrong was correct when he predicted Christ's imminent return "in 15 to 20 short years."

Looking at Pastor Shaddock, I asked the question that, in my mind, would make him either a "true believer" or a "false Christian." Having failed the pork test, he didn't stand much of a chance on the bigger question I was lobbing his way.

"So when do you think Christ is going to return?" I asked.

"Well, Tommy, it could be several hundred years," Pastor Shaddock replied. "No one really knows."

This, in fact, was a good answer because Christ Himself said no one knows the time of His return except the Father in heaven. But Pastor Shaddock's answer did it for me! Now I knew that he, too, was on the wrong path and could no longer lead me. I thanked him for his time and left absolutely convinced that my spiritual insight was infinitely greater than that of this poor pastor and that Herbert W. Armstrong was truly God's man. Why didn't my pastor know the truth about pork, Christmas, Easter, and the time of Christ's return? The Bible spoke plainly about all these issues.

My theological arguments had come from the pages of *The Plain Truth*. Whenever I presented my (actually, Armstrong's) case on issues such as Christmas, Easter, and pork only to find superficial and shallow responses, my confidence in the Baptist church was further eroded. I developed a spiritual "big head." The church was deceived and had deceived me, but Armstrong was bringing the "plain truth." I was one of the elect few privileged to share in it. My youthful experiences with adult Christians now remind me of Peter's words:

> Always be prepared to give an answer to everyone who asks you to give the reason for the hope that you have. (1 Peter 3:15)

I recently discussed this point with Pastor George Mather. He commented that many Christians are ill-prepared to defend their faith. Our understanding of the faith is so superficial that, when challenged, we fail to give the reasonable answer that Peter exhorts believers to be prepared to give. This only weakens the appeal of historic orthodox Christianity in the eyes of a spiritual babe who is facing the often-enticing appeals of a cult. Mr. Armstrong had answers that were quick, definite, authoritative, and black and white. Naturally, he had his own scriptural "exegesis" to support his points of view. Unless a spiritual babe meets a Christian who is solidly grounded in the faith and able, with patience and love, to argue convincingly for the truth, the cult often will win the battle for the heart and mind of the one not yet rooted in biblical truth.

That is what happened in my case. Neither my parents, Sunday school teachers, pastor, nor school teachers could give reasonable answers to my questions. They either would say that they did not know—without offering to find out and get back to me or to put me in contact with someone who did know—or the answers were so shallow and unsatisfactory that even I, a young teenager, could see them for what they were. Sometimes the response I received was exasperation accompanied by comments such as, "What makes *you* think you know the answer? Is everyone wrong except *you*?" But to those who are being taken in by a cult, that is *exactly* what they think! Everyone else *is* wrong!

Armstrong would proclaim on the radio and write in all caps in *The Plain Truth* that Christianity was deceived. God had shown him the truth. For 1,900 years, the truth had been hidden, and now, in the last times, God had raised him up to trumpet the truth throughout the world. Armstrong was God's end-time apostle, the Ezekiel messenger. He was to prepare the way for the return of the Lord. Bold, audacious claims, but when the Christians you know cannot refute someone like Armstrong with anything other than half-baked answers or ridicule, it only makes such claims more believable. Derision and *ad hominem* attacks to disprove another's point of view only underscore one's inability to argue scripturally and logically.

Another contributing factor to my susceptibility to this cult was my home life, which at times was stormy. Dad was always at work. He was a master at commercial air-conditioning and refrigeration, a trade he had learned while in the Merchant Marines. Because compressors in supermarket freezers and coolers can and do break at all hours, Dad was frequently awakened in the wee hours of the morning by a panicked grocer who needed him to fix a problem. Somehow Dad would manage to stir himself, dress, and be gone long before daylight. Rain or shine, sleet or hail, hot or cold, my dad would go. Consequently, my sister and I did not see a lot of him, but he often would wake us for school and prepare breakfast so we would have the opportunity to visit over oatmeal and toast. Although he was gone a lot, my dad did sacrifice for our family, and I appreciate it to this day. My dad did not have the benefit of much instruction on family, child training, nurturing, etc. What he did know was from his experience as a boy. He came from a broken home and was determined to stop the cycle of misery in his generation. Although he and Mom had their trying moments, they remained faithful to their vows and provided a family for my sister and me. It's important to demonstrate faithfulness to one's wedding vows and to work at a marriage, especially when the going gets tough. My parents did that, and I thank and respect them for it.

Mom was a stereotypical 1950s woman who stayed home with the kids. Only years later did I realize this was not entirely her first choice. She had struggled with her own personal problems for some time, which caused hurt and pain for all of us. Frequently, stormy, hurtful words were heard in our home. Despite these personal battles, Mom and Dad always made sure we had three square meals a day, clean beds, and nicely pressed clothes.

The turmoil at home resulted in underlying feelings of insecurity and worthlessness, which led me to overcompensate in areas such as sports, academics, and religion. I was a regular baseball fanatic. I always strove for straight As and often achieved it. I also loved foreign languages and studied Spanish and German extensively. I also dabbled in Russian, Polish, Greek, Italian, and Hebrew. My love of languages served me well in my later experiences with the Worldwide Church of God and Ambassador College.

Religion became my secret garden. Through the teaching of the Radio Church of God and Herbert Armstrong, I found my special place in this wicked world. I began to see myself as a member of the elect few who were privileged to have been found worthy to understand "the truth." Of course, my "truth" was not the great plan of salvation fulfilled in the life, death, and resurrection of Christ. Rather, my "truth" taught, among other things, that the United States was the descendant of Manasseh—one of the 10 lost tribes of Israel; that God was going to use Nazis who had gone underground in Germany and Argentina to attack and punish the United States for its sin, especially the sin of Sabbath-breaking; and that Sunday worship was the mark of the beast. Knowing these esoteric "truths" made me feel special, loved, worthy, and spiritually superior. My susceptibility to these errors demonstrates the absolute necessity that young Christians be taught the historic Christian faith as encapsulated in the great ecumenical creeds. Otherwise new believers are easily susceptible to being "tossed to and fro" by every nutty idea espoused by some self-appointed prophet.

For me, becoming part of the Radio Church of God and a follower of God's end-time witness, Herbert W. Armstrong, was like having the "keys to the kingdom." I would be vindicated by God in the eyes of all those who ridiculed and made light of Mr. Armstrong's "true gospel." Now, some 35 years later, I shake my head incredulously and ask, "How could I have fallen for all this?" This same question may be asked of those who are involved in groups such as the Mormons, the Jehovah's Witnesses, and splinter groups of the Worldwide Church of God. Like me, they may have "swallowed the bait." But many of them are, like me, probably predisposed to the appeal that these seemingly "Christian" groups have.

I was predisposed to accept the teaching of Mr. Armstrong and the Radio Church of God. I don't absolve myself of any personal responsibility, however. I was not hypnotized or drugged. I made my own choices, both ignorantly and with great zeal. In fact, the actual degree of ignorance and height of zeal astounds me. (The one seems directly proportional to the other.) I think that many who join cults experience some kind of inculcating process that prepares them to make the choice to join the group. Note my use of the word *choice*. I chose freely to join the Worldwide Church of God. My decision was not a divinely inspired leading of the Holy Spirit. Many members of the WCG believe that God placed them in that particular church. This understanding was drummed into our heads from day one, so it is not surprising that many believed it. But would God lead me into error so He could later enlighten me? Would He burden me with legalism and works righteousness so He could then show me the Gospel? Would He place me in a group that denied and decried His identity as Triune, castigating this truth as a pagan falsehood? The answer is obvious. God, who is truth and in whom is no shadow of deceit, does not employ falsehoods, deceptions, and heresy to lead His children to truth.

As believing Christians who are grounded in the historic orthodox Christian faith, we can be aware of friends and loved ones who are being led astray into some pseudo-Christian movement. We need to look for ways to help them. We need to be ready to give an answer to questions about the faith delivered to the apostolic church. We need to be patient and gentle when engaging in dialogue with others about their beliefs. Putdowns and ridicule only drive people further away and root them deeper in their error. Most important, we need to remember it is the Holy Spirit who opens our minds and leads us into truth. Jesus promised He would send the Spirit to us to "guide [us] into all truth" (John 16:13).

Now I'd like to take you back to the old tobacco farm in tidewater North Carolina and introduce you to my grandfather, Joe Bradham. He was a key figure in my life who helped put me on the road to Mt. Sinai.

ENDNOTES

1 Warren Mueller, *Homemade* (May 1990).

Chapter 2

Ripe for the Picking

From all false doctrine, heresy, and schism, Good Lord, deliver us.—The Litany (*Book of Common Prayer*)

My father met my mother in Wilmington, North Carolina, just before World War II. They were married in June 1939. After the war, my sister and I were two among the millions later to be known as Baby Boomers. We were both born in Wilmington—my sister, Susan, in 1947, and I followed in 1949. We moved to Richmond, Virginia, in 1951.

Mom's parents, Joe and RobertAnne Bradham, lived in North Carolina in the little town of Chinquapin. It was not much more than a single asphalt road with a few stores and a gas station. It was rural North Carolina at its finest. Life was slow and easy. Most folks lived on farms, raising tobacco as a cash crop, corn for feed, and vegetables and livestock for their own consumption.

Every summer our family would either load up in dad's work van or take the Silver Meteor train to my grandparent's farm. Actually, the farm was owned by my grandfather's brother Van. Granddad was a sharecropper. He paid his rent by giving Van a share of the crops he raised.

The weeks with my grandparents in North Carolina were memorable. When we rolled into the front yard of their farm, we knew Grandma would have lemon meringue pie and coconut and pineapple upside-down cakes waiting for my sister and me to gobble up. Another bonus was the biscuits Grandma baked from scratch every morning. They came piping hot out of the old cast iron oven and onto the table, where they quickly disappeared into the tummies of two little "piggies" from the city.

Granddad was special because of the time that he spent telling me stories. Every day after his work was done, he would sit in his rocking chair on the wood-slat front porch that faced the dirt road that ran in front of the house. The sun would set behind us, so it was shady and cool in the dank North Carolina twilight as we rocked together. We listened to crickets chirping, bobwhites calling from the grassy field across the road, and the cow in the barn singing out her slow resolute moos. Granddad would tell me stories from the Bible, and I loved them. When Granddad told a story in his uncomplicated North Carolina accent, his eyes twinkled with excitement as he smiled at me. He was short and portly, not terribly overweight, but just enough to give him a little girth. His hair was white as snow, which afforded a wonderful color contrast to his blue denim overalls. Sometimes I would sit on his lap; sometimes I would rock in a chair beside him or sit on the wooden porch steps. Other times we would swing together on the front porch swing. As Grandpa's rocking chair creaked and the porch's wooden planks groaned under the rhythm of his back-and-forth motion, he would tell me about God, His love for me, heaven with its mansions, and hell and its torments. He spoke of David and Goliath, Noah and his ark, faithful Abraham, and Jesus of Nazareth. It was his stories that made the Bible come alive. It was his encouragement that later prompted me to live for God.

Despite his interest in the Bible, Joe Bradham was not a regular churchgoer. He was Baptist by confession, but something must have happened because he did not regularly attend church. I fondly remember Sunday mornings at his house. Granddad would begin his shaving ritual. He took out his shaving mug, mixed a batch of soapy lather with his wood-handled horsehair shaving brush. After lathering his face, he would take a straight razor and go to work. This Sunday rite took place by the iron pot-bellied stove on which he had placed his radio. A preacher's voice would blast from the radio. His favorite was Preacher Green from somewhere in South Carolina. After Reverend Green came another and maybe another before Grandma would run him out. I would sit with Granddad throughout his ritual, listening to the radio as he commented either positively or negatively about what was said. Granddad was my idol; therefore, his comments were gospel to me.

My grandfather was, in fact, a religious "dabbler" who was not well grounded in theology. He loved to read the Bible, listen to preachers of all stripes, and eclectically piece together his own theology from the various ideas he gathered. As far as I was concerned, I adored him and thought he could do no wrong. To me, he spoke only the truth regarding the Bible. If Granddad said it, it had to be true.

One summer night I remained at the dinner table after everyone else. Granddad looked at me and asked, "Do you know who the Americans are?" I was about 11 years old, so I had no clue who we were or why he was asking me this question. Nor could I possibly have been prepared for his next statement. "We are descendants of the ancient tribes of Israel. The United States is the tribe of Manasseh."

I was not sure what this meant, but the almost hushed tone of Granddad's voice signaled this was a hefty revelation. "How do you know that, Granddaddy?" I asked.

He said that he had studied the matter. Granddad was not immediately forthcoming with a source of authority for this audacious claim, but that was okay with me. If Granddad said we were descendants of the Israelite tribe of Manasseh, then we were. He could have said we were descendants of Martians and I probably would have believed him! He had said it, I believed it, and that settled the matter! I did not know that Granddad had been receiving a regular subscription to Armstrong's *The Plain Truth*, as well as assorted literature from the Radio Church of God.

During the next summer, Granddad asked me, "Have you ever heard of Herbert W. Armstrong?" I told him I had not. "If any man knows his Bible, it's Herbert Armstrong. He comes on the radio. You should listen to him," Granddad said.

I asked if he had any written material from Mr. Armstrong, and Granddad produced two pamphlets: *The Resurrection Was Not on Sunday!* and *Easter Is Pagan!* I immediately devoured the contents and was convinced Granddad was right. I doubt that I would have come to any other conclusion because that would have been an assault on the wisdom of my beloved grandfather. So I concluded this Armstrong fellow really knew his Bible. Was I excited! I asked Granddad if he had anything else from Mr. Armstrong. He disappeared into his bedroom for a few minutes, then emerged with a stack of *Plain Truth* magazines. I spent the rest of my vacation reading through these magazines. I read all the way back to Richmond in the family station wagon, totally absorbed in this "new truth" that was beginning to take root in my all too open mind.

For the next several weeks, I read until I thought my eyeballs would pop. "New truth" after "new truth" was revealed through the pages of *The Plain Truth*. I learned hidden truths about the mark of the beast; the paganism of Christmas; how eating pork was a sin; the diabolical plans of the Nazis who were waiting underground in Germany and Argentina to launch the final revival of the Holy Roman Empire and attack the United States; the union of the Chinese and Soviets as Gog and Magog to oppose the beast power of Europe; the wickedness of the apostate Roman Catholic Church, whose pope would soon move to Jerusalem to reside as the "abomination of desolation"; and, of course, the apostasy of the Protestant churches, the harlot daughters of the great whore of Rome. This was fantastic information for a 12-year-old boy in Richmond, Virginia. I had discovered wonderful hidden "truths" from Mr. Herbert Armstrong.

During a conversation about truth, a friend from another denomination quoted the book of Jude: "I felt I had to write and urge you to contend for the faith that was once for all entrusted to the saints" (Jude 3). He pointed out that the truth of God was delivered to the apostles in the first century. There are no "new truths" today. He said, "If it's new, it's probably not true." This thinking flew in the face of what we believed in the WCG at the time. Instead, we held the conviction that truth had been lost and now in these last days was being revealed through God's special emissary, Herbert W. Armstrong. Such thinking was not confined to the WCG. Other groups, such as the Mormons and the followers of Jim Jones and David Koresh, have claimed some degree of the same thing. There is a certain measure of self-satisfaction and old-fashioned self-righteousness when you believe you belong to God's elite who are privy to special long-lost insights that have been newly revealed.

If it's new, it's probably not true. Maybe not an axiom, but it is a caution worth remembering. My 35 years in the Worldwide Church of God was punctuated constantly with proclamations of "new truth." This jargon denoted a new doctrinal understanding that had been "revealed" to Mr. Armstrong. "New truths" included the correct day to keep Pentecost, a different administration of divorce and remarriage within the church, our incredible human potential to be born as gods into the God-family, among others. We were excited about and lived in anticipation of the next "new truth" that God would show to Mr. Armstrong. Even as the Worldwide Church of God struggles to regain its momentum after doctrinal changes of historic proportions, one can hear some old-timers speak of these changes as "new truth" or "new understanding." It is difficult for some current WCG members (and almost impossible for those who have splintered off) to accept this gracious work of the Holy Spirit not as "new truth," but as the ancient historic truth delivered to the apostles and the first-century church. It may be new to them, but it is not new to the centuries-old professing Christian church that never lost it.

The elevation of Mr. Armstrong to near prophetic dimensions made him seem like a special tool of God who had received this "new truth" in some mysterious way. Unfortunately, there was no way to test Armstrong's proclamations internally. There was no committee of scholars skilled in biblical languages and hermeneutical training to review, debate, and weigh the biblical veracity of Mr. Armstrong's claims. He said it came from God, so we assumed it did. After all, Armstrong claimed to be God's only "end-time apostle." He needed only to speak, to give his scriptural "proof," and it was accepted as God's revelation.

Granddad also told me to listen to Mr. Armstrong on the radio. I searched *The Plain Truth* until I found a radio log. It pointed me to 50,000 watt WWVA in Wheeling, West Virginia. I started tuning in each evening at 10 P.M. to hear *The World Tomorrow*, Mr. Armstrong's radio program. His voice was authoritative; there was no backpeddling. Everything sounded cut and dried. Here was God's end-time man, not unlike Ezekiel (which Armstrong called himself), telling things just the way they were. He challenged listeners: "Blow the dust off your Bible. Don't believe me; believe your own Bible!" So almost every night, I sat at my desk alone in my room with my Bible, notepaper, and pen, and I followed along. Sure enough, just as Granddad had said, Armstrong was proclaiming the "truth" right from the Bible. However, to find Armstrong wrong would have forced me to admit my granddad was wrong. My love for Granddad was so great that it blinded me to his and Armstrong's errors. At age 12, I was ripe for the picking—and picked I was.

I sent for and received dozens of booklets and roughly 70 lessons in the *Ambassador College Bible Correspondence Course*. Mr. Armstrong never asked for a cent. He even boasted on the radio and in print, "You can't buy this magazine." This was impressive. In fact, if you sent money for the literature, it would be returned with a polite letter that stated no one could pay for a subscription. Behind the scenes, a heavily burdened Worldwide Church of God membership made great financial sacrifices so this "free" literature could be offered. Eventually I joined the ranks of those who gave heavily by "command of God" to keep the giant wheels of the Armstrong empire greased and running.

My adventure of discovery gradually carried me deeper into study. I learned in the pages of WCG literature that true Christians tithed for the "work of God" being done by the "true Church of God." The logical question was *Which is the true church of God?* It did not take a lot of deductive reasoning to put two and two together and realize that God's true church must be the Worldwide Church of God, which was led by God's own apostle,

Herbert W. Armstrong. My responsibility became immediately clear. I needed to send money to Pasadena, California, to support this great crusade. After I had sent a few money orders to the WCG, my parents stepped in and said this religious business was getting out of hand. After all, didn't I know that only religious nuts were in Southern California? (No, I had never heard that before.)

I was in a real bind because I knew I had to obey my parents. But I believed I was commanded to pay the tithe—or else. I figured the "or else" was certain financial punishment from God. During my years in the WCG, I heard enough and read enough to be convinced that tithing was the way to certain financial blessing. If a WCG member was having financial problems, the first speculation was that the person had not been faithful in tithing. It was called "robbing God," and we cited Malachi 3:8–10:

> "Will a man rob God? Yet you rob Me. But you ask, 'How do we rob You?' In tithes and offerings. You are under a curse—the whole nation of you—because you are robbing Me. Bring the whole tithe into the storehouse, that there may be food in My house. Test me in this," says the LORD Almighty, "and see if I will not throw open the floodgates of heaven and pour out so much blessing that you will not have room enough for it."

Those members who were financially successful were held up as living proof that tithing was a living law of God. They had "tested" God's faithfulness and been rewarded. To obey the command to tithe provided assurance of financial success because we knew God would open heaven and rain down blessings (mostly material things, of course). Thus, the motivators to give were either fear or desire to please God—and sometimes a combination of both. It wasn't only fear that motivated me to give, it was also an enthusiastic belief. I believed in what Mr. Armstrong was doing. His message was clear, and his vision was something to which I subscribed wholeheartedly. Besides, giving to support God's church was something I had learned as a little boy. I wanted to give.

There also was the reality of my life situation. My parents provided for all my needs, so any money I had was pretty much mine to spend. I started faithfully putting a tithe of all I earned into a glass jar, which I hid in my sock drawer. When the sum became substantial ($20 or $30), I deposited it in the bank. I kept careful records of God's tithe, looking forward to the day when I could send it to Pasadena. When I entered Ambassador College in Big Sandy, Texas, several years later, I turned in this accumulated tithe to the WCG business office. It amounted to approximately $300, which was a good-sized contribution in 1967, especially for a 17-year-old.

Many who have become disillusioned with the Worldwide Church of God or with their own church have ceased to give, citing one reason or another for withholding contributions. Some are even bitter about the money they have donated to the church. Some disenchanted WCG members tried to sue to have the church return years of tithes. But this seems ridiculous. Although tithing is a part of the Old Covenant and is no longer binding on Christians, it is still an acceptable practice of Christian stewardship. We don't give out of compulsion nor from what we don't have; instead, we give according to the blessings the Lord has given to us. Giving is an act of worship between my God and me. I give to Him as an acknowledgement of His generosity to me, returning what is His anyway. If I claim to be a member of a particular church, I feel compelled by Christian conscience to support it financially. If I believed this church no longer preached the truth or was misrepresenting the Word of God, I would withdraw my membership and support another ministry. But to consume all of one's income without giving to further God's work misses the point of Christian stewardship. As one man said, such is the mark of real poverty. Sadly, many who claim the name of Christ and call on Him for every blessing withhold support from His church or give a mere pittance dredged from their pockets in a last-minute frantic effort to "throw something in the plate" so they won't look bad in front of others. Now I give according to what I have, thankful that I may give, and acknowledging that all

I have or ever will have comes as a gift from a most generous Lord.

Today's Worldwide Church of God has come a long way in the area of stewardship. Years ago the leadership spent money like they were pouring water out of a pitcher. Mr. Armstrong liked nice things and felt God wanted him to set a standard of quality. With that as his premise, Armstrong built splendid buildings at the church's Pasadena headquarters. He gave expensive gifts of Steuben crystal to the world leaders he visited. He had a small fleet of planes and limousines. And Armstrong and his top executives lived in expensively decorated homes along Pasadena's fashionable Orange Grove Boulevard. Most members accepted this lifestyle as normal for God's apostle and his top ministers. However, a small percentage of members were irritated by this high living and felt money was being squandered. When Mr. Armstrong heard such criticism, he angrily chided the doubters for questioning his motives. He often reminded us that he had lost everything in his call from God, living many years in desperate poverty while serving God faithfully. He would plainly state, "I've been faithful, and God is now rewarding me, so how dare you question God's doing?" This shut down most critics, or they eventually got mad and left.

Mr. Armstrong's successor, Joseph Tkach Sr., gradually began to cut back on the lavish excesses of his predecessor. After major doctrinal reforms were instituted in 1993, income began to fall dramatically, which forced Mr. Tkach to eliminate many past luxuries. Out went some of the limousines. Silver and gold table settings were auctioned off along with fine artwork. Mr. Tkach sold the Gulfstream III jet soon after he took office in the wake of Mr. Armstrong's death in January 1986. Mr. Tkach complained about its expense (it cost around $16 million). It was sold for a good price, and he bought a used BAC 111 for a few million dollars. It was larger than the Gulfstream and allowed Mr. Tkach to carry a much larger staff when he traveled, which he enjoyed doing. Finally, even the BAC—which the church spent thousands to upgrade, refit, and operate—was put on the chopping block. It didn't sell until after Mr. Tkach's death, but when it did, we rejoiced. Ridding ourselves of the jet and limousines was symbolic of our separation from a past approach to ministry that was more corporate life than Christian ministry. Joe Tkach Jr., who was appointed to succeed his father in September 1995, continues to promote a more modest and appropriate Christian ministry within the Worldwide Church of God.

Another early discovery I made as a young teenager reading WCG literature was the nature of the "true Sabbath." In fact, one cannot talk about the Worldwide Church of God without mentioning the Sabbath. WCG tradition and teaching until December 1994 was strict observance of the weekly Sabbath from Friday sundown until Saturday sundown. Every WCG member was keenly aware of the setting sun on Friday evening and the need to wrap up work and get home before the golden orb disappeared over the horizon. As a rule, members were in their homes with family by the time the sun set. On Friday evening the best meal of the week was served, and we would guide our conversations along biblical or spiritual themes. In our home, my wife would bring out candles, serve on the best china, and pour that special bottle of wine. It was a great time, and many in the WCG fellowship still practice such family togetherness on the eve of the Sabbath.

Saturday was truly a day of rest. We did no work, refrained from entertainment, and focused on prayer, study, and fellowship. Some members even left dishes in the sink to wash on Saturday night so they would not profane the Sabbath. "Heavy" cooking was done on Friday, the "preparation" day, so little food was actually prepared on Saturday.

Saturday was also church day. We dressed in our finest to appear before God in worship. And we drove whatever distance it took to meet with like-minded people. In the early years of the WCG, some people would drive three, four, or more hours roundtrip to be present for a worship service. Why such dedication when neighborhood churches were much closer? Armstrong had convinced us that we were the "one true church" and that his ministers were "true" ministers of God. This effectively relegated all other churches to the category of false Christianity. Besides, we figured it would be a sin to visit another church because they were "Satan-inspired harlot daughters of the Babylonian whore [the Roman Catholic Church]." So we kept to ourselves and were happy to do so. We were shining lights set on a hill to illuminate God's only true way—at least that is what we thought of ourselves. In reality, we were faulty blinking lights that blinded one another. Perhaps this feeling of exclusivity in the WCG helps explain why we would drive enormous distances—sometimes more than 100 miles in one direction—to attend church services on Sabbath. This is in stark contrast to people I hear who complain that a 15- to 20-minute drive in to attend a Gospel-centered church service is too far! Some would rather stay home than drive a little to attend a Christ-centered service. No wonder cult members, who typically are zealous, look negatively at Christians who often put such low priority on church selection and attendance.

In my early years of the WCG, there was a real joy in getting together. Everyone was scattered geographically, so weekly meetings gave us the opportunity to visit, encourage, and update one another on the events of our lives. Our fellowship was a close-knit group. We believed the same way and faced many of the same obstacles in dealing with a world that saw us as somewhere between slightly and completely daft. We came to church because we wanted to and because of the scriptural command, "Let us not give up meeting together, as some are in the habit of doing, but let us encourage one another—and all the more as you see the Day approaching" (Hebrews 10:25). There also was the ever-present fear factor. If you missed church for any but the most serious of reasons, you feared both the wrath of God and the wrath of the minister. In many cases, the fear of the minister was a bit greater because he did not often let things slide by without discipline.

Part of the Sabbath observance was to wear our finest clothes, not unlike the custom followed by many Sunday observers. Because we were appearing before the King of the Universe in worship, we had to look our best. Some ministers even recommended that members should come before God properly clothed and groomed even in one's private home devotions. I doubt many people did that, but it illustrates how we revered

God and sought to please Him in our religious observances. For a woman to appear in church wearing anything other than a dress or for a man to appear without coat and tie was a noticeable offense. To add to the offense would have been for women to wear miniskirts or tight clothing or for men to have long hair. And a woman's haircut couldn't be too short. Sometimes those who were not properly attired were turned away at the church door by zealous deacons and greeters. If admittance was granted, the improperly groomed or dressed person was made to understand by well-meaning members that one should spruce up before returning the following week. This turned off some people, but those who had made it through the church doors usually were willing to conform to "God's" standard. To make an issue of dress leads to the establishment of standards, which leads to enforcement issues. Then legalism comes to full bloom. Now WCG members are more relaxed in their dress code; however, you probably still will find WCG members dressed nicely for their weekly worship service. In my work today, most people come to church presentably dressed. Those that don't usually self-adjust to the Sunday environment.

Why were members of the WCG so geographically scattered? After all, the average church draws on the immediate geographic area for members. Most people won't drive more than 15 minutes to attend church. But WCG members were spread out and willing to drive hundreds of miles to central locations to worship. Why?

The short answer is the power of radio, which broadcasts its message over a wide area like a farmer sowing seed. Mr. Armstrong's ministry began on a small radio station with a limited broadcast range in Eugene, Oregon, around 1934. He had been offered a few minutes of airtime by the station owner, who was looking for a minister to fill a daily devotional spot. Mr. Armstrong did so well that a nice response of mail and calls came in to the station. The manager was impressed and offered him a regular spot. Armstrong accepted and launched a brilliant radio ministry. Soon he was syndicated on 50,000-watt radio stations heard over several states. During the 1930s, 1940s, and into the

1950s, radio was the number one entertainment medium in America. And there weren't hundreds of stations either, so chances were good that a lot of people would hear you if you could get on the air. Eventually millions heard the crisp, booming voice of Herbert Armstrong on *The World Tomorrow* program. Of those who heard, some believed. They wrote for literature and requested a visit from a minister. By the early 1950s, Ambassador College was sending baptizing teams to visit interested people to baptize them. The two-man teams traveled throughout the United States and Canada for most of the summer. They visited, counseled, and baptized scores of people. It was then that the Radio Church of God began to take root in communities across North America. When there were enough people within a "reasonable" driving distance, Pasadena assigned a minister to a central point and founded a local congregation. Not only did members have to drive a lot, but ministers virtually lived on the road. In-home visitation was a significant part of the ministry, so ministers easily drove at least 50,000 miles per year to keep in touch with and check up on members. One long-time minister drove weekly between Kansas City, Chicago, and St. Louis to preach and visit.

I must have been 15 years old and in the 10th grade when the Sabbath command became clearer to me. Venerable Street Baptist Church was still my church home, so my understanding of "Sabbath" always had been Sunday. It never dawned on me that Sabbath meant Saturday. So when the commandment "to remember the Sabbath day to keep it holy" became clearer, I thought I'd better do something.

Once while on vacation at the North Carolina farm, I thought I would surprise Granddad and mow the grass for him. It was a beautiful bright Sunday morning, and the dew lay heavy on the grass. I pulled out the old push mower with the cylindrical blades and with a mighty grunt set off to work. I thought Granddad would be pleased with me. Not more than five minutes later, I heard the screen door swing open and suddenly slam shut. I turned to see Granddad standing on the back porch shouting at me. "Tommy, it's Sunday—the Lord's day. Put that mower away, and stop that work!" That incident stuck in my mind.

Years later I put two and two together, came up with five, and realized I must prepare for my next assault on my parents. One spring Sunday, my dad told me to mow the yard. This was the moment of truth. Remembering how I had dealt with the pork issue so well, I knew I had to be consistent with the Sabbath issue. With a pounding heart, I told Dad I wouldn't be working in the yard on Sunday anymore. He became visibly upset and said I had taken things too far, but he didn't push too hard. He walked off in a cold, steely silence, cranked up our gasoline-powered mower, and began to mow. I sat on the back porch while he worked. My increased "orthodoxy" certainly didn't make me easier to live with around the house. What's amazing is the patience my parents exhibited with me. In some contemporary families, such behavior would have resulted in many trips to a professional counselor or a psychiatrist in the hopes of "detoxing" me.

The real surprise came when I read a WCG booklet titled *Which Day Is the Christian Sabbath?* There it was—plain as day. Saturday was the Sabbath, and the pernicious Catholic Church had changed the day in A.D. 325 at the Council of Nicea. Keeping Sunday somewhat holy was struggle enough, but keeping Saturday holy was going to be a real challenge. First, my dad had gotten me my first job at Koslow's Supermarket. During the school year, I worked Friday nights, Saturdays, and Sundays. The Sunday Sabbath conviction that I first held didn't lead me to quit my job. (I just couldn't do yard work—you can see I wasn't always consistent or logical.) But after reading Mr. Armstrong's exegesis on Saturday Sabbath, I was more deeply convicted, so I quit my job. In his booklet, Mr. Armstrong wrote of the Sabbath as the "sign" between God and His people. It was a test commandment of obedience to God. It was the identifying mark of the true believer.

Quitting Koslow's upset my dad for several reasons. First, he saw the move as religious fanaticism, and he may not have been far off the mark. Second, Mr. Koslow was his friend, and this didn't make my dad look good. Third, he knew it would hurt me in the pocketbook because I was saving money for college. Again, Dad's non-scriptural arguments were to no avail. Besides, I told him about my decision only after I had quit the job. Because I was on my own as I tried to figure out daily application of these marvelous insights from Mr. Armstrong, I made many mistakes and hurt my parents deeply, which sincerely grieves me.

One of the great challenges of any new believer is applying truth to everyday life. I made awkward stabs at it, and soon I was faced with yet another application dilemma. Baseball was my teenage passion. As you know, Saturday is a big baseball day for most kids. In reading Scripture, it was clear to me that the Sabbath was to be a "delight" and I was not to profane it by working. In my 16-year-old brain, that meant baseball on the Sabbath was okay because it was a delightful thing and it certainly wasn't work. That line of reasoning carried me through one school season, during which I played on the varsity team, and through summer Babe Ruth League. By the beginning of my senior year, however, it became clear that my reasoning was off the mark. According to Mr. Armstrong's understanding of the Sabbath, playing sports also was prohibited.

This was a real problem. I was 17 years old, a senior, and a member of the varsity baseball team. For the previous two years, Steve had beaten me out for the first-string position at third base. Because he had graduated, the field was clear in my senior year to start at third. Spring training was going great. I was smacking the ball all over the park and seldom ever striking out. My glove was hot as I scooped up everything that came my way. It was a dream come true. All the years of drills, scrimmage games, and workouts were finally paying off. Our games were after school on Tuesdays and Thursdays, so there would be no conflict with the Sabbath. Then came the announcement that the coach expected us to play a scrimmage game on Saturday morning. This was a dilemma.

As some of the guys dropped me off at home after Friday's practice, one of them asked, "Well, Tom, are you coming to Saturday's scrimmage?" He didn't know about my newfound beliefs about the Sabbath. It was a moment of truth, and I mulled over what, if anything, I would say. In that '56 Chevy Bel-Aire, all eyes were on me, waiting for a response. "Well, are you coming or not?" the question was repeated.

"No, guess I won't be," I replied.

A surprised teammate asked why I wouldn't be there. I muttered some incoherent statement about Saturday being the Sabbath and that I couldn't come. There was a brief moment of stunned silence that was broken by a guy who simply stated, "The coach is gonna kill ya'." The next hours were pure torment. What could I do?

It's amazing how—when caught between the proverbial rock and the hard place—the human mind manages to find a solution in favor of what it wants to do. That's what happened to me on that Friday night. *Surely playing baseball on Saturday can't be a sin,* I thought. *Why, didn't Christ say that the Sabbath was made for man and not man for the Sabbath?* Eureka! That was the solution that almost cleared my conscience. At least it paved the way for me to appear at the high school baseball field the next morning.

There I was, with an almost clear conscience on a sunny Saturday morning, ready to play baseball. The coach lined us up, did role call, then made a devastating announcement. "Guys, before we play ball today, we need to do a little work on the field. First, we are going to drag it with the screen, then pick up rocks on the infield."

I couldn't believe my ears! Did he say that four-letter word *work*? He must have because the next thing I remember was guys pulling the screen across the infield and finding myself propelled along with my teammates to clear the field of rocks. My tender conscience was getting darker as I found myself totally dumbfounded by the turn of events. I did not have a clue about how to wiggle out of the situation. We must have scrimmaged after we worked, but I don't remember anything other than having transgressed the holy Sabbath, the covenant sign of God. Even my otherwise dependable emergency exegesis couldn't blow away the cloud of sin that had gathered over my head. This ominous cloud enveloped me all weekend, totally consuming my every moment. I felt guilt—no, I knew I was guilty before God.

During our regular practice on Monday afternoon, it became painfully obvious that something wasn't right. Routine ground balls would not stay in my glove! Instead, the ball would bounce off my glove, bounce off my chest, or sail through my legs. This was unbelievable! The golden glove had turned to ash. Embarrassment was heaped on embarrassment when I took batting practice. The week before I had been on a hot streak, hitting solidly all over the field. Now, if I connected at all, I swung ahead of the ball and knocked it foul. I was like Mighty Casey—great swats with the bat, but strike out after strike out. God was dealing with me now! I knew He was intervening in my baseball life to cause me to mess up, which was the most severe punishment I could imagine. My baseball prowess was broken for all to see. The coach couldn't figure it out, but I knew the real score. Breaking the Sabbath had exacted a painful penalty in my life. Two weeks went by with no visible improvement in my abysmal fielding and batting performance. Then came the call to report to the coach's office after practice.

With a sad tone in his voice, my coach said, "Tom, you're just not cutting it out there. As much as I hate to do this, seeing as you are a senior and all, I'm going to have to cut you from the squad." To say I was stunned is an understatement. The unthinkable had just happened. After being on the squad for two years, I had been cut. In my heart, I knew God Himself was punishing me.

My conclusion was the logical extension of legalistic, Old Covenant thinking. In the Old Covenant, God speaks of blessings and cursings—blessings for obedience to His laws and curses for disobedience. Leviticus 26 outlines the blessings God promises to pour out on His people for obedience: rain in due season, good harvests, peace in the land, victory over enemies, population growth. If people disobeyed, God would bring disease and fever, defeat by one's enemies, drought, failed crops, decimation, plagues. Now, it looked like the curses extended to getting axed from the varsity baseball squad! I had heard Mr. Armstrong preach about these curses on WWVA, and I was convinced God's punishment had been visited not only on the United States, but on this struggling third baseman at Highland Springs High School. Recently, the Worldwide Church of God has come to see that contrary to the teaching of Mr. Armstrong, Christians are under the new covenant of grace and forgiveness. But as one of my former bosses at WCG headquarters in Pasadena once told me, perception is reality. My perception was that I had sinned and God was punishing me for that sin.

But what sign does God give that we are His? Is it something outward, something that we do? Or is it something inward, something hidden from the world? Paul wrote in Romans 8:14 that those who have been granted the Holy Spirit are God's own. Regeneration by the Holy Spirit is not outwardly defined by the observation of a particular day of worship. However, the Holy Spirit does produce a noticeable effect in the believer's life. Jesus said, "By this all men will know you are My disciples, if you love one another" (John 13:35). But I was so engrossed in externals, in the letter of the Law, that I missed the internal, the spirit of the Law. This obsession with external signs produced an ingrained legalistic thinking that convinced me my works could assuage God. The more I obeyed, the better I obeyed, the greater the detail of my obedience, the more pleasure God would have in me, or so I thought. Such thinking resulted in two things. First, I completely missed what Paul wrote in Romans 3:28: "For we maintain that a man is justified by faith apart from observing the law." I did not live by faith and through faith believe in God's forgiveness for Christ's sake; instead, I lived by the Law, which did its work in my heart. The Law put me under a dark cloud of fear, uncertainty, and guilt. Second, the more I tried to win God's approval by following the dos and don'ts of Armstrong's religion, the further I slipped away from God. My conscience was not free. It was bound by the certain knowledge that I had not obeyed God perfectly, whether in tithing, Sabbath-keeping, avoiding pork, or whatever other law there was. I was like Martin Luther—inwardly terrified by God. Unfortunately, legalism plagues every denomination to some extent. Depending on our performance to please God and to move Him to forgive us is much easier than to believe that we are "saved by grace through faith" (Ephesians 2:8). For many, faith is too difficult because it does not appeal to our human reason, which tells us that we can contribute to our salvation. How far removed this thinking is from the simple truth of the Gospel that those who believe in Christ as Savior are indeed saved (John 3:16).

This baseball incident in my formative years illustrates how legalism robs the believer of the assurance of forgiveness. Legalism and its works-righteousness falls short of a full understanding of the grace and forgiveness of God through His Son, Jesus. Paul wrote in Ephesians 1:7–8: "In Him we have redemption through His blood, the forgiveness of sins, in accordance with the riches of God's grace that He lavished on us with all wisdom and understanding." Peter echoes the same thought in Acts 10:43: "All the prophets testify about Him that everyone who believes in Him receives forgiveness of sins through His name." Perhaps Mr. Armstrong talked about such concepts on *The World Tomorrow*, but I missed them. What I do recall is his focus on sin as the disobedience of God's Law and the certain punishment of evil-doers.

After reading all the material Granddad had given me and ordering stacks of my own, I decided at about age 13 that I would attend Ambassador College. It was clear no other college or university in the world could offer me the education that Ambassador would provide. At least that is what Armstrong claimed, and I had taken the hook pretty hard. Armstrong often spoke or wrote about the abysmal state of the education system, which was based on paganism and not on the "true values" of God. Ambassador College's motto was "recapture true values." It became obvious to me that Ambassador was the only educational institution that I should attend. Out the door went my previous thoughts about enrolling at the University of Richmond or the University of Virginia. No, God's truth and true values were being taught at "God's very own college"—Ambassador College.

After ordering and meticulously reading the Ambassador College catalog, I prayed, "Dear God, if You get me into Ambassador College, I will serve You the rest of my life." I didn't know you weren't supposed to bargain with God. After all, I had read in WCG literature that Jacob had bargained with God, offering a tithe of all his future wealth if God would protect him and return him home safely. That seemed a safe model to follow in petitioning God for my educational desires.

After hearing my granddad, listening to Armstrong on WWVA, and reading an enormous amount of WCG literature, I wanted some of my closest friends to know this new and esoteric "truth." My best friend, Steve, lived in the house behind me, our yards separated only by a wire fence. Gene, another good friend, lived about a half block away. I began to tell them the wonderful truths I had learned: German Nazis were in hiding, preparing a vengeful sneak attack on the United States; the United States was really the lost Israelite tribe of Manasseh; the Soviets would mount a preemptive strike against the German-led United States of Europe; the pope, who was clearly the false prophet of Revelation, would move his headquarters to Jerusalem; together with the European dictator (the prophetic "beast" and most probably a German), the pope would prepare to launch the final battle—Armageddon. All Gene and Steve needed to do was to believe this truth and obey God's laws and they would be saved with me.

Incredibly, Gene and Steve didn't grab on to this revelation! They pooh-poohed the entire idea, but we remained friends. Now Gus, who lived across the street, was not one of my friends—in fact, he was the neighborhood pariah. During Thanksgiving school break, my dad had me doing some work around the house when Gus asked what Steve, Gene, and I had been talking about in recent weeks. "I can't tell you, Gus," I replied.

"Why not?" he shot back.

"Because if I do, then you will be held accountable by God," I answered. That's the way I understood the program. If I told someone the "truth" and that person refused it, he or she was in serious spiritual peril. Although I didn't like Gus that much, I didn't want to see the guy under God's curse. Gus spent hours with me over the next several days as I worked. He kept bugging me to tell him my secret. Finally, worn down by his incessant badgering, I solemnly declared, "If I tell you this and you don't believe, then it's your responsibility before God, not mine."

"Okay, okay," said Gus.

For the next several days I instructed Gus in the mysterious biblical prophecies and secret truths that would show us how to be spared from the coming world catastrophe. To my utter disbelief, Gus turned out to be a believer! This probably was not so incredible because Gus and I had similar struggles at home. He also lived under the curse of an equally devastating inferiority complex. For Gus this new knowledge must have seemed to be truly a God-send, giving him a measure of self worth. First, he was "in the know." Second, he had been accepted by one the neighborhood kids. After his indoctrination, Gus and I became good friends and have remained so to this day, though Gus has long since left the Worldwide Church of God and all churches for that matter.

Gus was my only "convert" during my teenage years, and he also decided to attend Ambassador College. Of course, a lot of time and water would go under the bridge between eighth grade and high school graduation. During those intervening years, I determined that if I didn't make it into Ambassador, I would join the military. At first I wanted to be an Air Force fighter pilot, but my vision deteriorated from the required 20/20. Then I wanted to be a Navy frogman, which progressed to a desire to join the Marines and become one of the "few good men." Finally, because of my interest in foreign language, I opted for the Army because its language training program at Monterrey, California, was the best. Besides, by the time I was 17 years old, it was 1967 and the Vietnam War was going full blast. I decided that slogging through the jungle was not for me. My plan was to become a Russian interpreter and be shipped off to Europe. The military was my plan B if Ambassador didn't materialize.

Throughout high school, I worked hard to qualify for Ambassador. My goal was to earn straight As, thus making myself a top candidate for Ambassador College. I still have my high school report card and a certificate congratulating me on maintaining an average grade of 94 for my years at Highland Springs High. My zealous goal-orientation sprang from a strong need for recognition and its accompanying feelings of self-worth. This inspired me to excel and achieve both academic and athletic goals.

In those days, prospective students could not apply to Ambassador College until the December prior to their first fall semester. So in December of my senior year, I sent to Pasadena my application to attend the Big Sandy, Texas, campus of Ambassador College. The campus was about 100 miles east of Dallas. By December all my friends who were going to college had long since been accepted for the coming fall, yet I was just submitting my application. But who cared about those other colleges?! They taught a pagan-based education. So I waited and waited and waited for Pasadena to respond to my application. Month after month rolled by. Each day I rushed home after school to find out if anything had come from Ambassador. You can imagine how excited my parents were about me going to this "fruits and nuts" college. By this time the skirmishes with my parents had become progressively worse. One day Mom even took all my WCG literature to the burn barrel in the backyard and set it ablaze! That only deepened my resolve to pursue the path that I was convinced God had chosen for me.

Time was ticking away, so I began to crank up plan B. I visited my local Army recruiter in downtown Richmond. He began the testing process. One day of written tests; another day spent in my underwear, running from station to station to have my body parts checked. And finally, I took a language test at Ft. Lee, Virginia. I scored extremely high. The sergeant assured me that I would qualify for the Army Security Agency (ASA), and he prepared my enlistment papers. I was only 17, so Dad had to sign so I could enlist. He consented, probably thinking that Uncle Sam could jar my now very lopsided brain back into normal functioning capacity.

For me, joining the military was the most logical thing in the world. It was my duty to my country. After all, my Dad had served in the Merchant Marines during World War II. And I had heard Garner Ted Armstrong—Herbert W. Armstrong's son—speak on the radio about his Navy days. I had no idea that the Worldwide Church of God was pacifist. Only later at Ambassador did I learn of this pacifist position after I submitted a question about the biblical teaching on military service for discussion at a Friday night Bible study. Garner Ted presided that evening and explained that war was not God's way and that a Christian should not become involved in killing. This sounded fine to me, especially as I watched the news about the Vietnam War and saw young men shipped out to Southeast Asia.

I believe the Worldwide Church of God's strong pre-millennial orientation led it into formulating a pacifist theology. Believing the world to be desperately wicked and that only Christ's return could sort out the myriad problems and conflicts of people and nations, WCG members saw it as their Christian duty to refuse to bear arms in defense of their country. The Old Testament stories that told how God fought for the Israelites when they trusted Him were quoted as evidence. It was only when the Israelites rejected God that He let them make war and suffer its consequences. Besides, Jesus said in John 18:36: "My kingdom is not of this world. If it were, My servants would fight . . ." Because our allegiance was to the kingdom of God in heaven, we felt it would be a sin to go to war. Historically, men in the WCG have done either alternative civil service, which the United States and some other governments allow, or they have served only in non-combatant roles in those countries where alternative service was not available. Many courageous WCG members have stood by their convictions and suffered verbal abuse and even jail sentences to remain faithful to this interpretation of God's will. Although the church's position has moderated on military service, many WCG men around the world still take only non-combatant positions. I salute all who, based on deep personal conviction, have suffered because they followed their conscience before God. But one's conscience should be shaped by the full counsel of God, not selected passages pulled out of context. Part of "rendering to Caesar what is Caesar's" is the fulfillment of one's civic duties, which includes a readiness to love our neighbors enough to defend them from bodily harm, even to the point of laying down our lives. God provides the "sword" of government for just such service. This sword includes civil institutions such as the police, the militia, and the military.

By May of my senior year, I still had not heard from Ambassador. I sent a letter to the registrar that said I would be joining the Army to become a Russian interpreter in a few weeks. If I was be accepted into Ambassador, it had to happen soon or I would be in boot camp. That seemed to do the trick. Within a few days, I received a letter from Ambassador College in Pasadena congratulating me on my acceptance into the freshman class at Big Sandy, Texas. That was good news for me, but not so good news for my parents. Mom was upset and said I would be far better off in the Army. Dad didn't say much at all. He probably realized he had lost the battle and resigned himself to the inevitable. When I told Granddad about my acceptance at Ambassador, he was happy and congratulated me heartily. Mom later chastised him for getting me "mixed up with Armstrong," but that didn't seem to faze Granddad.

Sometime during my second year at Ambassador College, my granddad died. Mom did not tell me of his death until sometime after the fact. Maybe she wanted to spare me the pain, but I mourned the passing of my grandfather with great sorrow and a sense of real loss. I loved him dearly. As I grew older, I learned Joe Bradham had many faults, but they have never mattered to me. Granddad loved me unconditionally. He spent time with me. He taught me about God and Jesus. He always encouraged me. All I have left of his is a bone-handled pocketknife, which my mom gave to me to remember him. It is one of my greatest treasures. My grandfather is often in my thoughts. Just as Joe Bradham loved and guided me, I want to do the same for my grandchildren when God blesses me with them.

Chapter 3

Entering the Twilight

The heresy of the pious: to cut the arms off the cross and leave nothing but a pole, a vertical relationship with God with no outreach toward one's suffering fellow man.—Paul Calvin Payne

Before complete darkness covers the face of the earth, twilight enters that period somewhere between light and darkness. By the time I was 18 years old, I had stepped into the "shadows," that spiritual realm of delusion and confusion between orthodoxy and complete heresy. I left my home in Virginia for Ambassador College in Big Sandy, Texas. What I experienced at Ambassador College, which was under the auspices of the Worldwide Church of God, can only be described as a surreal experience that took me deeper into the twilight zone of a cult.

The last weeks at home in Richmond with my parents were not particularly pleasant. Dad and I got along well enough because I spent the summer helping him at DeWitt's Refrigeration. We spent hours together, driving all over town, working on jobs, and having some good times. During this time together, I got to know my dad much better. He even helped me to purchase things I needed for school. We bought a footlocker to ship my things ahead of me to Texas. He took me to Robert Hall's men's clothing store in Richmond to buy a dark blue suit and plain sport coat with slacks.

Things with my mom were not going so well. Maybe the thought of losing her only son to some far-off place affected her more than I knew. I remember the last 10 days in particular as rather stormy. She fussed and fumed, and it seemed as if every little thing led to a verbal confrontation. I had long since adopted the policy of avoidance; however, on one occasion I did give in to my lowly human nature because I felt the verbal assault was becoming too intense. I said, "You only have 10 more days to yell at me, so do the best you can because after that I'm gone." That remark, of course, fanned the flames, so I retired from the front lines and tried to keep my mouth shut as I counted the days till departure. By the time I left, the relationship with my mother was at an all-time low.

My self-righteousness and elitism had driven both of my parents to the edge of sanity. Mom's verbal attacks on me succeeded only in hardening the wall between us. To my shame, I confess my feelings toward my parents had started to border on hatred. I have long since repented, realizing such behavior and emotions were nowhere close to what Christ would have me do. Seeing my sin was part of my first-semester repentance experience at Ambassador College. I thank the ministers there who, through their preaching and teaching, set me straight on this important point. Countless others in the WCG have been estranged from loved ones because of uncompromising positions on what were considered major doctrinal issues, including not celebrating birthdays or even accepting birthday cards from others. In the last few years, many in the WCG have returned to alienated family and friends and asked forgiveness. In so doing, bridges have been mended that had been broken down for too long.

God places a high degree of value on family relationships, including His will for families in the Ten Commandments where He states that we are to honor and obey our parents. When one's religious zeal disturbs family ties, it is advisable to seek counsel from a Christian pastor or a state-certified Christian family counselor. In my case, the chief problem in our relationships was my belief in anti-Christian teachings, which understandably drove a wedge between my parents and me. It is a classic tactic (whether deliberate or unwitting) of cults and radical religious groups to alienate "true believers" from friends and families. Those who were once closest to us are characterized as "unbelievers," "lost," people who could not possibly understand us anymore because we have been "enlightened" and they have not been. The members of your newfound church become your family, which only makes exiting the group more difficult. But just because a religious group makes you feel "at home" or acts "just like family" does not mean the Holy Spirit is working the truth of Christ in the group. Virtually every cult or sect will offer a familial atmosphere. And for people like me who are starving for a warm, loving, understanding, and accepting family, the bait is tempting. Once the hook is set, it's a simple matter to be reeled in.

The big day was a hot, sultry Thursday afternoon in August 1967. I left home and headed for "God's" college, which was a common expression in the WCG (and other cultish circles) for its center of learning. I remember sitting in the Greyhound bus, waving good-bye to my parents and sister, and thinking I would probably never see them again. At that time I did not really want to see them again. They were "of the devil" because they refused to believe the murky message I had been trying to communicate to them for years. They were unbelievers destined for the Great Tribulation, a time immediately before Christ's return when the last great crisis would strike all humankind and leave billions dead in its wake. Their time would come in a resurrection to physical life after the 1000-year reign of Christ. Until then, I knew, there was no hope for them. As I waved good-bye, I felt no great warmth of love, only a terrible anger that approached hatred. This lack of love for people was an attitude I had unconsciously picked up from Herbert Armstrong's materials. Although he did not overtly encourage such feelings, they seemed to be a by-product of adopting his belief system.

Where did such an aloof coolness and a self-righteous arrogance toward those who did not follow Armstrong come from? I believe it came from our strong pre-millennial beliefs. We believed we were in the "last days" only a few short years before Christ's return. The whole world except us few elect had become apostate and turned completely toward evil. There was no way to save them. Any efforts to do so were too little too late. Only Christ Himself could turn things around and bring peace, love, and harmony to a sick and dying world. Our role as God's chosen was not to try to change the world for the better, but to warn the world of its sin and coming punishment while proclaiming the promised return of Christ to set up His 1,000-year earthly reign. Preceding this reign, the government of God on earth was to begin with a great tribulation that would last three and a half years. This tribulation would be the most terrible time of world crisis, war, deception, disease, and famine in all of human history. The physical descendants of the tribes of Israel (the United States, Great Britain, and Great Britain's white, English-speaking Commonwealth countries) would suffer the brunt of the crisis. The prophet Jeremiah spoke of this time as "Jacob's troubles," which would come on the modern descendants of Israel the United States and the British Commonwealth. These nations would be taken into slavery by a resurrected Nazi-like empire in Europe, which Armstrong claimed biblical prophecy referred to as "the beast." The beast would derive its power and inspiration from a supreme religious leader headquartered in Jerusalem (the pope, who would move there from Rome).

As fantastic and "twilight zone" as this may sound, it is exactly what members of the WCG believed and what we taught. It is not far from the teachings of some pre-millennial groups today. We knew that most people would die during the great tribulation so the human population would be greatly diminished when Christ reappeared to take charge of the world and to force peace on everyone. Those who "lived over" into the millennium would most likely repent and accept Christ and the Law of Moses, especially the observation of the Sabbath and holy days.

But what about everyone who had died in ignorance during the tribulation before they had a chance to know God's laws? And what about everyone who had ever lived and died without this knowledge? Mr. Armstrong found the answer to these questions in Revelation 20, Isaiah 65:20, and Ezekiel 38. By examining these texts and applying his exegetical method of "here a little, there a little" (which meant one must piece together God's revelation by combining various biblical texts), Armstrong concluded that during the millennium those alive in the flesh would be given their first opportunity to hear the truth, and after the millennium, there would be a second resurrection to physical life. The first resurrection would occur when Christ returned and called back to spiritual life the dead saints. The second resurrection would follow the 1000-year rule of Christ on earth. According to Mr. Armstrong's interpretation of the vision of the dry bones in Ezekiel, those who had died without the "truth" would come back in the flesh. Then, for about 100 years, they would be taught who Christ is, what His laws are, and the need to observe the Sabbath. The WCG taught that this period would be called "the Great White Throne Judgment."

Understanding this "truth" affected me in several ways as it did many in the Worldwide Church of God. First, we became pacifists. Because only Christ could straighten out this sick and warring world, what could we do to improve things now? Nothing! The die was cast, and to struggle against the predetermined future was futile. Second, we lacked concern for our neighbor's spiritual condition. If God didn't call our neighbor now to reveal these hidden truths to him, then God would give him a chance either in the millennium—should he live through the horrors ahead (in which case he would be ready to pay attention!)—or in the second resurrection. In either case, it eased our consciences to know that God would make sure everyone heard His truth in His own time. This view made us less concerned about evangelizing unbelievers and, I think, less concerned about unbelievers altogether. Those in our fellowship were of more immediate importance than those who were not, which led us to develop and maintain a certain callousness toward the non-believer.

This hardness of heart even affected our dealings with one another inside the fellowship. Some have accused the WCG of "shooting their wounded," which seemed to be the case in far too many situations. Because "the Work" (the broadcast of *The World Tomorrow,* the publication and distribution of *The Plain Truth*, the Ambassador College system, and Mr. Armstrong's visits to world leaders) was the most important thing, when members developed personal problems that interfered with their ability to support the effort, ways were found to dispense with these members. This might include loss of a job, dismissal from Ambassador College, or suspension or disfellowship from the WCG. This "shooting of the wounded" did not happen to everybody, but it did happen to too many, including myself. The personal problems that would really get you into trouble were having a bad attitude or showing any sign of disloyalty. For example, a bad attitude was ascribed to disagreeing with Mr. Armstrong, a minister, or a college professor. If you disagreed, it was understood that you were rebelling and had to be dealt with accordingly. Either you came around to the party line or you were dismissed. To criticize anyone in authority was not only exhibiting a bad attitude, it was an obvious sign of disloyalty. Mr. Armstrong made it clear that God Almighty had placed him as apostle over this church and to criticize him was tantamount to criticizing God. Loyalty to Armstrong and "the Work" were top priorities in our church's life. Armstrong's decisions were hailed as "God-inspired," thus any doubt or criticism of the decision or the process by which the decision had been made was viewed as disloyalty or rebellion and incurred swift consequences. This extreme sensitivity to criticism has carried over into subsequent administrations. However, the censure one can expect has become milder.

The inability to voice criticism has been labeled spiritual abuse by some,[1] especially when those in spiritual authority cause harm to the spiritual well-being of those under them. Spiritual abuse is not confined to cults; it can appear in evangelical and orthodox circles as well. There are those holding offices in any number of denominations who see criticism as questioning their authority. In some cases, criticism is extrapolated to imply an assault on God's own authority. To suggest something is wrong opens the criticizer to charges of rebellion or disloyalty. This individual may be declared "spiritually sick," thus the tables are quickly turned and the criticizer becomes "the problem." If the complainer doesn't quickly join in lockstep with the leader, he or she will become discredited in the church and feel compelled to leave. Such departures are often spiritualized as "God's pruning," but in fact the individual has been driven out by a spiritual midget who is more concerned with programs and self-image than spiritual welfare. Although the person leveling the criticism may have been labeled a "wolf," in actuality it is the leader who is shouting "wolf" who is quietly devouring those in his flock. Mr. Joseph Tkach Sr., Armstrong's successor, used to label such carnivorous leaders "sheriffs." They had no concept of their role as undershepherds of Christ, but were driven by an oversized ego to abuse Christ's little ones. Instead, they harmed themselves spiritually and caused havoc in God's church.

My perception of service in the WCG crystallized in the 1980s when I served in Switzerland. I believed that as long as I performed well, those in authority over me were happy, but when I stumbled, I could expect an invitation to an expeditious departure out the back door. Many in the WCG would take exception to that statement, but that is how I felt and, indeed, how I had been treated on one occasion. It also is how others were dealt with over the years. Today this attitude toward those expressing dissenting opinions has become more in line with what one would expect of Christians: love and charity toward all. Employees, students at Ambassador University, ministers, and members are treated with more respect, and significant effort is made to help people with problems rather than ushering them to the door.

After 36 incredibly long hours of sheer boredom and inability to sleep on the bus, we finally rolled into either Gladewater or Big Sandy, Texas. At long last I was close to my goal. It was around 10 P.M. when I disembarked. I was met by two nicely dressed young men, Otto and Bob. Both wore dark suits, white shirts, and ties. As they greeted me, they also welcomed Laura, who had been on the same bus and was also a new Ambassador student. She had boarded the bus somewhere in the Midwest, but only at the end of the line did I meet her. Later, we became good friends and remain so to this day, though she left the WCG to join one of its many splinter groups.

I was euphoric to arrive at Ambassador College. I felt as though I was on top of the world. After years of planning, praying, and worrying, I had made it to God's college. Now I would learn "truth" firsthand from "God's very own ministers." I wanted to be a sponge and soak up everything, both words and examples. As the four of us drove onto the 1,500-acre campus, I saw the first buildings. The fieldhouse was straight ahead as we drove down the main road. This building served as the student dining hall, the gym, and held some classrooms and some business offices, including the office of the college president. We dropped Laura at one of the modern, low-lying brick-and-glass women's dorms and proceeded to the identical-looking men's dorm where I would live. The four men's dorms and four women's dorms, which made generous use of huge glass windows, were separated by a stream that ran through a narrow ravine, which was crossed by a wooden bridge. We entered the dorm through the glass door at the front of the building. The lounge we entered was spacious, tastefully decorated in orange and blues, and featured comfortable couches and chairs. The focal point of the lounge was a large fireplace. The rooms were typical college dorm rooms—rectangular in shape with four beds, one in each corner of the room. Between every two rooms there was a study room with eight built-in desks. In the center of the dorm was the communal shower and laundry area. Basically, it was a high-quality living environment.

Mr. Armstrong stressed quality. He believed, and I still agree, that a pleasant environment enhances learning. Further, Armstrong believed that God is a God of quality and His people should strive for quality in their lives—quality character and quality possessions. He did not encourage us to go into debt to maintain appearances, but we were to purchase the best we could afford. Armstrong taught that this would be less expensive in the long run. My experience has proven him right on this point. Armstrong may have gone overboard in his acquisitions of works of art, jets, cars, and more, but the WCG did not lose much money on these things in the long run. When it came time to sell them, their high quality brought a good price and, in most cases, more than initially spent to purchase them. In some years, the sale of these articles helped the WCG meet its budget.

The first person I met in the dorm was Rod, a senior. As I walked into the study area, he sat at his desk, which was closest to the open sliding glass door that led to the patio. He wore a white, sleeveless T-shirt. His dark short-cropped hair was slicked straight back, which was the style among many of the Ambassador men. Perspiration ran down his forehead on that sultry August evening. Either the air-conditioning was not working or maybe Rod wanted to be hot. Rod greeted me warmly, welcoming me to Ambassador. Bob and Otto left, and Rod gave me a tour of the dorm. After the tour, he said, as diplomatically as he could, "If you smoke, you will have to go off campus because smoking is not allowed." I had no idea why he would tell me that because I was an avid non-smoker. I discovered later that he shared this information because after 36 hours on a bus with passengers who were smoking, I smelled like a smoker. In those days, the Worldwide Church of God viewed smoking as a sin because it violated Paul's statement in 1 Corinthians that the body is the temple of the Holy Spirit and the Christian is to keep the body holy. This made sense to me, and because I did not smoke anyway, it was no big deal. The WCG still discourages smoking.

Armstrong distinguished between "physical" and "spiritual" sin. For Armstrong, physical sin was transgressing a physical law, such as defying gravity by stepping off a roof or smoking, which was injurious to one's health. If someone broke a physical law such as smoking, there would a price to pay physically. This teaching had its greatest consequences in the area of healing. Sickness was considered the result of the transgression of some physical law, hence it was a "physical sin." The WCG further taught that healing was the forgiveness of that physical sin. Healing was believed possible through the sacrifice of Christ, the result being a dual benefit. The first part of the sacrifice was Christ's physical body on which He bore the stripes (1 Peter 2:24) of the pre-crucifixion beating so our "physical" sins could be for-given. The second component was Christ's blood, which was shed for the forgiveness of our spiritual sins. But Armstrong could not have been more wrong. Christ gave His body and blood as a sacrifice for our sins, which are *spiritual* in nature. In His body, Christ obeyed the Law of God perfectly on our behalf. With His blood, Christ paid the penalty of our sin, which is death. Hence the elements of bread and wine in the Lord's Supper, emblems of His obedience and suffering.

Armstrong's interpretation of sickness and healing led most of us to avoid doctors or medicine because the use of medical knowledge was viewed as lack of faith in God, as well as depre-cating Christ's sacrifice on the cross. Most of us refused to let our children be vaccinated or to receive much, if any, medical atten-tion. Some members of the WCG have even died rather than seek medical help. Mr. Armstrong's first wife, Loma, died an untimely death in the spring of 1967 from an internal blockage of the bow-els. She had relied fully on God for healing. One amazing thing about this situation was the great mercy God shed on us. There were some astounding miracles in which the Lord mercifully intervened and healed people of various illnesses. The other amazing thing is the infrequency of lawsuits that resulted from this doctrine on healing. Often when it looked as though some-one were going to die or suffer severe physical consequences without medical attention, an appeal would be made to Mr. Armstrong for guidance. I am told he would suggest the party seek medical help. This was a wise approach that undoubtedly helped avoid screaming headlines that decried the death of adults and children because of refusal to seek medical attention.

Many WCG members still may not know that in the years before Mr. Armstrong's death, he availed himself of every avail-able medical resource. He had a nurse, doctors visited him regu-larly, and he took prescribed medicines. Those who knew of this wondered about this apparent inconsistency while others debat-ed if such stories were true. Mr. Armstrong himself reported what he was doing, at least in broad terms. Armstrong's successor, Mr. Joseph Tkach Sr., told me that before Mr. Armstrong's death, the issue of healing came up in one of their conversations. Mr. Armstrong apparently was not happy with how the healing doctrine was understood and practiced within the WCG fellowship. He wondered how members could reject the use of doctors and medicine because this was not his opinion or practice. But how Armstrong came to his conclusion that WCG members had misunderstood his teaching on healing is intriguing. In reading Armstrong's booklet on the subject of healing, one could hardly have arrived at any other conclusion.

Double standards often arose in the WCG regarding the official teaching and what Mr. Armstrong did. The area of medical treatments was one such example. After Armstrong died, the doctrine of healing was one of the first to be revised. In the revision, the taboo on seeking medical help was lifted and the doctrine of "physical" sin was studied and rejected. The WCG explained that Mr. Armstrong's understanding of physical sin was based on a conclusion he drew from a false premise. This caused no small stir in the WCG because physical healing was one of those outward badges of God's approval that could be proudly worn. Being healed is a wonderful blessing of God's grace, which He bestows as He wills. It is not based on an individual's righteousness; rather, it is based on God's love and mercy. The WCG lost few members over its doctrinal change regarding healing because, I believe, most members had already arrived at a more balanced view based on their own personal experiences.

After the smoking issue was handled, I remember that Rod showed me my room and the bed I was to have. I began to stow my things and noticed Rod preparing for sleep. Instead of hopping into his bed, Rod laid a bedroll on the floor and lay down to sleep. I did not think it appropriate to question a senior at "God's college" about why he was doing what to many would have appeared as strange. Instead, I assumed this man of God was following the example of Jacob, who on his flight from home to avoid Esau's wrath slept on the ground, taking a rock for a pillow. I was ready to follow such a godly example, so I prepared my own bed on the floor (minus a rock pillow) and stretched out to enjoy my first evening growing closer to God. The night was miserable because the floor was incredibly hard. I tossed and turned all night and awoke with a stiff back. But this did not deter me from walking in the footsteps of the patriarchs. I spent night number two in the same manner. Finally, on day three, when I realized that my poor back could not bear another night of such pious activity, I gave up and retreated to the soft comfort of my bed.

A few days later, I mustered the courage to ask Rod why he slept on the floor. I fully expected him to give me the spiritual answer that I had been surmising. Much to my dismay, he said, "I've got some real back problems, and sleeping on the floor is the only way I can get relief." What a disappointing surprise! Rod was not a holy patriarch after all, but a normal guy with a bad back.

The next morning was Saturday, the Sabbath. I was excited to see how the Sabbath was supposed to be observed because I had visited a Worldwide Church of God service only once. This visit had taken place in Richmond a few weeks before I left for Texas. The local WCG minister called and said he had received word of my acceptance to Ambassador College. He thought I might find it helpful to visit the church once before heading off to Texas. This sounded like a good idea. I don't remember much about that service except that the members were friendly. So here at Ambassador, I expected to see the model of how this special day was to be celebrated. I woke shortly before dawn, unable to sleep because of sheer excitement. After reading the Bible and watching the squirrels scamper around outside the dorm, I prepared to go to brunch at the fieldhouse where the student dining hall was located. Rod told me that this was a coat and tie affair. I slipped into my best clothes and walked about a quarter mile in the sultry early morning air. Not only did I not know what to expect from the worship service, I had no idea what a brunch was either. This only heightened the excitement. It was about 10 A.M. on a clear August morning when I stepped into the dining hall. Many students already were milling around the room, but no one was seated at the tables, which were nicely set for the meal. Paper plates and cups and plastic utensils were used because no dishes were washed on the Sabbath. This day was devoted to prayer,

Bible study, fellowship, and the church service, which I learned to appreciate and look forward to as the years rolled by.

Soon a member of the senior class took a microphone and welcomed us. He asked us to remain silently standing while he asked the blessing on the meal. An often-repeated request during the blessings in those early years was that God would remove all impurities from the food. Where this notion of asking God to remove impurities from food came from, I do not know, but it continued for several years until eventually the WCG found it to be meaningless and recommended that it be dropped. After the "amen," we took our seats. We ate boiled eggs, a fruit cocktail, and sweet rolls. Across the table from me was a sophomore. He had blond hair and was deeply tanned from working in the sun. He introduced himself as Ken and proved to be a very gracious person. He chatted warmly and cordially with everyone at the table. Ken became a dear friend and to this day faithfully serves as a regional pastor of the WCG in the northeast.

Around 11 o'clock, an announcement was made that we could move to the gymnasium through a door at the rear of the dining hall and participate in "Sabbath singing." Another surprise! I wanted to see and do everything, so I joined the crowd that moved into the gymnasium. The gym was a multipurpose facility that served not only for basketball, volleyball, weightlifting, etc, but doubled as an assembly hall. Here students gathered during the week, but on Saturday afternoons, church services were held for students and church members in the Big Sandy area. On a stage that served as the speaker's platform, an upperclassman welcomed us and asked us to take a hymnal and join in the singing. Accompanied by the pianist on the stage, we began to sing songs that were, for the most part, new to me. Most of the songs in the WCG hymnal were composed by Dwight L. Armstrong, brother of Herbert W. Armstrong. Dwight used psalms for many of his hymn texts, setting them to music. Because the Protestant churches were the "harlot daughters" of the false Catholic church, it was obvious their hymns would be unsuitable. Thus, like many other things in the WCG, we recreated the wheel and wrote our own hymns. Dwight's hymns weren't bad, but this inability to use music from other denominations meant the loss of much wonderful Christ-centered hymnody. This was just one element that kept the WCG firmly rooted on Mt. Sinai, facing the smoking mountain with our backs partially turned to Calvary's cross. Since that time, the WCG hymnal has been reworked. Russ Jutsum, a music professor at Ambassador College, composed many new hymns that have helped to bring a New Testament focus to the hymnody of the WCG.

After the first young man led two or three songs, he asked for volunteers from the audience to lead several more. This was repeated several times over the next hour, making a couple points clear to me. First, this was a male thing because none of the women in attendance volunteered nor were asked to lead. Second, I could be called on to lead! That would be a personal catastrophe because I had no concept of what to do. For the rest of the hour, I hovered near the periphery to ensure the possibility of a quick escape should the fickle finger of fate point to me. Later, I learned that typically junior and senior men performed this function. A couple years later, while on an archeological project in Jerusalem sponsored by Ambassador College, I finally mustered the nerve to lead songs before a small group of fellow students after a Sabbath morning brunch. Learning to lead hymns was an important part of training if you expected to go "out into the field" (to serve as a ministerial trainee or pastor's assistant). Most Ambassador men learned this skill, which was later taught to willing appointees (men selected by the ministry for this honor) in the local congregations so we always would have a certain quality of song leaders for church services.

On my first Saturday afternoon, we assembled again in the fieldhouse gymnasium for Sabbath services. Why did we meet in a gymnasium for worship? Actually, the Worldwide Church of God owned few pieces of property because Mr. Armstrong was driven by a vision to preach his gospel to the entire world as a witness before the end came (Matthew 24:14). He expected the end to come no later than 1975, so there was no need to invest money in real estate. According to Armstrong's logic, WCG money was invested in publishing the message of the church in

The Plain Truth and broadcasting it over the airwaves. In the 1980s *The Plain Truth* reached a peak monthly circulation of eight million copies in seven languages. At this same time, broadcasts of *The World Tomorrow* could be heard on hundreds of radio and television stations around the world. In comparison to its size, the media impact of the WCG was enormous. But the downside of this exposure is that more than 25 years after the unfulfilled prophecy of the 1975 arrival of the end-time, the WCG has little to show for its investment in the media. Today WCG members meet in rented facilities such as lodges, Masonic halls, school cafeterias, auditoriums, theaters, and the like. In recent years, some congregations have started to rent from other churches, but most still meet in multi-use settings. Therefore, the WCG is virtually invisible in most communities. WCG members, who usually commute to a central location to worship, do not have a sense of belonging in the local community. The rented hall does not readily lend itself either in facility or ambience to a worshipful atmosphere. Even the luxurious Ambassador Auditorium on the WCG's Pasadena, California, property was designed as a concert hall, not as a worship facility. I believe Mr. Armstrong's decision regarding local church property underscores the relative unimportance he assigned to the local church. We were taught by Armstrong that we were in a local church only to support him in his special role as God's end-time messenger. Joseph Tkach Sr. desired to correct this imbalance and even proposed a building plan to provide local congregations with worship centers. However, like so many other grand proposals, this was short-lived because of a continuing decline in income and greater financial commitments to Ambassador College, *The Plain Truth*, salaries, upkeep on the Pasadena property, hall rentals, Plain Truth Ministries, gratuitous retirement assistance (to date there is no formal retirement fund for employees), and various other administrative expenses. Consequently, local WCG congregations find themselves in an economically disadvantaged or impoverished circumstance because all contributions are sent to WCG headquarters in Pasadena and redistributed from the central office.

That first Sabbath service in Big Sandy was a joyous occasion for me. There must have been 900 people assembled in the hall— all dressed in their finest. Huge fans were mounted on the walls to keep the air circulating and offer a little comfort in the hot, humid room. The men carried their briefcases, which held Bibles, note pads, and writing instruments. The married women would have kids in tow, arms full of blankets for the children to sleep on and toys or coloring books to keep them quiet and busy when they were awake. There was no special service for the kids because children were expected to be in service with their parents. In the last 15 years, efforts have been made in the WCG to offer the children biblical instruction on their level.

The Sabbath service began with hymns, which were unfamiliar to me. Following the hymns was an opening prayer and a sermonette. (In the WCG at this time, the sermonette was a 10- to 15-minute message on a particular topic such as an explanation of difficult passage of Scripture, a lesson on Christian living, or perhaps a spiritual insight from the life of a biblical character. Many contemporary WCG congregations have dispensed with sermonettes.) The sermonette was followed by another song, a long period of announcements, a musical performance by the choir or soloist, and finally a long sermon. I do not remember the topic of that first sermon, but I do recall checking my watch frequently to see if it had stopped. The sermon seemed to go on forever. When the last amen was spoken, the service had lasted two hours. That was a real surprise because Venerable Street Baptist had managed to wrap up everything in an hour. But the people around me seemed content with the two-hour format, and I quickly realized that I would have to be as well.

In the early 1990s, I was asked to pilot a new worship format in a small WCG congregation near Pasadena. It had become obvious to the WCG leadership that the time for change had arrived. The sermon was shortened to 45 minutes, more music and prayer was added, and the resulting service format lasted about 90 minutes. The WCG has gone through a state of flux regarding its worship service, which caused additional stress on the membership, but it appears to have settled into a non-liturgical evangelical worship format that emphasizes praise hymns and centers on the sermon.

The issue of worship is one that concerns many thoughtful Christians. Much of what passes for worship today is human-centered, driven by a conscious or unconscious desire to offer an experience with elements of entertainment that will make it more "culturally sensitive." Such practices are in sharp contrast to traditional worship, which is viewed as *Gottesdienst*, or God's service to the worshiper through the Word and Sacrament. Central to traditional worship is the objective justification won by Christ. This is in contrast to contemporary worship, which is based on the subjective side of justification—the sanctification of the individual. In most contemporary worship formats, the worshiper is viewed as "serving God" while concentrating on ways to become more God-pleasing. There is a saying that "prayer shapes faith"— that the way we worship will impact our doctrine and our doctrine will determine how we worship. The first Christians were mostly Jewish converts. They clung to many traditions of the synagogue worship, though in "Christianized" form. As the church grew and spread, different traditions, church festivals, and forms of worship were developed to provide a structured framework for proclaiming, teaching, and sharing the Good News of Jesus Christ. Unfortunately, so much of contemporary worship is driven by worshipers' feelings and emotions instead of a need to hear objective scriptural truth about what God has done for us in Christ.

Sometime during my first week at Ambassador College, all new freshmen were assembled for an orientation speech by Mr. Armstrong. We gathered in the large meeting area formed by opening the partitions between the small rooms at the back of the dining hall. This was the first time I laid eyes on Mr. Armstrong. He was about 5-feet, 6- or 7-inches tall. He was pleasantly portly with white hair and round-rimmed glasses. After one look, you knew he was a man of authority who possessed self-confidence and a knowledge of where he was going in life. His suit was visibly well tailored, and everything on his person was immaculate and neat. As Mr. Armstrong spoke, his deep voice resonated with warmth and friendliness, and he put us at ease with his welcoming words. He spoke for at least 30 minutes about the church and its work and the opportunities that awaited us as Ambassador students. The only thing that has stuck with me over the years was his statement: "You will have travel opportunities beyond your wildest dreams." This was exciting and hard to imagine because I had just traveled 1,500 miles from Virginia to Texas—the longest trip I had made in my life. Mr. Armstrong's statement certainly came true for me. In 30 years with the WCG, I traveled to many parts of the world and was privileged to visit many congregations, foreign offices, and ministers. Mr. Armstrong believed that travel was an important part of education, so he made certain that hundreds of Ambassador students had the opportunity to visit many parts of the world.

As a student, I saw Mr. Armstrong fairly regularly, especially during my final two years, which I spent at the church's English campus in Brickett Wood, Hertsfordshire, just north of London. Mr. Armstrong had a special love for England and enjoyed visiting the Brickett Wood campus. We would see him strolling around the campus, hear him at student assemblies, or listen to him at Sabbath services. Students had fairly easy access to Mr. Armstrong. He did not mind if someone joined him on a stroll or sat with him at a student activity. He seemed to enjoy the company of the students and always spoke to us in a warm and fatherly manner. It sometimes astonished me to consider how open he was when speaking to me, after all, I was a lowly student! But from what many have said about him, Armstrong was open with most people, which was a strength that endeared him to many people. It was common for Mr. Armstrong to share his thoughts about doctrinal matters with us after church services. Or he would present his ideas about new directions for the "Work." This openness earned him our trust and confidence because we never felt as though he were holding out on us or had some secret agenda. It was easy to believe in Mr. Armstrong because he was willing to share with us, including some of the mistakes he had made. On such occasions, he would apologize and accept responsibility for things that had gone wrong. Subsequent administrations have been less forthcoming with such admissions of error.

During orientation week, students registered for classes, which was the opportunity for which I had been waiting. One of my early interests was the study of foreign languages. In my sophomore and junior years in high school, I took Spanish and became quite proficient. Then I bought books and records (those were the days before audiocassettes) to study Russian, Greek, Italian, and Esperanto. I had a special interest in German, but it was not offered in high school, so I studied on my own with the help of my neighbor Mr. Marx. But here in Texas, I could begin formal training in German under the tutelage of the dean of students. He helped launch my career in the WCG Foreign Service and helped sponsor my transfer to the English campus, which brought about my first contact with the German regional director of the WCG.

When I left Richmond, I also left my girlfriend, Lynn, who had promised to follow me to Big Sandy after a year. Alas, as true love among teenagers often does with a little time and distance, Lynn and I drifted apart, and she went to a women's college in Virginia. We wrote each other for a while, but the relationship eventually faded, and the girls at Ambassador became more interesting. Eventually I learned that the girls at Ambassador or in the larger Worldwide Church of God were not only more interesting, they also were the only option. Armstrong understood Paul's admonition in Corinthians not to be unequally yoked with unbelievers as a statement against dating or marrying someone of another faith. Because the Worldwide Church of God was "the one and only true church," the logical extension of that reasoning was that WCG members could date and marry only one another. This prohibition on marrying Christians of other denominations has since been lifted.

At Ambassador, there were some clear rules on dating. First, underclassmen were allowed only one date per semester with the same person. As upperclassmen, the frequency was increased to three times a semester with the same person. During your last semester as a senior, you could date as often as you wanted. If you exceeded the limit, somebody always would make sure a faculty member heard of the infraction. Then you would receive an invitation for a chat with the dean of students or another faculty member. Each dorm had a monitor chosen from among the upperclassmen. The girls had to sign out and note who they were with when they left the dorm at night. If the girl was honest, and most were, it was easy to see when a couple was spending "too much" time together. One reason for the strict dating rules was to prevent senior men from marrying freshmen and sophomore girls. Apparently several men heading into the ministry had married younger women, which Mr. Armstrong deemed problematic because he wanted a minister's wife to have at least three full years at Ambassador so she could better serve with her husband. The big question was what constituted a date. I had considered a date to be a guy asking a girl to a dance, movie, etc. Ambassador faculty, however, defined a date as spending time together. This definition did not leave much wiggle room when it came to spending time with a young woman. But we developed clever ways to walk with someone between classes, or eat together in the dining hall, or visit in the library while "researching." Of course, the faculty was not dumb, and if one persisted in pushing the limits, an invitation to a private conference was forthcoming. We were advised that it was best to date widely and not become involved romantically before the time was right. On the surface this sounds reasonable, but in practice the faculty members became police officers, who not uncommonly extended their involvement to the role of matchmaker. The matchmaking took place in the senior year when the faculty strove to help the "right" people get together. This oppressive and intrusive involvement in people's lives made life miserable as young people "perfect" for each other married on the advice of well-meaning faculty members, but were divorced years later.

There were all kinds of rules regarding dating, including signing in and out when one left campus, how late one could be out, holding hands, kissing, etc. Holding hands was definitely out. And if you kissed someone before the second semester of the senior year, you could easily be expelled. Some of us referred to this as "the kiss of death." In my four years at Ambassador, only a few people were caught breaking the rule, and they were expelled.

Dating was not the only part of campus life that occurred under close supervision. Another was dress. The women had to be careful of skirt length. In the late 1960s, miniskirts were the rage, but not at Ambassador. Mr. Armstrong believed that modesty called for skirts to be no more than one and one-half inches above a woman's knee. Either the dorm mother or the young women themselves measured the skirts to make sure the rule was followed. My wife tells me that everyone was careful on this point lest they receive a tongue lashing for their impropriety. Make-up was out as well because that was viewed as tantamount to harlotry.

One can learn from these experiences that legalistic control does not change a person's heart and often leads one to break the laws. This results in personal feelings of guilt and shame, as well as public censure if caught. I have found that people usually will live up to the level of trust placed in them or, conversely, will sink to the level of distrust. But the guiding principle at Ambassador seemed to follow an old German expression that roughly translates to: "Trust is good, but control is better."

This Orwellian effort was made to ensure that we lived godly and moral lives. The theory was great, but some people were burned along the way. This spiritual "sheriffing" is practiced in countless congregations. Well-meaning pastors, priests, and church elders seek not only to define, but also to police our walk with Christ. No end of ingenious means are employed, including "rules of accountability" and public signing of covenants and pledges. It seems we have little faith in Christ through the power of the Holy Spirit to transform our lives to become God-pleasing. Thus we establish our own "heavenly police squad" to enforce godly living in all, similar to what John Calvin attempted in his conversion of Geneva into a model Christian city. The result, however was the creation of a christianized Big Brother society.

Building character, being humble, and having a good attitude were trumpeted constantly at Ambassador College. The motto was "recapturing true values." However, I never recall any-one defining exactly what those "true values" were. We assumed that all those things we were made to do on the road to perfec-tion constituted the true values. Since our understanding was that eternal life depended not only on Christ's sacrifice, but also on our own efforts to build character, we strove to chisel away at any character flaw, real or imagined, that might stand in the way of entering the kingdom of God when Christ returned to earth. Part of the godly character that we strove for was humility. To assist freshmen in the acquisition of humility, we were assigned the lowliest of tasks. Everyone had to work at least 20 hours a week for the college at minimum wage, which helped pay off our tuition and expenses. This was actually a great program and helped many students, including me, work their way through school.

My first assignment was to the janitor crew. No one asked me what I could do or would like to do; I was assigned to the jan-itor crew. (The alternative for freshmen was landscaping.) I found myself scrubbing the toilets in the men's restroom in the dining hall. I worked alongside Marty, a man probably in his mid-20s, who held a master's degree in mathematics from Michigan State University. He had a fabulous attitude as he performed this hum-bling chore. As I worked, I complained to Marty that I was an A-student, a varsity baseball player, a top student in my high school class of 245 students, and I had traveled 1,500 miles to swab out toilets. Marty would only smile and tell me this was a necessary part of our training. If we could work at such a lowly job and keep a good attitude, then we were learning important kingdom lessons. As I consider St. Paul's words that we should be content in whatever state we find ourselves (Philippians 4:12), I think Marty probably was right. The problem with the Ambassador (and the WCG) approach was that circumstances were construct-ed specifically to test us. We were placed in circumstances that would "build" character. Throughout these experiences, we were closely observed to determine whether we had a good or bad atti-tude. A bad attitude was broadly defined as a frame of mind that resisted, resented, or opposed the treatment we were given. It did not take long to get a reputation around campus for possessing either a "good" or "bad" attitude. Those with good attitudes were given greater opportunities. Those with bad attitudes were passed over for promotion, publicly ridiculed, or, in extreme cases, served with dismissal. To be dismissed from "God's college" was tantamount to being cast out of the kingdom, so we suffered much abuse in the name of godly character-building so we could remain at Ambassador.

Now, years later, I see that many described as possessing great attitudes were, in fact, people like me who gave themselves over to the system, agreeing unconditionally with everything that was said and modeling themselves after everything that was done by the ministry and faculty. The word and example of those in leadership positions was considered above reproach, and these leaders were there to serve as our self-appointed spiritual guardians. Many past detractors of the WCG referred to Ambassador students as "Ambassadroids," which implies a certain mindless obedience to those in authority. In many respects, these detractors were right. Mr. Armstrong had sought, at least theoretically, to found a college that would be a bastion of intellectual freedom and thought. He would publicly make fun of state schools, saying that what was passed off as education was merely funneling in knowledge that had to be repeated back without question. But this was how Ambassador operated for most, if not all, of its existence. In the end, we "Ambassadroids" came out of the other end of the system with a great smile, a good attitude, and were ready to unquestionably follow the instructions of Mr. Armstrong and his executives.

This approach to learning was readily observable in our Bible classes. The main emphasis was to learn the "truth," which turned out to be the doctrine of the Worldwide Church of God. Our classes on the life and teachings of Jesus, the epistles of Paul, survey of the Old Testament, and others were used as platforms to teach and reinforce the doctrines of the WCG. Wide reading was not encouraged in the theological areas of soteriology, christology, pneumatology, ecclesiology, etc. because we understood that the authors were deceived and had nothing of value to offer.

Rather, our instructors—who were ministers who held bachelor's and sometimes master's degrees from Ambassador—were considered to possess the true knowledge of God, which may explain why it would have been ludicrous for us to challenge anything these men said. As mostly 18- and 19-year-olds, we did not know much anyway. Most Ambassador students were from WCG families and had grown up in the basic ethos of the church. Ambassador, therefore, only added to and reinforced already-established religious, world, and life views. Within the first couple months on the WCG East Texas campus, I found out that I belonged to the small group of non-WCG students known to the WCG students and faculty as the "black sheep." There were only eight of us in my class, so we were far outnumbered by the church kids, yet we managed to march to the same drummer that they did.

I enjoyed all my Bible classes. Because I was ignorant of the bigger theological and psychological picture, I enjoyed four blissful years of college. It was fun to learn the "correct" interpretations of Scripture. We wrote laborious notes in our wide-margined Bibles, copying statements from Mr. Armstrong and other leading ministers as they expounded on Holy Writ. The most difficult passages of Scripture were addressed in the so-called 900-series letters, which many of us young men in speech class committed to memory. Through a system of Bible marking, I was able to chain reference a response to a "difficult" passage throughout the pages of my Bible. What was a difficult passage of Scripture? In broad terms, it was a text that seemed to contradict what the church taught. But there was always an explanation, we were assured, and one was always found. The fact that Mr. Armstrong and the faculty of Ambassador College seemed to know all the answers impressed me! They never seemed to be stumped by any question, regardless of its difficulty. Even the vaguest prophetic material offered little challenge to the "keen" biblical insight that had been given to the leadership of the Worldwide Church of God. This became further proof for the veracity of the claim that the Worldwide Church of God was God's one and only true church.

Speech training was a core part of my Ambassador experience. All male students had two years of public speech training. Female students were required to participate for only one year. As a male student, if you were proficient in oral communication, did well in Bible class, and had a good attitude, then you could be admitted to advanced speech classes designed to prepare students for the pulpit. Of everything Ambassador College offered, the courses on public speaking have been of lasting value to all graduates. Even some who attended Ambassador and later left the WCG to become critics of the fellowship often admit that the speech training helped them greatly.

We learned to speak powerfully and persuasively in the most difficult situations. For example, in the second-year speech class at the British campus, the men had to give a speech at London's Hyde Park. That was the ultimate challenge! The speaker would stand on a platform and hail passing pedestrians. In the English tradition, this sort of activity is regarded with cynical delight as a public sport. The audience loves to listen and respond with catcalls and "hear, hear!" At the Texas campus, we had to give the "disinterested audience" speech to classmates who had been instructed to be rude, noisy, and disruptive. We also had to deliver an "attack" speech in which we selected some evil in society and railed against it. One humorous example of an attack speech happened shortly before I arrived at Ambassador. The young man was attacking the evils of pornography, and to underscore the heinousness of this sin, he unfolded a large full-color picture of an attractive nude woman. It was quite a showstopper!

As part of the speech training, we learned to evaluate speaking. We looked for interesting introductions; clear, specific purpose statements; logical content development; and an appropriate conclusion. We also studied body language, tone of voice, and the proper attitude to accompany a speech. The evaluation process had positive and negative results. Positively, we were taught to think critically when listening to a speaker. Whether what was said was true was easily determined by how the message corresponded to our worldview. Negatively, we had to focus on attitude, which was difficult to evaluate. Because attitude is purely subjective and no one can know another person's heart, we were being prepared for a lifelong penchant for judging others. We considered ourselves to be insightful in discerning another person's attitude based on body language, word choice, and voice inflection. Later in my ministry, I realized how damaging this was in our interpersonal relationships.

Another part of the speech training for men was compulsory participation in an evening activity called Ambassador Club, which was modeled after Toastmaster's Club. Once each week we continued to strive to become excellent speakers. It was at one of these gatherings that I had my first experience with beer, which was allowed at certain activities. Drinking in moderation was allowed because the Bible calls drunkenness a sin, not the consumption of alcohol. However, if someone became intoxicated, he or she was immediately expelled, which happened a couple times during my Ambassador experience. I knew a couple of guys who overdid it and disappeared from college immediately. We would ask one another, "Hey, what happened to . . . ?" Soon someone would know the story and tell everyone. Such overnight disappearances struck fear in my heart and made me all the more determined not to step over the line.

One evening in the Ambassador Club, along with our meal each of us received a can of Budweiser. I didn't know what to do because I had never had a beer and had grown up with a dim view of the substance. Some of my friends saw my puzzlement and offered to relieve me of my problem. I gave the beer to the first guy who asked me for it, but I didn't know what I should do in the future. The future took care of itself when my roommates realized I needed to be initiated into the fine art of beer drinking and made sure over the next weeks that I acquired a taste for Bud.

Ambassador's policy on alcohol changed periodically, vacillating between prohibition and freedom. We were "wet" for most of my first year until the freshman class sponsored a dance. In our enthusiasm to do a first-class job, we made sure several kegs of beer were available. All went well until some students imbibed a little too much and allowed themselves the liberty of dancing more closely with their dates than the faculty thought appropriate. Although no one became intoxicated, within days the student body was raked over the coals for its libertine behavior and we freshmen were told that we were the worst class to appear at Ambassador. Without knowing better, some of us took that comment as a mark of distinction. Prohibition was then enforced and remained so until some point during my sophomore year.

During September of my freshman year, I noticed a huge tent being erected on a large asphalt parking area near a campground called Piney Woods. I didn't know what was happening, so I was amazed when I heard the college was going to take a two-week break within a matter of days. Finally, curiosity got the better of me, so I asked my work supervisor what was happening. "We're getting ready for the Feast of Tabernacles," he responded.

"What's that?" I asked, absolutely puzzled. My 20-something boss patiently explained in some detail that the Feast of Tabernacles was an eight-day religious festival. I eventually learned that by keeping the Feast of Tabernacles, along with the other holy days of Leviticus 23, Armstrong claimed to have understood the entire plan of salvation. In fact, Armstrong said that only in observing the holy days of the Old Testament could one grasp God's plan of salvation. In my mind, this was more "proof" of how right he was and how wrong the rest of Christianity was.

To better understand the Worldwide Church of God, one needs to have a familiarity with their previous understanding of the Old Testament holy days. Mr. Armstrong considered the knowledge of the holy days to be an important revelation of God to him. Early in his ministry, Mr. Armstrong and his wife, Loma, became convinced through his study of the Bible that God would have them keep the seven holy days of ancient Israel. In reality, however, Mr. Armstrong came upon his revelation through study of other writings and became convinced that observing these days was God's will for a true Christian. For seven years, he and Loma observed these holy days by themselves, unable to convince those in the fellowship of their church, the Church of God (Seventh-Day), that they should follow suit. As the Radio Church of God took form, Mr. Armstrong taught his followers that God commanded all true believers to celebrate the holy days according to the Hebrew calendar. Consequently, the Worldwide Church of God still observes the seven annual feast days of Leviticus. Admittedly, the WCG today no longer mandates the observance of these days and certainly has ceased to connect them to the apocalyptic events of Revelation. The WCG is making an effort instead to connect them to Christ and His ministry, however tenuous the link may be.

The following is the manner in which Mr. Armstrong explained the various feast days. The first three feast days fell in the spring of the year, which corresponded to the early rains and spring harvest in Palestine.

PASSOVER

This was the first holy day of the Hebrew calendar. As Israel was delivered from slavery in Egypt by the power of God, so we Christians are delivered from sin through the sacrifice of Christ, the New Testament Lamb of God. This is the one time in the year when WCG members take the elements of the Lord's Supper (unleavened bread and wine) and practice foot washing. Today the WCG allows more flexibility in the frequency a congregation may partake of the Lord's Supper.

The Passover observance is preceded by what the Bible calls the "Night to Be Much Remembered," which commemorates the night on which Israel left Egypt. We never understood this evening to be "holy." Rather, it was an occasion ordained by God so Israel's freedom would not be forgotten. Somehow the logic does not hold that the evening's observation could be commanded, yet not pronounced holy. However, illogic never stopped us from faithfully observing and doing those things we believed to be God's will. Members generally gathered in one another's homes for a common meal. In later years, the church permitted members to gather at a restaurant if private accommodations were available. The host was encouraged to remind everyone at the table why they were gathered. In later years, this format was revised to permit only the host to ask a blessing on the meal, lest he overstep his boundaries and assume a ministerial posture. The WCG had a real concern that someone would "lift himself up" and preach at his guests. Further, it was felt this type of instruction was more appropriately the role of an elder, not a layperson. To a Jew, the evening would have seemed similar to the celebration of the Passover Seder. I always enjoyed the evening as we gathered with other church members to celebrate and look forward to the festival days.

THE DAYS OF UNLEAVENED BREAD

The Israelites were to put all leavened products out of their dwellings during the seven days of this festival. In the Bible, leaven is understood as a symbol for sin. Christians, then, are to put sin out of their lives. For members of the WCG, the Feast of Unleavened Bread was and is spoken of in the short form of "UB." Members traditionally put all leavened products out of their homes and eat only unleavened bread for seven days, outwardly symbolizing their inward desire to rid themselves of sin. UB traditionally has been a time of intense self-examination and repentance. Orthodox Christians understand this season in light of Lent, but the major difference is the emphasis on Christ's work, not our own. In the Lenten season, we remember the faithfulness of Christ in working purification in us through forgiveness, which He won for us on Calvary. Past WCG practice focused on individuals' efforts to cleanse themselves of sin, prompting a works-righteousness approach to personal holiness.

The custom WCG members had of casting out leaven always brings to mind the extremes of some people as they observe the letter of Law. One friend even soaked his toaster in water and threw out his oven to make absolutely sure no breadcrumbs remained in his apartment! This was an extreme and the vast majority of the WCG membership were not so fanatical. The word "thorough" better describes most members. We did remind members, though, not to forget to look in the freezer, the car, the cuffs of men's trousers, and certainly not to forget the vacuum cleaner bag! Our understanding of removing leaven from our lives for seven days did present some interesting questions regarding what is really leavened. For example, what about beer (brewer's yeast), whipped cream (like leaven, it is "puffed up," which is what sin does to us), or dog food with leavening? What if you work in a restaurant and must serve bread? What if your mate is a non-believer? The church provided answers to all these questions and many others regarding leaven. This may appear a bit odd, but through this rigorous approach to obedience, we were given a clear focus on sin and the need to put it out of our lives. Just as God had intended, we sought to find the "leaven" of sin in our lives, repent of it, and with God's help seek to expunge it. This activity also highlighted the human penchant for works-righteousness rather than resting in the assurance of forgiveness of sin through Jesus' perfect work. As humans, we find it difficult to accept the simple offer of forgiveness in Christ without connecting it to the need to do something ourselves. To imagine that we could add to the work of Christ by performing some type of penance diminishes the power and efficacy of His sacrifice. But the Holy Spirit calls us to confident faith in the statement of Christ: "Whoever believes in Him is not condemned" (John 3:18).

In the early years of the WCG, Mr. Armstrong had all the members gather at a central location for seven days to celebrate Passover and UB. By the time I arrived at Ambassador, this practice had been dropped because of the hardship it caused members who could not be absent from jobs for an extended period of time. The binding guideline at the time I arrived at Ambassador in 1967 was that we had to gather on first and last holy days of the seven-day feast.

PENTECOST

This feast follows 50 days after the weekly Sabbath that falls during the seven-day Feast of Unleavened Bread. (The counting of Pentecost became a divisive issue within the WCG in the early 1970s.) For the WCG, this day symbolized the coming of the Holy Spirit and the harvest of the firstfruits of God's salvation plan. The Holy Spirit was viewed not as a Person of the Trinity, rather

He was the "power of God" that would enable people to get sin out of their lives and keep God's law more perfectly. We considered ourselves to be the firstfruits, believing that all others would come to salvation at a later time, which was depicted in the holy days celebrated during the fall.

The autumn holy days were four in number and symbolized the completion of God's plan of salvation when all humankind, with the exception of a very few, would receive salvation. Members of the WCG looked forward to these days because they involved travel to a nice place, renewing contact with old friends, and making new friends, and being charged up by powerful sermons that pointed to exciting prophecies that would be fulfilled "just around the corner."

THE DAY OF ATONEMENT

This feast was certainly not our favorite holy day because we had to fast, spending 24 hours without food or water. We saw the prophetic fulfillment of the Atonement ceremonies pictured in Deuteronomy 16 where the priest took two goats, confessed over their heads the sins of Israel, sacrificed one, and sent the other into the wilderness at the hand of a strong man. Armstrong's interpretation was that the sacrificed goat represented Jesus, the Lamb of God, and the banished Azazel goat represented Satan, who received just judgment for his role in our sins. This was the fulfillment of Revelation 20 where the mighty angel of God chains Satan and casts him into the bottomless pit for a thousand years (Revelation 20:1–3). (The fact that this interpretation found no support in any reputable commentary did not slow down such exegesis.) This event was supposed to take place after the Great Tribulation at Christ's return to usher in His 1,000-year millennial reign on earth.

Fasting was required if one were not to be "cut off from Israel." We did have practical questions to deal with, including what to do about diabetics, young children, and nursing mothers. But Mr. Armstrong conferred with his top ministers and gave guidelines to deal with all the questions that came up. WCG children were not forced to fast, but they were encouraged to follow their parents' example when they felt ready. As children, my sons, Rhett and Dustin, tried it, but Rhett vomited the first time he attempted it. The next couple times, he made it and was quite proud of himself. Our younger son, Dustin, accomplished the fast as well. As time went on, our sons lost interest in fasting, and we did not push them nor make them feel guilty for not going the distance. Because they were not yet converted anyway, we believed God would take that into consideration.

Day of Trumpets

In the WCG, this feast foreshadowed the return of Christ to the sound of the angels' trumpet blasts as described in Revelation. It was a day that depicted the horrors of the end-time struggle between Christ and the beast power of Europe. All people would suffer from God's plagues because of their defiance of His laws and refusal to repent. Billions would die horrible deaths because of the plagues God would rain on the wicked. At the sound of the trumpet, the dead in Christ would rise from their sleep and meet the returning Christ in the clouds. Those of us still alive at the time would be changed in a "twinkling of an eye" to join the ascending saints to welcome back Christ. Christ, with His holy angels and born-again children (born into the God family as gods), would touch down on the Mount of Olives, which would cleave in two to the north and the south.

Where would the righteous be during this end-time intervention of heavenly plagues and the preceding Great Tribulation? Those in the Christian community who hold a pre-tribulation view of millennialism say the righteous would have been raptured to heaven. Mr. Armstrong rightly rejected the rapture as unbiblical. Instead, he taught the error that God's people would be protected in a "place of safety" on earth. After some study of the prophets, Mr. Armstrong became "almost" convinced that this place of safety would be the ancient deserted Rock City of Petra in Jordan. I say "almost" because Armstrong would never say publicly that Petra was definitely the place of safety.

There were numerous theories about how we would get to Petra. One leading evangelist in the 1960s believed God would take the elect there on "the wings of an eagle," which he interpreted to be a fleet of 747 jets. These jets would fly around the world to pick up God's elect and transport them to the safety of the Trans-Jordanian Desert Mountains. This was heady stuff! I was excited beyond imagination at the prospect of camping in the desert rocks of Petra and receiving three-and-a-half years of final training before Christ's return. This same evangelist, at Mr. Armstrong's instruction, traveled around the world for years, visiting all the WCG congregations to spell out in great detail how the future was going to be and the major role we would play. He spoke for three or four hours, holding us spellbound with his prophetic insights. He also reinforced Herbert Armstrong's key role in God's plan and exhorted us continually to stay faithful to God's man and thus ensure our escape of the coming horrors. Loyalty to Mr. Armstrong was a large part of our Christian life and gave us the confidence of following God and enjoying His blessings and protection. Such loyalty to one man is another insidious earmark of a religious movement gone astray. Later, Joseph Tkach Sr. "retired" this particular evangelist, cut back his speaking engagements, and put restraints on his subject matter. These changes were too much for this man who was consumed by his own religious fantasies. He eventually left the WCG and joined one of its splinter groups more compatible with his prophetic worldview.

Regarding this "place of safety," the WCG experienced the extremes that such prophecy/fulfillment motifs can engender. Some people would stockpile food and have clothes packed and ready to go. One couple even secured visas for a trip to Jordan. By the early 1970s, Garner Ted Armstrong, Herbert's youngest son, was speculating openly that there was no single place of safety, rather God would protect His people wherever they were. This made sense, but it poured cold water on our excitement about the coming years of training in Petra. Most discounted Ted's view and sided with the elder Armstrong, who continued to support the Petra position.

During Armstrong's extensive world travels, he met with King Hussein of Jordan on one or two occasions. And until the mid-1990s, the WCG-supported Ambassador Foundation also participated in a project to help handicapped children outside of Amman, Jordan. We expected Mr. Armstrong to be led by God to negotiate an agreement with King Hussein to grant us access to Petra. Or at least we listened eagerly for some news that the king had started a massive building project that would house us for the three-and-a-half years we would be there. But nothing ever came of these meetings, and the WCG leadership eventually rejected the entire concept of the place of safety in general and Petra in particular. There are, no doubt, still WCG members who hope of an escape to a place of safety wherever it may be. I would encourage them to focus on Jesus Christ, the author and finisher of their faith, who tells us through St. Paul to keep our eyes on things above, not on things below (Colossians 3:1). Men and women of God in the New Testament are rarely concerned with escaping the trials and tribulations of this world; rather, they trust their Lord to see them through the tough times, believing that when they close their eyes for the last time, they will be received into the arms of the Son of God.

FEAST OF TABERNACLES

This was the grandest of the feast days because it meant leaving home and traveling to a resort area for seven days plus an eighth day known as the Last Great Day. The children loved it because they got out of school, traveled, and saw new and different things. In its heyday, some 150,000 WCG members and families gathered at more than 100 festival sites all over the world. During this feast, we envisioned Christ setting up the 1,000-year millennial kingdom on earth with His elect (the baptized members of the WCG) taking responsible positions of rulership in His government. Our not-yet-converted teenagers would remain in the flesh and assume important positions of leadership in the New World. This was the government of God ruled by Christ Himself with all of us newly born "gods" (we believed we would be born as gods into eternity) as co-heirs and co-regents. Christ, with our help, would bring this sick world into its Adamic perfection. Based on Armstrong's booklet *The Wonderful World Tomorrow—What It Will Be Like,* we imagined a world ruled by a God's rod of iron and in which the remaining humans would be "forced to be happy" by learning and submitting to the laws of God. There would be no more crime, sickness, war, unemployment, or other negative social woes. The new temple in Jerusalem would be built, and Christ Himself would be present there as rivers of living water would rush out to the east and west to renew the face of a devastated planet, bringing forth life where death had reigned. Sacrifices would be re-introduced by the re-established Levitical priesthood so the physical humans could better understand God's plan of salvation. One language would be taught and learned worldwide (probably a version of English purified of all of its vulgar and pagan expressions), and all people would go to Jerusalem each year to keep the Feast of Tabernacles. Those who refused would suffer drought, and it looked liked the Egyptians would refuse and thus serve as an example for the rest of the nations (Zechariah 14:12–19). This was the time the prophet Isaiah spoke of when he said the lion would lie down with the lamb and a little child would lead them (Isaiah 11). This wonderful picture of the "world tomorrow" became the official seal of the church and Ambassador College. (In recent years, the WCG has adopted a new and more befitting seal—a globe within which stands the cross of Christ.) The prophets spoke of this coming kingdom of God in great detail; and we believed all these prophetic accounts would be *literally* fulfilled. There are still those in the Worldwide Church of God who believe some or all of this description of the end-time.

The Last Great Day

John wrote that Jesus stood in the temple to speak on "the last great day of the feast" at the end of the Feast of Tabernacles. The first day of the Feast of Tabernacles (the WCG acronym is FOT) is an annual holy day as is the eighth day. It was on this day that Jesus declared He was the living water of life and all who would come and drink of Him would have eternal life. The WCG understood this feast day to represent the second of three resurrections. The first resurrection was of the saints like ourselves (1 Thessalonians 4:13–18), the second resurrection would be those who had died without the opportunity for salvation (Ezekiel 37:1–14), and the third resurrection would be those condemned to burn to ashes in the lake of fire (Malachi 4:1–3).

Because of Armstrong's unique reading of Revelation 20, his unique interpretation of Ezekiel's vision of the valley of dry bones (Ezekiel 37), and his reading of an obscure verse in Isaiah 65, he understood the Last Great Day would be a period of approximately 100 years following the millennium. There would be billions raised to physical life that would have the Book of Life opened to them for the first time. This is a comforting doctrine that assumes the absolute goodness and fairness of God toward all people and answers nicely the question of what happens to those who have never heard the Gospel.

Several years after Herbert Armstrong's death, the new leadership of the Worldwide Church of God recognized that the meanings he had assigned to these feast days were somewhat fabricated and could not stand the test of biblical scrutiny. Over the last few years, current WCG leadership has tried to move the membership to a more Christocentric view of these feast days. In 1996, for example, they called the Feast of Tabernacles a "Feast of Salvation," referring to the salvation we have in Christ. The WCG no longer teaches that keeping these feast days is a requirement of God for all true Christians, rather that they were fulfilled in Christ. Some success in making these feasts Christ-centered has been achieved, but old habits die hard among some "old-timers" in the fellowship.

It would appear that the WCG will continue to observe these Old Testament holy days as non-binding worship occasions. In recent years, the WCG has introduced traditional Christian celebrations of Christmas and Easter into their church year. Despite mixed feelings about the preservation of such Old Testament celebrations in the WCG, I recognize that as long as these days are not taught as commands, nor seen as meritorious for salvation, and are clearly Christ-centered, the WCG has the Christian liberty to celebrate or not celebrate these feasts. But some members still cling to the former teachings regarding these days. On a positive note, as long as people attend these celebrations, the reformed pastors within the WCG have a platform from which to proclaim Christ, the true Son of God to whom all these Old Testament days pointed.

Armstrong taught that only in knowing and keeping these holy days could one really understand God's plan of salvation. Some WCG members may still believe this. During a 1996 visit to a WCG congregation in Berlin, Germany, some members told me the holy days were "pearls" that God had given to the WCG so they could have a clearer understanding of God's plan of salvation and be of help to the rest of Christendom by sharing such insights. I told them this view of the holy days was false. I related that Christians are able to comprehend God's plan of salvation through Jesus Christ by seeing the deep spiritual message of Christmas, Easter (including Good Friday), and Pentecost. On Christmas we have the message of God coming in the flesh to save mankind from sin; on Good Friday, God in Christ gave Himself for us; on Easter, He rose from the grave to defeat death and assure us of eternal life; and on Pentecost we receive the Holy Spirit, who grafts us into the body of Christ and preserves us to glory. This is the heart of the Gospel.

Attendance at the holy days used to be a "must" in the WCG. If you were a member and failed to attend, it could be grounds for disfellowship (excommunication). Skipping a holy day was, to most WCG ministers, a clear indication of rebellion toward God. Therefore, the individual had to be dealt with lest others grow lax in their obedience to God on this vital point. In the 1980s, I received instructions to address firmly those who had skipped the feast. Regrettably, I disfellowshiped one older woman who, instead of going to the Feast of Tabernacles, fulfilled a life-long wish and accepted the offer of her sons to take an all-expenses paid trip to Israel. I told her that her actions were wrong (so I thought) and that repentance would be appropriate. She was more than 80 years old, her deceased husband had been a missionary, and she could not comprehend what I was saying. Even when I disfellowshiped her, she did not understand the problem. Eventually, she regretted what she had done and I allowed her to return to the congregation. I regret my actions and would have apologized to her for them, but she passed away before I came to see my error.

I was assigned to help set up chairs for the Feast of Tabernacles (FOT) during my first month at Ambassador College. We had to set up about 10,000 chairs. It seemed as though we worked for days, hauling and setting up chairs. My dreams even were about setting up chairs! Early one morning, about 4 A.M., a call came for volunteers to help unload a truckload of metal folding chairs. I was so physically and mentally exhausted from days of work in the tent that I pretended to sleep as some guys answered the call to duty. There was a brief feeling of guilt, but I managed to deal with it nicely and drop off into blissful repose. Finally, after a week or more of preparation, the tent and its more than 10,000 chairs was ready for the arrival of members.

One day before the feast was to begin, it was announced that all freshman students who had need of "second tithe" should come to the business office and receive financial assistance. I learned the second tithe was a second 10 percent that WCG members saved from their gross income to finance their festival expenses. An additional "tithe of a tithe" of that sum was sent to headquarters to pay for the expense of putting on the feast (tent, hall rental, chairs, and a hundred other administrative costs). This "tithe of the tithe" (taken from Nehemiah, I believe) was like a convention registration fee. Of course, I had not saved any festival tithe and had little personal money. This entire holy day and festival tithe teaching was new to me. The business office gave each "black sheep" freshman $20 as a feast gift, which in 1967 was a nice sum. The guys in my room chipped in and gave me another $20. I was loaded! But what would I use this money for? Mr. Armstrong had a clear answer for that question too. Based on his understanding of Deuteronomy 14 and other Bible passages regarding tithing, he instructed us that the second tithe could be used only for consumable festival expenses such as food, drink, and shelter. If you wanted to spend it on something else—clothes, gifts, etc.—it was advisable to check with your minister first. By the late 1980s, that ruling was relaxed and members were allowed to spend their money on whatever they wished. One humorous statement made by a WCG minister in response to the question of whether it would be permissible to buy a wristwatch with one's second tithe was, "Sure, if you can eat it!" After all, everything we spent our money on had to be consumable within eight days. Especially in later years, it became difficult for some members to consume a full tenth of their annual income during the spring and fall holy days, but as opportunities to visit international feast sites opened up, it was more easily accomplished.

During that first Feast of Tabernacles, I had no idea what I would do with so much festival tithe money. I bought extra food for myself and the guys in the dorm—lots of fruit, cheese, crackers, nuts, and more were stockpiled for the eight days of rejoicing. My dorm buddies put in a generous store of beer as well. In fact, many guys were buying booze by the caseload. The college sent a bus into town once a week for shopping, and many men would stop at a liquor store as well as the grocery store. Members also would buy generous supplies of alcoholic beverages for the feast. A few overdid the drinking, but surprisingly almost everyone stayed within the bounds of moderation, though to an outsider it looked more like the Feast of Booze instead of the Feast of Booths, which was another Old Testament name for the Feast of Tabernacles. We were told there were rumors in Big Sandy, a largely Baptist community, that Ambassador students had mountains of beer cans outside the dorms, that they engaged in animal sacrifices, and that there was wild fornication. Because we had little contact with the local populace other than at the liquor and grocery stores, the atmosphere was ripe for such exaggeration

It was at either my first or second feast at Big Sandy that I remember an impressive incident involving Garner Ted Armstrong. A strong wind had arisen during the morning service, and it was announced that a storm was heading directly for the college campus and the tent. Garner Ted led us in prayer, asking

God to spare us from harm and allow us to continue to meet in peace. As he prayed, the wind whipped up and scores of the light bulbs strung above us in the tent starting popping, showering us with glass fragments. We left for lunch and came back for the afternoon service under dark, foreboding skies. Again Ted and others led us in prayer, begging God to have mercy on us. Shortly thereafter the wind died down and the skies cleared. We learned later that the storm had split to the north and south as it approached us from the west. It had severely damaged crops and property on both sides of our campus, but we were spared. This fact impressed me and constituted further proof in my mind that God was with us. In fact, I still believe that in His mercy He was. I have learned in the course of my own spiritual journey that our dear Lord is far more gracious and merciful than I could ever imagine. Undoubtedly many in the Worldwide Church of God wonder if God was with us in those years in shadow. I experienced that an erroneous, even heretical, understanding of biblical truths does not hinder God in showering His mercies on those whom He will. In all that we did, such as our scrupulous attention to keeping some of the ancient ceremonial laws of the Old Testament and adhering to the strict observance of the Israelite holy days, we did everything with all of our hearts to serve our Lord. Perhaps that is one reason why He mercifully has brought us out of the shadows of Mount Sinai into the clear light of the cross on a hill called Calvary.

During those first two years in Big Sandy, I had little contact with Garner Ted Armstrong. He was on the campus often. It was rumored that he liked Texas better than Pasadena, where he had his office. When he was in town, Ted often played basketball on the faculty team. At college dances or singalongs, Ted sometimes would attend to sing with us and for us. He was a good singer and had many other talents and gifts. The church provided him with a lovely house among the other faculty members' beautiful ranch-style brick homes on faculty row. All the homes had a view of Lake Loma, named after Mrs. Armstrong. Ted's home enjoyed an especially nice view from atop a small bluff. Ted also loved to fly, and he even became qualified as a co-pilot on the WCG's

Falcon jet. In addition to the Falcon, the church owned a KingAir twin-engine propeller plane and a smaller single-engine propeller-driven aircraft. There was an airstrip on the college property so the executives could land and take off on campus, which was simply grand to us students. I never once thought about the enormous costs involved in this nor did I question why a church would need all those planes. Later, when I worked at Kellogg's and Johnson Wax, I saw surprising similarities between the way things were run in a big corporation and in Armstrong's WCG. As time passed, I grew uncomfortable with the "corporate image" we portrayed. Joe Tkach Jr., who succeeded his father as pastor general of the WCG, has fairly well erased the last vestiges of the corporate enterprise image from the WCG.

Although Ted Armstrong was popular with the students, when I heard people debate whom they would follow if Ted and his father split, they almost always came down for Herbert Armstrong. Why did this question arise? Perhaps even in the late 1960s there was friction between Ted and Herbert that caused such speculation. A parting of the ways between the Armstrongs did occur late in the 1970s, which was a sad chapter in the history of the Worldwide Church of God. About 1978, Garner Ted was disfellowshiped for the final time from the WCG. He moved to eastern Texas and founded his own church, the Church of God International. Today no one in the Worldwide Church of God pays much attention to him. Garner Ted Armstrong has gone his own way and has had his own battles.

Another interesting and often-forgotten episode in the history of the WCG and Ambassador College in particular was Mr. Armstrong's great interest in health and nutrition. He had studied a little about these topics, and he wrote quite often on the subject in the 1950s and 1960s. One of Armstrong's booklets, *The Seven Laws to Radiant Health,* encouraged us to eat whole-grain bread, avoid refined sugar, and consume lots of fruits and vegetables. At Ambassador College, Armstrong sponsored agricultural research on its own farm with some wonderful results. Through the studies, experiments, and efforts of a knowledgeable and able faculty member who managed the agricultural department, we grew high-quality grains and vegetables on what had once been worthless soil. The food in the dining hall was excellent. We had our own beef, chicken, fresh milk, eggs, vegetables, and freshly baked bread. The Texas campus even supplied food to WCG headquarters in Pasadena. As a result of this emphasis on health and wise eating habits, it seemed that we were a healthy group of people. But legalism knows no bounds, and health, too, became a measure of one's righteousness. To eat white bread or sugar was bordering on sin! Much judging and condemning occurred regarding eating habits, so the church dropped the whole thing, closed the agricultural program, and nothing is said about health in the WCG fellowship today.

During my freshman year at Ambassador, I began to give serious thought to the subject of baptism. My desire to be baptized had never waned, and now, away from home and 18 years old, I realized I could finally take this step. Students were told that if we felt "qualified" for baptism, we should make an appointment with a faculty member who was a minister and undergo counseling. After considerable prayer and wrestling with the reality of my own sinfulness, I called the treasurer's office, which was managed by an evangelist, to arrange an appointment. The day arrived, and I appeared in his office not sure what to say other than I wanted to be baptized. The treasurer put me at ease and talked to me about repentance, the meaning of baptism, and the lifelong commitment I was about to make. He suggested that many who were about to take this important step would fast so they would be better prepared spiritually to seek God's face. I thought that was a good suggestion and wanted to do everything anyone told me to do. After fasting, reading suggested church literature on the subject (including *Just What Do You Mean Water Baptism?*), and undergoing two more sessions with the college treasurer, he said I was ready to be baptized. Naturally, I was overjoyed at this opportunity to have all my sins washed away, receive the Holy Spirit, and begin a new life as a "begotten" son of God. Mr. Armstrong taught that baptism was like being begotten of the Holy Spirit, but rebirth would come at the resurrection of the saints at Christ's return. Although his theology was in error, I did understand that I was a sinner and desperately in need of Christ's atoning sacrifice for my salvation. My life was God's without reservation. An appointment was made for me to be baptized by total immersion near the end of December during my freshman year. It was a few days before Christmas.

The evangelist who had counseled me was not available to perform the ceremony, but the dean of students came in his place. Another freshman girl was to be baptized also. The three of us stood in our street clothes behind the Redwood Building by a large galvanized water tank similar to those ranchers use to water livestock. No one else was present. The temperature was in the 60s. The dean took us one at a time, asking us to step into the water, which was somewhat on the cool side. He spoke the traditional WCG formula to the baptismal candidate. It went something like this: *What is your full name?* (The candidate would answer.) *John Thomas Lapacka, have you repented of all of your sins?* (The candidate usually would answer yes; however, I did have one young man who said he wasn't sure. I suggested we get out of the pool and talk further.) *Have you accepted Jesus Christ as your Savior, High Priest, and soon-coming King?* (The candidate would answer yes.) *Because you have repented of your sins, which is the breaking of God's holy and righteous law, and accepted Jesus Christ as your Savior, High Priest, and soon-coming King, I now baptize you not into a sect but into the name of the Father, Son, and the Holy Spirit for the remission of your sins.*

After we both were completely immersed in the tank, we quickly moved inside the Redwood Building and dried off. The dean then laid hands on each of our heads, praying for us individually and asking God to grant us His Holy Spirit through this act. Our understanding of the laying on of hands to receive the Holy Spirit was based on Acts 9, in which the Samaritans received the Holy Spirit through the laying on of hands. In WCG practice, the literal view of the Bible was the governing norm. Such practice was rooted in a fervent zeal to please God through a diligent and careful observance of His Word as we understood it. Unfortunately, at the time of my baptism the WCG did not understand a lot about baptism.

Looking back on that overcast December day, I am grateful that the Lord led me to repentance at age 12 and kept me until age 18 when I could follow His call to be baptized. I do regret that baptisms in the WCG have not been witnessed nor celebrated by the congregation; rather, they are usually private affairs to which only friends and family are invited. Because the WCG has few church buildings of its own, and those they do own are not designed for public baptism, new members are usually baptized wherever they can find enough water to do the job. I recall how moving the ceremony was at Venerable Street Baptist Church as the congregation witnessed and rejoiced as a spiritual community in a special baptismal service, which celebrated the repentance and rebirth of a sinner.

During the 1960s, Ambassador College offered scholarships for qualifying students from the Pasadena and Texas campuses so they could transfer and study at the English campus in Brickett Wood. Before I left for college, my friend Gus, who lived across the street, and I sat in his backyard swing in Richmond and dreamed about our future plans. Because I was a year older, I would go to Ambassador first, and Gus would follow me to Texas, which he did. Somehow I would get to England so I could continue to study German and spend time in Germany. Gus would follow once again. He was interested in studying French and wanted to go to Paris. We both did exactly as we had planned. In my sophomore year, after hearing the announcement that sophomores could apply for the Brickett Wood scholarship, I did so. Then I fervently prayed that God would grant my desire. During a Sabbath service in the spring semester of 1969, it was announced that selections had been made for two students to go to England. I did not know who had applied other than me and my friend Laura, whom I had nagged until she reluctantly agreed to apply. I held my breath as the minister milked the suspense for all it was worth. Then I heard the sweetest words a person can hear—my name. I heard Laura's name too! (Later I learned that we were the only ones who had applied.) Either right after that Sabbath service or the next week, Laura and I were invited to Herbert Armstrong's house on the Big Sandy campus. I was floating on a cloud as Laura and I were ushered into his living room. There he sat, the white-haired "apostle of God," welcoming us and bidding us to be seated. After that I don't remember any more of what he said. It was probably something about the wonderful opportunity we were receiving.

I was so excited that I called to tell my parents. Although I had left home in a rather un-Christian frame of mind, I had maintained contact with my parents by phone and letter. After my first year, I even went back to visit for a few weeks during the summer. Our relationship had normalized somewhat. In fact, my folks even sent me spending money occasionally, for which I was and am still grateful. Instead of the excitement I had anticipated from my mother, she pleaded with me not to go. She felt it was unsafe. At the time I thought my mother was being unfair. Now as a parent myself, I have experienced the same hesitations when my 20-year-old son, Dustin, called from his Alaskan airbase to say that Uncle Sam was sending him on a 90-day tour to Saudi Arabia.

My father had gone to sea at around 19, so I was preparing to follow in his footsteps. At age 19, I was poised to strike out into the world of international travel and see what God would have me do. In fact, international travel became a large part of my experience with the Worldwide Church of God. But in the summer of 1969, I was prepared to "go into all the world."

ENDNOTES

1 Johnson, David, and Jeff Vanvonderen, *The Subtle Power of Spiritual Abuse* (Minneapolis: Bethany House, 1977).

Chapter 4

Go into All the World

Ignorance is the mark of the heathen, knowledge the mark of the true church, and conceit the mark of the heretics.—Clement of Alexandria (*Stromateis I*)

I spent the last days of my sophomore year preparing for the trip overseas. For Laura and me, going to Europe was a first. We had to get passports, money orders, complete last-minute shopping, etc. Part of the scholarship included a four-day stop in New York City, where we met four other Ambassador students from the Pasadena campus (two men and two women). Traveling abroad and experiencing a multitude of cultures was consistent with Mr. Armstrong's desire for Ambassador students to be well rounded and able to hold their own in any social setting. Although not every Ambassador student achieved this trait, many developed social skills that continue to enable them to conduct themselves appropriately at most social levels.

When the big day arrived, Laura and I went to Dallas to catch a flight to New York City. I had said good-bye to Chrisie, the girlfriend I was not supposed to have. Because dating was controlled at Ambassador, having a "steady" as a sophomore was certainly out of bounds for me. But love conquers all—or ignores all! Chrisie had tried to talk me out of leaving her, but my heart was set on adventure. Neither love nor money could keep me on American soil with such an opportunity at hand. We parted with heavy hearts, promised to write, and had the understanding that I would come back for her in two years. We probably both had vague thoughts of matrimony, but at 19 years old, one often has hazy ideas about many things.

Once in New York, Laura and I met Tom, Marsha, Zenda, and Bob. With the exception of Bob, we became and remained close friends for years. (Bob left the WCG in the 1970s and spent much of his time and personal resources attacking the WCG.) The days in New York City were a blur of sightseeing, which was led by a faculty member who had been sent as a chaperon. We saw the Empire State Building, Rockefeller Center, the United Nations, the harbor—all the while staying in the Waldorf Astoria Hotel in Manhattan. One evening we were treated to dinner at an exquisite restaurant by the WCG's German regional director, who happened to be in the city on his way from Pasadena to Germany. It was a great experience, and I began to grow more excited about the prospects of world travel. I wanted to see everything, which is not unusual for a 19-year-old. No one gave much thought to the expense, nor did we wonder if this adventure was something the church members would mind funding. In Mr. Armstrong's opinion, which he repeated more than once over the years, it was the members' job to pray and support the church financially. He alone would decide how the money would be spent. To question him was like questioning God because he was God's apostle. Because Mr. Armstrong was not accountable to an elected board, he was able to conduct himself in any manner he saw fit. If someone questioned the propriety of Armstrong's actions or decisions, he usually would explode, chastising the person for being rebellious. We were taught that if Mr. Armstrong makes a wrong decision, it's God's responsibility to take care of it, which He will do in His own time. This attitude has mostly disappeared from the WCG under the leadership of Joe Tkach Jr. Now many WCG members are like other Christians who withhold financial support if they disagree with the direction of church leadership—

which is not necessarily the most spiritual way of handling a disagreement either.

The issue of church government has periodically prompted questions among WCG laity and ministry. Originally Mr. Armstrong was not so hierarchical in his thinking. In the 1940s, Mr. Armstrong published a document under the auspices of the Radio Church of God entitled *Fundamentals of Belief*. Article 14 articulates a more congregational polity, which is what Mr. Armstrong initially had in mind.

> We believe the Church is merely that body of believers who have, and are being led by the Holy Spirit; that the true Church of God is not a denomination, an organization or a political machine; and while each local congregation is to be organized, there is no Bible authority for any super-organization with authority over local Churches . . . In the New Testament, the only organization further than this is a cooperative fellowship based on *love*.

In my opinion, this is sound biblical position. As time progressed, however, Armstrong stated that the correct form of God's government was one of the 18 truths given to him by God. This "revelation" was pretty straightforward. He, Herbert W. Armstrong, was in charge, had absolute authority over the administration of the church headquarters and the local congregations, and was accountable to no one but Almighty God Himself. The practical exercise of "God's government" meant that Armstrong could not be removed from office regardless of his conduct or lack of competency. He could, in turn, remove from or place into office any person in any position anywhere in the worldwide organization of the church. His decisions were final with no appeal to any group, council, board, or body. All major financial, doctrinal, and strategic decisions were his to make. Appointments to executive positions rested with Armstrong and were based on his judgment. He did not believe in committees and felt God personally led him to make decisions in accordance with the Lord's greater will. Criticism or any form of opposition was futile and was dealt with swiftly and completely. The worst punishment imaginable was disfellowshipment (or excommunication, which is to be cast out of the fellowship of God's "one true church"). When someone at the higher executive levels fell from grace, the individual often was "reassigned" to the WCG's United Kingdom office or some other equally faraway site. The new position was lauded publicly as a promotion, but in reality this was a polite means of banishment.

This form of government was passed on to Mr. Joseph Tkach Sr. and has been changed little, if any, in the bylaws. After Armstrong's death in 1986, however, Mr. Tkach Sr. did begin to administer the church more gently and kindly, giving it a more "human" face. For example, Mr. Tkach Sr. felt members had been oppressed by Mr. Armstrong's almost continual demands for contributions. Mr. Tkach Sr. refused to pressure members to give beyond their normal tithes and offerings. Some criticized this position, but Mr. Tkach held steadfastly to this principle. When the financial situation in the church was difficult, he remained tactful and careful in his appeal to members. Having risen through the ranks in the church, Mr. Tkach Sr. entered the office of pastor general with a keen feel for the circumstances of the average church member. Members picked up on this and loved him for his attitude. However, Mr. Tkach Sr., like Mr. Armstrong, was given to occasional angry outbursts from the pulpit when he learned of critical comments about his administration. Although Mr. Tkach Sr. did not want to become pastor general, he felt God had put him in the office and he did the best he knew how to do. He was sincere in his efforts, but he, like all of us, struggled with his human nature. It must have been difficult for him to maintain his composure when some of his most loyal and dedicated people would tear him down. During Mr. Tkach Sr.'s administration, I began to hear more people complain openly about the pastor general's approach toward his critics. This was practically unheard of during the tenure of Herbert Armstrong, who ruled with an iron hand. Unfortunately, like Mr. Armstrong, Mr. Tkach Sr. would occasionally fall prey to the temptation to use the pulpit to claim exclusive autonomy and to castigate his critics. This exemplifies what can and does happen in most organizations when absolute power falls into the hands of one man who makes himself accountable to no one but God. Such lack of accountability in the office of pastor general has been an Achilles' heel in the polity of the WCG, leading to abuse of authority and unilateral decisions, some of which have had long-term negative consequences for the church.

In the fall of 1994, Joe Tkach Jr. succeeded his father as pastor general of the WCG. Although he has the same absolute authority as his predecessors, he does not rule with the iron hand of Mr. Armstrong nor attack his critics from the pulpit. He is far more accessible and ready to hear criticism without losing control of his emotions. Mr. Tkach Jr. has said several times that he plans to change the current bylaws as soon as it is prudent and already has sought legal counsel on the matter. I feel that many in the Worldwide Church of God would welcome significant changes in the government of the church and a clear system of accountability, which would be healthier for the organization.

When our plane touched down at Heathrow in England, we were tired but extremely excited about our future at the church's Bricket Wood campus. The campus in England was opened in the early 1960s. Mr. Armstrong had traveled to Europe shortly after World War II, looking for a promising site for a European college. He envisioned a place of learning that would prepare men and women from all over the world to be trained for international assignments within the church. Despite his doctrinal shortcomings, Mr. Armstrong was a man of vision who continually looked to the future and saw a clear picture of where the church should be going. Through his charismatic personality, persuasive speaking ability, and a good amount of bullying, he could marshal the troops to support his vision. Part of Armstrong's vision was a worldwide "work" that would reach out in several languages to spread the message of the coming return of Jesus to set up His millennial rule. Through his tireless efforts at vision casting, Armstrong was able to rally the membership behind his vision; thus, to a large extent, his dreams became reality.

In his autobiography published in the 1960s, Armstrong wrote that during this exploratory trip, he had found a chateau and property on the shores of a lake in southern Switzerland.

Negotiations to purchase the property began, but for some reason, things did not work out, and the European branch of Ambassador College had to wait until the early 1960s to open. By then, circumstances looked more promising in England, where Armstrong secured a lovely property about 20 miles north of London in Hertsfordshire, near St. Albans. The grounds were crowned with a stately mansion, which had beautiful Japanese rose gardens and majestic cedars of Lebanon just behind it. The church built a modern women's dorm and a sports complex with gymnasium, natatorium, and soccer field/track. The property's rather large stables had been converted into livable housing for the male students. The campus also had a small lake, which bordered the long lane leading from the main road to the buildings that formed the administration complex.

As we rolled on to the campus in the college's coach (English for *tour bus*), it was early June and the campus grounds were in full splendor. The sun shone brightly and everything was a lush green, accented by multitudes of flowers in full bloom. There was an international track and field meet taking place on the campus among teams from all three Ambassador campuses (Pasadena, California; Big Sandy, Texas; and Bricket Wood, United Kingdom). For most of its history, Ambassador College did not participate in intercollegiate sports. Mr. Armstrong believed that Ambassador's high standards of sportsmanship would be compromised through such participation. Therefore, our sporting activities were only intramural, except for an occasional flirtation with intercollegiate play. This restriction didn't bother me nor do I recall many other students complaining about it. Our desires were simple—to be able to participate in sports on a regular basis. We enjoyed wonderful facilities and opportunities for basketball, soccer, tennis, racquetball, weightlifting, swimming, and many other sports. There was a certain rivalry among the campuses, but nothing mean-spirited. (Some Pasadena students occasionally made comments about their campus being the "hub" of God's Work, which was a bit irritating.)

The international track meet was a wonderful success and a great opportunity for travel and crosscultural exchanges. The

English campus offered the added benefit of being the favorite college for church kids from the British Commonwealth and Europe. There were students from India, Australia, New Zealand, South Africa, Scotland, Wales, England, and all over Europe. Noticeably absent were any African or African American students. This fact was the result of the church's teaching concerning race. Mr. Armstrong believed that God forbade interracial marriages. Armstrong was not opposed to integration and fraternization, but he felt the Bible clearly taught that marriage between races was a sin. To afford African and African American students an opportunity at an Ambassador education, they were allowed admission only to the Pasadena campus. Here the problem of interracial dating could be dealt with more easily—students of color were permitted to date only one another. This led to some knotty problems when the occasional student of mixed race came to campus. To solve such social difficulties, an effort was made by the faculty to determine to what racial group a student of mixed-race belonged. This sometimes caused some hair-splitting, but when one lives by every letter of the law, in good Pharisaic fashion, the smallest amount of mint and cumin must be counted and tithed. At Bricket Wood, I was surprised to see, for example, a beautiful but dark-complected East Indian woman. She dated and eventually married another darker skinned man who also was Indian. All this seems bizarre now, but at the time it was part of what we learned to accept as "God's truth." Having personally come from a segregated environment in Richmond, Virginia, I did not find the church's teaching on race to be that foreign. Of course, those affected by these teachings would have a different perspective regarding this shameful era of WCG history. In the early 1990s, one of the first reforms that Mr. Tkach Sr. introduced was a total abandonment of racial discrimination. He rightly taught that interracial marriage is a personal decision, which has no bearing on one's spiritual standing. All previous dating restrictions regarding race were rescinded, both at the college and in the church. Perhaps some WCG members expected a flood of interracial marriages, which did not happen. Race has become a non-issue within the WCG fellowship. If anything, the fellowship currently strives for racial reconciliation in its congregations.

This matter of race and the WCG's past beliefs and teachings leads into the identity of nations and particularly the knowledge of the identity of the 10 lost tribes of Israel. My grandfather first introduced me to this issue when he told me that Americans (white Americans) were descendants of the lost Israelite tribe of Manasseh. Mr. Armstrong was convinced of this "revelation" regarding the tribes of Israel before he founded the Radio Church of God. While he still belonged to the Church of God (Seventh Day), Armstrong studied materials published by others, especially *Judah's Scepter and Joseph's Birthright* by J. H. Allen. As a result of his studies, Armstrong produced a manuscript that eventually became one of the WCG's most popular pieces of literature, *The United States and the British Commonwealth in Prophecy.* Armstrong told the story of how he submitted this work to the leadership of the Church of God (Seventh Day), urging the church to adopt this "new truth" as an article of faith. In his book, Herbert Armstrong sought to prove the modern identity of the 10 Israelite tribes that had separated from Judah, Levi, and Benjamin during the reign of King Solomon's son Reheboam. Jereboam rebelled against the heavy hand of Rehoboam, leading the 10 tribes to establish a separate kingdom of Israel in northern Palestine. King Jereboam led the 10 tribes into idolatry, and they were carried away into Assyrian slavery about 722 B.C. According to Mr. Armstrong, the land of captivity was north and east of Israel and few of these Israelites ever returned to Palestine. Over the centuries, these "lost tribes of Israel" migrated north and west and eventually settled in areas of northern Europe. Mr. Armstrong offered no sources and only thin linguistic parallels to support his claim that "ancient traditions" proved that the descendants of Joseph's children, Ephraim and Manasseh, migrated to the British Isles. From there, the Manassites settled the New World. By looking at God's promises of race and grace given to Abraham and his descendants, Armstrong saw the fulfillment of the prophecy that Ephraim (Great Britain) and Manasseh (the United States) would inherit much of the world's vast riches. Looking at the world of the 1960s and its recent history, Armstrong saw that Anglo-Saxons did seem to have most of the world's wealth and prime real estate, as well as military superiority. Thus, his position seemed to make sense to the WCG membership. Furthermore, Armstrong contended that unless one understood the role and identity of Israel in prophecy, the prophets' predictions of the future could not be interpreted correctly. With this "key" to prophetic understanding, Armstrong was able to state rather dogmatically the biblical identity of modern nations. It's interesting to study the "who's who" of nations in Armstrong's identification of nations. The following is a brief listing.

United States = Manasseh
English-speaking British Commonwealth = Ephraim
Wales = Simeon
Ireland/Denmark = Dan
Norway = Benjamin
Sweden = Naphtali
Finland = Issachar
Holland = Zebulon
France = Reuben
Switzerland = Gad
Israel = Judah
Belgium = Asher
Levi = scattered among the tribes
Germany = Assyria
Soviet Union = Gog
China = Magog
Greece = Javin

Given this interpretation and worldview, we believed ourselves to be empowered to understand the mysteries of the prophets, what had happened to the backsliding Israelites in the 8th-century B.C., and that history would repeat itself when the United States and Great Britain would fall in "10 to 15 short years." Modern Ephraim and Manasseh were prophesied to go into captivity at the hands of the German-led "Babylon revived," also known as the beast power of Revelation. The chief sins of America and Britain were said to be disobedience to the Ten

Commandments, especially ignoring the observance of the Sabbath (Saturday).

Mr. Armstrong was heavily influenced by the Adventist theology of the "third angel's message" of Revelation, which emphasizes proclaiming the law of God with particular regard to the Sabbath. Coupled with his adoption of Anglo-Israelism, this gave Armstrong a unique message, which he determined God wanted him to proclaim to the world. The leadership of the Church of God (Seventh Day) did not accept Armstrong's proposal to support the Anglo-Israelism doctrine. Mr. Armstrong claimed that this led to the break between him and the church. Several years ago, I met John, who was a contemporary of Herbert Armstrong's in the Church of God (Seventh Day). In fact, John had been an elder in the church. He said the Church of God leadership was willing to allow Mr. Armstrong's Anglo-Israelism view within the church body, though not adopt it as official church doctrine. According to John, Armstrong actually left the Church of God (Seventh Day) over the matter of the administration of tithes, not Anglo-Israelism. The Church of God leaders wanted all tithes to be sent to their central office. From there the bills would be paid, including ministers' salaries. John claims that Armstrong felt the tithe should be collected and administered locally.

Because both men are now dead, I do not know who is right. Perhaps the truth lies somewhere in the middle. As a result of this split, the WCG formulated an official theological position against the Church of God (Seventh Day). Mr. Armstrong believed that the Church of God was the "Sardis era" of God's church, which is one of the seven eras mentioned in Revelation 2 and 3. Armstrong claimed that the Church of God (Seventh Day) was "spiritually dead" because it had rejected "the truth"; thus, God was now working with the WCG, the "Philadelphian era" (the church characterized by "brotherly love"). Brotherly love, however, is not how I would characterize my experiences in the WCG. Historically, it has been more of a "I'll love you if you are one of us" church body.

Interesting and tragic in all this is the fact that from the beginning of Armstrong's ministry, he focused on prophecy and the keeping of the Law (Ten Commandments) rather than on the birth, crucifixion, and resurrection of our Lord—the Gospel. I believe that Herbert W. Armstrong was building a ministry right of center from the start. It was not that he *strayed* from the central message of the Gospel; rather, he never was fully grounded in it in the first place. Such a statement may upset some in the WCG; however, I'm not interested in vilifying Armstrong. I want to state scriptural fact. Many people have left the WCG to form splinter groups that adhere to Armstrong's teachings at some particular point in time. Because Herbert Armstrong believed and taught progressive revelation, his doctrines always were in a state of flux. Some splinter groups prefer the Armstrong of the 1950s; others say he had it right in the 1960s, and so on. Each group finds its own most desirable period when it is confident God had revealed the complete truth to Armstrong. After that magic line in the sand of time, each group says that Armstrong became overly influenced by those around him, thus changing truth for error. Many who left the WCG after its reformation in the early 1990s accuse the current leadership of not building on the foundation Mr. Armstrong laid. They are quite right. Armstrong built his theology on a false and ever-shifting foundation. On this foundation, he erected a theological house of cards. The house looked great on the surface and motivated people, but it could not stand the test of time nor withstand the intensity of scholarly scrutiny. I do not sit in judgment of Herbert Armstrong's soul, but I clearly state that his theology was heretical.

Darryl, one of the Bricket Wood students, met us as the bus stopped in front of the spacious track field that was situated in front of the men's dorm. Darryl was an American; in fact, about one third of the student body at Bricket Wood was American. Darryl showed me to my room in the dorm and directed Erich and Everett—two of my friends from Big Sandy who had come for the summer to tour Europe—to their guest rooms. After we settled in, we went to the men's lounge, pushed a few chairs aside, and started an old-fashioned Texas wrestling match. A small crowd gathered to watch this curious phenomenon. Then we heard a proper English-accented student exclaim, "I say, we don't do such things here in England." That killed the wrestling match and served as an introduction to a more rigorously controlled student life than at the Texas campus.

Adjusting to the new culture was somewhat difficult. Everything was strange, like not being allowed to wrestle in the dorm at will. Or at 5 P.M. being told it was time for tea. Upon hearing this, I told one British student that I was not interested in tea. I wanted supper. He looked puzzled, then realized he was in the company of a Yank. In his dry, disarming British manner, he informed me that "tea in England *is* what you Yanks call *supper.*" Despite these "slight" differences, the experience of living in a foreign country has proven invaluable in many ways.

In my first few days at Bricket Wood, I was reminded of the all-pervasive "government of God." I was told to check with the dean of students before I would be allowed to fly to Germany. At first this was puzzling, but it soon was followed by a slight panic attack. Arrangements had been made for me to go with Erich and Everett to Düsseldorf, Germany, to spend the summer at the church's office. I couldn't imagine why I had to "check this out" with the dean. When I spoke with the dean, I was informed that transferring students usually remained on campus throughout the summer so they could become acclimated in time for the start of the new year. All my dreams for a summer in Germany seemed to disintegrate before my eyes! It did not occur to me that this was an invasion of my privacy, but I did understand I had to do some fast talking—which I did. In general, I argued that I had come to England to improve my ability to speak German. Everything had been arranged with the German regional director through the dean's office in Big Sandy, Texas. After my brief filibuster, the Bricket Wood dean relented and allowed me to go to Germany. Within a few days, the three of us were off on an adventure that we have repeated dozens of times during the last 30 years.

As our plane touched down at the Düsseldorf airport, the sun was shining brightly and our spirits were soaring. Erich, Everett, and I—three aspiring students of the German language—were anxious to try our language skills and improve them. The German regional director met us at the airport in his black

Mercedes sedan with brown leather interior. He warmly welcomed us to Germany. As we drove to the church's German office, he pointed out some of the local sites. It is hard to describe the excitement and wonder of a young person who is experiencing the fulfillment of his dreams. Reading, or at least trying to read, the German street signs and billboards added to the excitement of arriving at an important marker in the pursuit of my life's goals. Meanwhile, my friend Gus had begun his Texas adventure one year before my departure for Bricket Wood. Just as he had planned, he jumped right into his French studies. Also as he had planned, Gus was awarded the Bricket Wood scholarship and he followed me to England the next year. From there, Gus traveled many times to Paris. He became fluent in French.

The summer passed quickly as I spent half of each day working in the regional director's garden and the other half in the office handling the mail. I met many German friends, with whom I still am close with today. The regional director was a generous man who made certain that we had a nice place to live and plenty of food. He also provided opportunity for us to travel with him each weekend to one of the German-speaking churches. It was his custom to visit the congregations on a regular basis to give a sermon. This man was of German heritage and had an optimistic, charismatic personality, not unlike Mr. Armstrong. Many called the regional director "Mr. Positive" because no matter how bad things would get, he always praised God for the trials and found a silver lining in the darkest of clouds. I remember one leading WCG minister saying, "If he were to drive his Mercedes off a bridge into the river, he'd come out declaring that this was truly a blessing from God." He apparently was impressed with my work, good attitude, and interest in German because before I left for England at the end of the summer, he told me, "Tom, you always have a home with us in Germany." That was a heartwarming thing for him to say and became an invitation that often led me back to Germany.

During my first year at Bricket Wood (my junior year), I met Linda Dorsey, who would later become my wife. Linda grew up in a WCG family in California, but that is not where she began her life. She was born to Don and Velma Dorsey in Amherst, Texas, a small town about 40 miles west of Lubbock. Don was a cotton farmer and Velma was a mother and housewife who enjoyed studying the Bible and listening to various preachers proclaim their religious ideas. She was a woman who sought to serve God with her whole heart and committed herself to do what she believed to be correct. When Linda was still a young girl, Velma came into contact with the teachings of Herbert Armstrong. She was convinced that he preached the truth. Velma and Don had each been married once before, and these previous marriages made it difficult as she attempted to join the Radio Church of God. From the 1940s until 1974, Mr. Armstrong believed that divorce was allowed in God's eyes only when a strict criterion was met. The criterion was broadly defined as "fraud," which had to be determined by the ministry after reviewing the details of one's marital situation. Fraud was considered to be a situation in which one mate would knowingly and intentionally conceal important personal information from another, such as previous sexual relationships. When such secrets became known to the unsuspecting mate, he or she could petition the church for permission to divorce. We called these "D&R Cases" (divorce and remarriage). Permission from the church to divorce was extremely difficult to obtain. Mr. Armstrong believed strongly in the sanctity of marriage and did all he felt proper to preserve marriage. When potential new members sought fellowship in the WCG, they were asked by the ministry about their marital situation. If there had been a divorce, as in the case of both Velma and Don, it was not uncommon for the minister to tell the prospective member he or she had to return to the first mate. If reunion with a previously divorced mate was no longer possible and the prospective member was now remarried, he or she was told fellowship with the church was not possible unless the current "adulterous" situation was resolved, which usually meant leaving the current mate. This led to the break-up of marriages and families that were ripped apart. The counseling Velma received encouraged her to leave Don and extricate herself from her "adulterous situation." So Velma decided to please God by faithful obedience to the law.

One day while Don was away, she loaded Linda and her other children into the car and left her husband. She drove across the state to Big Sandy, Texas, where she earlier had been baptized by Herbert W. Armstrong. This decision hurt and angered Don and made it extremely difficult for Velma, who now was the sole provider for her children. The WCG classified her as a "spiritual widow" because of her stand for "the truth." The truth, however, was that in leaving her mate, she was without a husband. Once settled in East Texas, Velma cleaned motel rooms and received meager financial assistance from the church to take care of her family. Despite her desperate financial situation, she believed she had followed God's will, which was worth all the sacrifices the decision brought with it. Linda and her brothers and sisters suffered in near poverty as involuntary participants in Velma's effort to live a godly life. Eventually Velma was given permission by the church to remarry a widowed man in the WCG. She moved with her new husband to Pasadena, California, where Linda continued her schooling at Imperial School, the WCG's private school for children in kindergarten through grade 12.

When a D&R Case came up, the local pastor was supposed to meet with both parties, if possible, and "write it up," which meant the pastor had to make a detailed investigation and report regarding the circumstances that had led to a divorce. This write-up was sent to Pasadena for review. There a team of two or three senior ministers would review the report and determine if the persons involved were bound to their previous spouses or not. This process could take months. Until a decision was made, the people were encouraged to avoid sexual relations so they would not exacerbate what might be an adulterous situation. If the word came back that a previous marriage was binding, families were ripped apart. This, indeed, is one of the saddest chapters in WCG history. I must assume that Herbert W. Armstrong meant well, but here was another case of a man with no theological training trying to figure out everything by himself. As "God's man," Armstrong had to decide, and he knew that what he "bound was bound in heaven" and whatever he "loosed was loosed in heaven." He believed this authority had been given to him by Christ as evidenced by Matthew 18, where Jesus speaks of the keys of the kingdom.

Garner Ted Armstrong began commenting during the early 1970s that the church's D&R position should be reviewed. In 1974, a major doctrinal change occurred that, in essence, stated that when one comes to repentance and forgiveness, all past sins are forgiven, including divorce. Thus new members did not have to leave their current mates to return to former spouses. This meant all those who had separated from their mates because of a previous marriage so they could join the WCG had done the wrong thing. For Velma and others like her, this was too much to bear. Her sacrifice had been too great. This doctrinal change—coupled with accusations circulating about improprieties in Garner Ted Armstrong's lifestyle—led her to leave the Worldwide Church of God and join one of its many splinter groups.

During the late 1960s and into the 1970s, Herbert W. Armstrong developed close ties with Teddy Kollek, who at the time was the mayor of Jerusalem. This relationship, along with personal connections by the WCG's Jerusalem office manager to Israeli archaeologists—including Professor Benjamin Mazar—led to an offer to Ambassador College to participate in an archeological excavation at the southern wall of the temple mount in Jerusalem. Ambassador College supplied the dig with hundreds of volunteers during its many years of involvement. In Bricket Wood, I heard about the opportunity to take part in the program and was immediately interested. To enhance my chances of selection, I took a course in modern Hebrew during my junior year. The offer to Bricket Wood students to take this archaeological trek to Israel was good. The college would pay for the trip to Israel, provide room and board, pay $1 a day for the work, provide one semester's tuition free, and offer college credit for participation in the program. I was picked to join the group of about 100 Ambassador students from all three campuses headed for Israel. This program was the start of long, close friendships between Mr. Armstrong and many Israeli officials. It also fit nicely with the church's prophetic views. We talked of finding the "throne of David," which Christ would ascend as the King of kings upon His return. We worked in full view of the Mount of Olives, where the prophet Zechariah wrote that Christ's feet would touch down on His return. Then this mountain would be torn asunder from the north and south. It was a great summer of hard work, touring, and fun. During that summer of 1969, I quite unexpectedly fell in love with Linda.

Falling in love was not something I had planned to do or even wished for at the time. I had had a bad experience with Chrisie, the young woman I had left behind in Texas. We had promised to wait for each other and get together after my two years abroad were finished. But word came to me that she was seriously dating another student in Texas. This upset me because I felt she was breaching our relationship of trust. In addition, I sensed general pressure from the college administration to avoid romantic involvements. We were warned that such involvement could negatively impact our future service to the church. Being an unbalanced zealot, I wrote Chrisie a one-paragraph "Dear Jane" letter that told her rather unceremoniously that our relationship was finished. Because I had been inconsiderate and tactless in dealing with her, another surprise soon greeted me. In my absence from the Texas campus, I did not know that Chrisie had become the dean's secretary. Upon receipt of my caustic "go jump in the lake" letter, she tearfully presented it to the dean, who happened to be a good friend of the dean at Bricket Wood. He sent my letter back across the ocean for review. One morning I received word that the dean was granting me an unsolicited audience. After inviting me to take a seat, the dean—a powerfully built man who could intimidate the most stalwart individual—pulled from his desk a letter, which he began to read to me. It sounded surprisingly like the one I had written to Chrisie. To my horror, it was the same letter! When he finished, he laid the letter aside and asked for my comment. All I could do was tell the truth—I was trying to clear the decks of an untidy romantic involvement. As my last weak syllable of defense faded into the silence of the office, the dean looked at me sternly and told me he had been shocked to receive such a letter. He was disappointed by my lack of tact. He added that if this had occurred in my senior year, the chances of being "used in the Work" would have been slim indeed. I gulped, sputtered, stuttered, apologized, promised to apologize to Chrisie, and left, feeling like the scum of the earth. I learned from this experience to be careful of involvement with women and never to put self-incriminating material in writing. I wrote a letter of apology to Chrisie, but the damage was done. Besides, I did not want to renew our relationship. Being a "disciple" in training, I did not want love for a young lady to cloud my vision or dampen my zeal.

So there I was, working under the hot Israeli sun, finding myself attracted to Linda Dorsey. To make matters worse, she was practically engaged to an Ambassador graduate who was serving as a ministerial assistant in the United States. I dealt with the realization of a possible romantic involvement in typical fashion—denial. I told myself there was no romantic involvement, only a close friendship. And close friends we became. We spent a lot of time together talking and getting to know each other. There was, of course, no hand holding or kissing, but there was a deepening friendship. This friendship concept worked well until the beginning of my senior year. During the Feast of Tabernacles, it became crystal clear that I loved Linda deeply. I knew there was no way she could possibly love me because I was a "nobody." I was not a student leader, not on the Visiting Program, and certainly not on the Sermonette List. (The Visiting Program was a short list of senior men who were allowed to accompany ministers on visits to members' homes. This was almost the highest honor a male student could have. One notch above the Visiting Program was the Sermonette List. This was a still shorter list of senior men who were privileged to give sermonettes in local WCG congregations.) By my senior year, my self-esteem was gone. I considered myself a lowly character who would be lucky to graduate. The loss of self-esteem is another terrible result of legalism with its never-ending list of dos and don'ts overseen by zealous spiritual guides. Many WCG members and Ambassador graduates suffered blows to their self-worth as they were driven to live perfect lives only to fall short time and time again—and be reminded constantly of how short we had come!

After the summer in Israel, I left the main body of Ambassador College students and flew to Paris to see Gus, who had arranged a summer work-study program in France through the WCG's French office. We drank a bottle of good French red wine to celebrate our reunion. After a day or two, I flew to Germany where I worked in the WCG's German office for three weeks to finish my summer vacation. As the start of the fall semester neared, I headed back to England to complete my final year of training. In October at the Feast of Tabernacles, I began to avoid Linda. I could not bring myself to tell her why because that would be too embarrassing. How could I tell my best friend that I had fallen in love with her? That would spoil our friendship. I chose not to talk with any faculty member about this because I expected they would jump on me for breaking the rules. Therefore, I suffered the agony of unrequited love alone. It proved to be a period of personal prayer for me because I sought the Lord's guidance in the matter. I read and prayed through the book of Psalms, which gave me a sense of calm and inner strength. My future seemed straightforward. I would graduate in June, probably move to Australia, and look for work. I wanted to go to Australia because of close friendships I had developed with many Aussies at Bricket Wood. At the time the Australian government was recruiting young able-bodied people to come to their country. There was no girl in my life other than Linda, and it was seemingly written in the stars that she would marry Ken, who had graduated from Bricket Wood the year before and at the time was serving in Washington, D.C.

A turning point in my stunted love life came during winter break of my senior year. Eight female students and a female advisor wanted to visit southern Spain for a week, but only two male students had agreed to go along. The faculty felt that at least two more male students were needed to serve as escorts. For some reason, the business manager stopped me on the way to class one morning and asked if I would be interested in going to Spain. I said yes, but my financial situation at the moment prevented such an adventure. He assured me that all my costs and that of another male student would be taken care of, if we agreed to chaperon the group, which included Linda. What a deal! So I headed off for Spain.

There on the sunny shores in the little town of Benedorm not far from Valencia, my conscience reached critical mass. I had to speak with Linda and get everything on the table. I would tell her I was helplessly in love with her, apologize, and understand totally when she announced that our friendship was over. I worked hard to prepare my speech, then invited her to the balcony sitting area of the hotel foyer. There we made small talk for a while before I finally mustered the courage to broach the subject at hand.

"Linda, I know you have wondered why I have avoided you so much in the last weeks. You see, I think of you as much more than a friend," I stated. That was as close to saying "I love you" that I dared come. I expected to see a flash of anger in her face and receive my deserved castigation for spoiling a perfectly good friendship with this love business.

Instead, Linda turned and said, "Thomas, I feel the same about you."

You could have knocked me over with a feather! Never in my wildest dreams had I expected such a response. An image of the dean's scowling face appeared in my mind's eye. A successful conclusion to my college career seemed doomed because of an unexpected romantic entanglement. With stunned surprise, my involuntary reply came, "Oh, this is worse than I thought." Another pearl of diplomatic tact had issued forth from my seemingly undisciplined tongue and empty head. I felt totally elated, overwhelmed, and at a complete loss for what to do next, which was somewhat out of character.

Before recounting my session with the dean, let's take a look at the subject of self-esteem. It has been WCG practice to discourage any and every form of vanity. For example, Linda is a beautiful woman and was a beautiful girl. When anyone made a comment about her beauty, her mother would quickly remind her, "Pretty is as pretty does." Compliments for a job well done were rare and, if given at all, were coupled with comments about how the job could have been improved. We were reminded constantly to "examine ourselves" for sin in our lives, especially in areas of non-compliance in keeping the law. We were sinners ever on the edge of "not making it" into the kingdom of God because of our weakness of character or our poor spiritual performance. Until only a few years before it closed in the early 1990s, children who attended the WCG's Imperial School were subject to public spanking—even in the high school years. Rhett, my older son, attended Imperial School for a couple of years. He chose on his own to inform the teachers that he would submit to neither public nor private spanking. Only his dad could give him swats; thus, he escaped this humiliation. Our lives were being evaluated constantly by those assigned to police our sanctification. Imperfections and shortcomings were pointed out constantly. We were told that God would not accept us the way we were and that we would have to change to find acceptance. The result was that many of us did not feel secure in our salvation and ended up thinking of ourselves as "worms." Although we were taught that God is love, the daily reality was that many of us felt less than loved and not particularly loveable. Although I do not feel qualified to enter the current debate in the Christian community regarding self-esteem, I do know the negative effects of a hyper-critical church atmosphere. Many of us lived under a dark cloud of guilt, not having fully experienced the joy of forgiveness and the assurance of salvation made possible by the love of God for us demonstrated in the sacrifice of His Son, Jesus Christ. There were precious few sermons about God's great love for us and His grace that frees us from the guilt associated with works righteousness. Instead, we were reminded continually of our need to keep God's commandments so we could please Him. Not everyone experienced the same impact from this approach to Christian living, but many, like Linda, ended up with a negative attitude about themselves, which virtually paralyzed their lives. Only in the last years, have we begun to recognize what this spiritual abuse did to her. With God's help, we have worked against its negativism. The Law—which is holy, righteous, and good (Romans 7:12)—describes and commands perfect righteousness, which we are to attain, but it provides no help in reaching that goal. Thus, we see ourselves condemned before God for our failure to be perfect. That's why repentant sinners need to hear the Gospel message of God's grace and forgiveness through Christ. This is wonderfully summarized in the following poem:

Do this and live, the Law commands.
But it gives me neither feet nor hands.
A better word the Gospel brings.
It bids me fly, and gives me wings.

Although my home life was basically negative, as a young boy and teenager I received from teachers and friends much positive encouragement and reinforcement. Although the WCG's general assault on my self-esteem took its toll, I had enough reserves from my pre-WCG life to give me basically a positive approach to life, though like most in the WCG, I did not have absolute assurance of salvation because I was reminded constantly of my sinful plight. I now understand that Christian self-esteem has to do with who I am in God's eyes because of Christ Jesus. In God's eyes, I am forgiven and justified solely by grace through faith in Christ's sacrifice on my behalf. Martin Luther called this passive righteousness, or alien righteousness, whereby God places a righteousness on us that is not ours, but His. Then He looks at us and does not see us at all, but He sees Jesus' blood that covers us. Therefore, God declares us righteous for Christ's sake, and we are, though we are at the same time sinners as Luther says, "*Simul justus et peccator*"—"the same time sinner and justified." This is the power of the Gospel, which is medicine for the soul. Through profession of faith and Baptism, I am united with Christ. As Paul said, I am "in Christ"; He is my identity, and His love for me gives me a positive self-image because my worth is wrapped up in God's love for me in Christ, not in my ability to keep the Law. I have preached often on God's love for us in Christ. Many who have heard this message have told me of the great comfort and assurance that it gives.

Because of my low self-esteem, I knew the dean would blast me as usual for my lack of spirituality when I told him about my love for Linda. However, the truth had to come out, and it was the right thing to do (according to the college's rules). With a lump in my throat, I began, "I have a little complication in my life that I would like to talk to you about."

With his characteristic raised eyebrows, the dean replied, "Oh?"

"Yes, sir," I continued. "You see, I have developed some deep feelings for a fellow student."

He played his part cool and noncommittal. "And who might that be?" he asked, as though he did not know.

Here was the moment of truth, when the name would have to be given and the entire Gordian Knot would be revealed. How could I possibly have fallen in love with a woman already spoken for by a successful graduate who was serving in the ministry? I was only a little grub with apparently no future in the church. I braced myself for the blast and spoke her name, "Linda Dorsey, sir."

To my surprise, the mention of that name did not unleash the hounds of hell. Instead, it was met with calm and understanding. "Well, you know Linda is currently involved with another guy," the dean said. "I think to be fair to him and Linda, you should stop dating Linda until she can determine what is going to become of that relationship."

That was it? The dean actually was a decent human being after all! We talked a bit more, I thanked him for his time, and left his office with my fragile ego and head in one piece. That was the easy part. What ensued in the following weeks was more difficult. I told Linda what the dean had said, and she agreed that we should stop dating until she could clear her head regarding Ken. Although we longed to spend time with each other, we obeyed the counsel of the dean and stayed apart, hardly even speaking to each other. During this time, I committed myself to a three-day fast so I could come closer to God and seek His help.

I called the rigors of Christian discipline that I learned in the Worldwide Church of God the 30/30/30 plan to righteousness. We were encouraged to pray 30 minutes a day, study the Bible 30 minutes a day, and fast one full day a month. This rather exact formula for righteous living gave us a measurable yardstick for our spiritual growth. Such yardsticks of righteousness are another hallmark of legalism. When I first heard this formula at Ambassador College's Big Sandy campus, I knew the 30 minutes each day for Bible study was no problem. I had several Bible classes in which we read Scripture during class and were assigned homework that required reading and studying the Bible. This easily consumed more than 30 minutes. Praying was a problem, though. It was not that I did not pray—I did. But my prayers were a few words given in thanks or short prayers at the end of the day requesting this or that of God. Ambassador dorms were equipped with "prayer booths"—closet-sized rooms with a wooden bench, sound-proof walls, a light, and a ventilator fan. These provided privacy to pursue our prayer lives. To face the daunting task of praying at least 30 minutes a day, I would take an alarm clock and pillow into the prayer closet and begin. It seemed I had prayed for hours as I praised God and asked for His help for this thing or that person or a particular difficulty in my life. During my prayer marathon, I would stop long enough to glance at the clock and note, to my chagrin, that only five minutes had elapsed. By the time I became a senior at Ambassador College, my prayer life had improved so the 30 minutes were no longer a problem. I still kept the clock close at hand to ensure the recommended 30 minutes were accomplished. Spending this daily time in prayer and study gave us a good feeling, despite the real value it may or may not have had. Despite the obvious legalistic approach to prayer and Bible study, both disciplines did become habits in my life. Now I approach prayer and Bible study from a desire to commune with my Lord, rather than to fulfill a legalistic requirement.

Fasting, on the other hand, was completely new to me. My first fast was on the Day of Atonement in 1967 at the Big Sandy campus. On this feast day, total abstinence from food and water was required so we would not "be cut off from Israel." We were given a last meal of fruit, cheese, bread, and drink around 4 or 5 P.M., just prior to the setting of the sun (Sabbaths and holy days were celebrated according to the biblical time of "even to even," which means the holy period starts at sundown and continues until sundown the following day). On that first fast day, I remember brushing my teeth at least six times so I could wash away the foul taste in my mouth and feel (but not drink!) the water. Once the day was over, we pigged out until our poor stomachs ached—such was the piety of budding spiritual giants! After that I began to fast voluntarily. These fasts were more difficult because I was doing them without the moral support of fellow students who were suffering with me. We were encouraged not to tell anyone that we were fasting lest we lose our heavenly reward. By the time that my second Day of Atonement rolled around in the sopho-more year, I was ready. In fact, on the day before Atonement, I ran a mile in the hot Texas sun and played a couple sets of tennis. Time got away from me, so I missed dinner and only had some water to drink before beginning the fast. That particular Day of Atonement was a killer! I thought I would die and go to heaven prematurely. After the fast, several of us went into town on a date. I embarrassed my companion by overindulging. After we had fin-ished a filet mignon, the waiter asked if he could bring me any-thing else. "You bet. Another one of those!" I responded. My date was overcome with embarrassment, but hunger was king over romance that evening. For some reason, she declined my future overtures.

By the time I arrived at Bricket Wood, I had the 30/30/30 program mastered. But there was one challenge I had yet to meet—the three-day fast. To me, that was the Mt. Everest of fast-ing! During this time of crisis in my romantic life, I determined to go the distance for a full 72 hours. Things went pretty well on day one. Day two began to get tougher. In fact, during the second night I was so hungry that I awoke and believed I saw a fried chicken leg hovering above my head. I reached for it, but it was only a mirage, so it vanished just as my trembling fingers sought to grasp it. Day three was insufferable, but I was determined that with God's help I would get through the day. Well, I did, then vowed never to do it again! And I never have.

My view on fasting has changed. After years of fasting once a month like clockwork, I have reached the point of burnout. New Testament admonitions to fast seem rather thin, but it may be good to do so occasionally as a spiritual discipline. I do not believe the only "acceptable" fast in God's eyes is one in which no food or drink is consumed. It probably is an issue of conscience and health rather than scriptural mandate. I do, however, seek the Lord regularly in prayer and enjoy reading His Word as I did when I was a boy. The Lord promises in His Word always to be near His people. My feeble and sometimes laughable efforts, however sincere, don't entice God to draw nearer to me. He is the one who reaches out to me through His Word and sacraments to draw and keep me close to Him. So much of what I had been taught and believed before placed the onus of salvation on my shoulders: *I* had to seek God; *I* had to become worthy to be received by God; *I* had to "qualify" to make it into His kingdom. With this mind-set, it is only a matter of time before spiritual exhaustion debilitates the individual. What a contrast to the promise of grace and help revealed to St. Paul in Romans 8: 28–35, 38–39:

> And we know that in all things God works for the good of those who love Him, who have been called according to His purpose. For those God foreknew He also predestined to be conformed to the likeness of His Son, that He might be the firstborn among many brothers. And those He predestined, He also called; those He called, He also justified; those He justified, He also glorified. What, then, shall we say in response to this? If God is for us, who can be against us? He who did not spare His own Son, but gave Him up for us all—how will He not also, along with Him, graciously give us all things? Who will bring any charge against those whom God has chosen? It is God who justifies. Who is He that condemns? Christ Jesus, who died— more than that, who was raised to life—is at the right hand of God and is also interceding for us. Who shall separate us from the love of Christ? Shall trouble or hardship or persecution or famine or nakedness or danger or sword? . . . For I am convinced that neither death nor life, neither angels nor demons, neither the present nor the future, nor any powers, neither height nor depth, nor anything else in all creation, will be able to separate us from the love of God that is in Christ Jesus our Lord.

It is passages such as this that give me hope because they make clear to me that my salvation does not depend on my efforts. God is the acting agent, working out His good will and salvation in our lives.

In the spring of my senior year, Linda received a letter from her boyfriend that made her doubt their relationship. She decided to break things off with Ken. It was painful for Linda and Ken, but she felt it was best. Ken eventually married a wonderful woman who has remained steadfastly by his side during many years of ministry. Once Linda told me her relationship with Ken was over, we began to date again. I knew this could mean marriage, but it did not settle in on me until I was with a group of students at a faculty member's home one evening. Our topic has long been forgotten, but something was said that triggered the realization that I was heading to the altar. When I heard wedding bells in my head, I became nervous and felt weak at the thought of the enormous responsibility I was about to assume at the age of 21. Overcome by these thoughts and feelings, I excused myself and walked out into the cool night air, needing to be alone. I walked down the lane back to the campus deep in thought about this life-changing decision. Despite feeling so overwrought, I was determined to go ahead with my plans. I knew in my heart that I loved Linda and wanted to marry her. After four years of dating young ladies from all over the world, I knew this beauty from Texas was for me. Over the years I had prayed that God would provide the wife He felt would best be suited for me. Nearly 30 years later, I can attest that Linda was and is a wonderful gift from the Lord.

In addition to the questions about marriage, there was still the lingering question about what I would do after graduation. My plans still called for a move to Perth, Australia. One night while playing basketball, a student delivered a message from the dean. He told me to get cleaned up and report immediately for an Ambassador Club session. I had no idea what the message meant; neither did the messenger. But to hear was to obey, so I headed to the showers, then to the clubroom. I was greeted by the dean, who introduced me as the new vice president of the club. What a shock! Not long thereafter, I was informed I had been selected for the Visiting Program. This was unthinkable! Suddenly, I was dressed up and calling on members with a local WCG minister. Cautiously, I started feeling better about myself. But I knew from experience that smooth sailing in God's church lasted only a while before the seas became stormy again. Then lightning struck a third time. Again while at a basketball game, the dean appeared behind me and quietly said, "Tom, we've decided to put you on the Sermonette List." This was absolutely too much! I was dumbstruck. What did this mean? In a few short weeks, I had gone from pretty much a nobody to one of the "big" men on campus.

How did all this come about? The answer is simple. The faculty held regular meetings each spring to discuss the current crop of senior men and women. The work of the WCG was still expanding in the early 1970s, which meant a great need for men to pastor churches and to take administrative positions. By my senior year, I had been carefully minding my Ps and Qs, plus I was doing well in my studies. In public speech training, I did exceptionally well as I moved into the area of homiletics (sermon preparation and delivery). Public speaking became one of my strong points. The combination of need, plus my own personal improvement (learning to comply) opened doors. Meanwhile, my thoughts about marrying Linda were vague at best. I did want to marry her, but my future was less than certain, which made it unclear how our romance could proceed to the final stage. We believed that somehow God would work things out for us according to His good pleasure, and He did!

I remember only a few incidents from my visiting and speaking experiences in England. After giving a sermonette, I was expected to ask the minister in charge for an evaluation. This opened the door to have my speaking critically evaluated, as well as my person and character. No one looked forward to this, but we knew "it was good for us." Besides, we could learn more about our imperfections and work to rid ourselves of them. The first minister with whom I shared the pulpit was an Australian. He was pleasant and encouraging. In fact, his advice has stuck with me. In response to my request for an evaluation, he said, "You just have to keep speaking. You'll only get better." The second pastor I worked with was an Englishman. He offered a bit of humor when he said, "My son told me that he wished I could speak as interestingly as you and then he would not go to sleep in church." The third evaluation came from an American minister. He shattered me with the following, "Everyone has a personality. Some are considered lively and outgoing, like myself, others more subdued and inward. But you have no personality." That hurt me deeply. Was it true? Was I cursed with zero personality? I had to know, so I asked my closest friends to describe my personality. My friends assured me that everyone had a personality—even me!

For the first time in my Worldwide Church of God experience, I found myself in disagreement with a minister of God. In fact, I felt a little anger and resentment toward him for such an unkind and ridiculous evaluation. But being hurt was part of the WCG experience. Repeatedly, Linda and I suffered personal evaluations that tore at our person, but we bore it all, thinking this was God's way of revealing character flaws we needed to address. Today I know what was done to us, and what I learned to do to others, was cruel and callous. Jesus is our Good Shepherd who seeks to love, heal, and strengthen us, not tear us down. But some churches tear you down because leaders constantly invoke the Law as the measure by which we are to live. We are crushed by the reality that we cannot attain that perfection, yet we are spurred on constantly by leaders to strive for perfection. When we fail, we are reminded how weak and sinful we are and how we must "try harder" or "wrestle with God" for the strength to be perfect so we might inherit eternal life. Where is the Gospel of grace and forgiveness? How many souls must be bruised, how much hope must be extinguished, how many tears must be shed before these spiritual sheriffs preach the tender mercies of God in Christ, who *already* has forgiven our sins and reconciled us to Himself by His Son (2 Corinthians 5:18–19; 1 John 3:16–17)? If you or someone you know is languishing in a church that burdens its members with Law, draining them of the joy in Christ, find a house of worship where the Gospel of forgiveness in Christ is the core of its preaching and teaching.

As the spring sun warmed the North Atlantic breezes that blew across our beautiful campus, Linda and I had become serious. I thought of buying her a ring, but first I had to seek advice from my close friends. Robert, an American, and Mark and David, two Englishmen, were student body leaders, so I respected their advice and knew they would be helpful and gentle. One night in Mark's room, Robert, David, and I were gathered to discuss the women in our lives. How could I be sure about my love for Linda? Was it the real thing, or was I only being led by boyish emotion? David asked two penetrating questions: "What is it about Linda that you love?" and "What about her do you not like?"

I went on for a while in my answer to the first question, but I could come up with nothing for the second question. Then David added, "Unless there is at least one thing you do not like about her, you don't really know her yet." *Point well made,* I thought. His statement caused me to think long and hard, trying desperately to come up with some flaw, any flaw. I did come up with some little thing, which I have long since forgotten. Whatever it was, it could not cast a shadow on my love for Linda. Even to this day, her virtues make insignificant any frailties she may have. I have learned to look at and praise her strengths rather than ponder her weaknesses. This keeps my fascination and love for her burning strongly.

Our courtship was a model of obeying the rules because we were model legalists by then. From the beginning, Linda and I agreed to follow the college's dating policies. We knew that one day we would look back on our dating and either be proud or ashamed. Our desire was to be pleasing to God in our conduct and to be able to set an example for our future children. I do not know whether our sons appreciate the high standard we strove for in our courtship, but maybe one day they will. As was allowed in the second semester of the senior year, we held hands, had our first quick kiss, which was as far as it went. I can say honestly, though some may find this hard to imagine, we did not desire to go any further. Our love and respect for each other and for God led us to stay within the bounds of virtue. I do not think we were alone in such conduct either. As far as I remember, all my friends conducted themselves in similar fashion. A strong code of conduct kept us on the straight and narrow. I think this was good, though it may sound archaic, even prehistoric, to many modern young people. For all the legalistic hardship imposed on us by the WCG, it did teach us a healthy and high regard for morality, fidelity, and spirituality. I am not saying that every Ambassador College graduate was or is a paragon of virtue, but many were and are to this day.

The last weeks of my senior year rolled by at blinding speed. A couple friends and their girlfriends went to London with Linda and me to shop for rings. Each of us men wanted our wife-to-be to have a part in selecting her ring. My parents had sent some money for graduation, which I used to buy Linda an engagement ring in preparation for the day that I would propose. I do not recall informing my parents of my budding romance; by my senior year, I had mostly shut them out of my life. We corresponded and they sent money occasionally for my essentials, and that was about it. Perhaps they could have given me good advice, but I never asked, so I will never know.

In the last weeks of college, one of our comrades blew it. He had one too many drinks in the Common Room (our lounge and game room) and was hauled home in a drunken stupor by some friends. That was the last I saw of him. What a sad ending for a nice guy, but there was zero tolerance for breaking certain rules, drunkenness being one of them. There was never anything said officially. In a couple days we heard that he had been sent home. Secrecy or information control is another hallmark of a cult. This helps maintain control through fear and intimidation of what "they" know, or what you think they know and might do with the information. Despite the attempt to cast a blanket of secrecy over unpleasant situations, we figured things out anyway. It probably would have been best to say something, but silence was the rule of thumb when dealing with fallen comrades. This would be my experience for most of the time I spent with the WCG. When someone fell from grace, he or she was quickly dispatched. Little or nothing was said officially. The troops knew the poor soul had transgressed and had been cast out. We would speak of it quietly and cautiously among ourselves, hoping not to be the next one to face the executioner. Humans were reduced to cogs in a wheel, and relationships became disposable. Ministry became villainy when people were subjected to tyranny, fear, and abuse. This is the sad truth and reality of the system created by Herbert W. Armstrong, which is still practiced among some WCG splinter groups that revere Armstrong as God's "true apostle." Are such tactics and abuse the sole propriety of Armstrongism? Unfortunately, some members of other Christian groups and denominations reach for the whip of intimidation in an attempt to control followers. May the Lord lead them to see their grievous error and repent so they may experience His grace and share it with those entrusted to their care.

Finally, it was time for our senior trip. For more than eight days, we rode the comfortable college bus through Europe, visiting Holland, Belgium, Germany, Switzerland, and France. It was a great trip, but one little incident almost became my Waterloo. We were staying in some Parisian pension (a small hotel) in which bathing facilities were limited. I needed a bath badly, and Linda and her roommate had a room with a bathtub, so I asked if I could use her tub. She agreed, drew me a bath, then went into her bedroom and locked the door behind her. We were alone in her room—myself locked in the bathroom and Linda locked in the bedroom. That seemed safe and above reproach to me. We were always mindful of avoiding even the appearance of evil. Well, I had a lovely bath, dressed, shouted my thanks to Linda, who remained safely locked behind her bedroom door, and left. No problem. Or so I thought. One senior girl became aware of this "scandal" and reported it immediately to the dean, who was chaperoning the trip. He cornered me in the hallway the next day and asked if it were true that I had been alone with Linda in her bedroom. Did that question ever ring badly in my ears! I explained exactly what had happened and assured him of our continence. He grimaced and asked me to be more circumspect in the future. Were my ears working? No blast, no scathing rebuke? The dean was turning out to be okay after all!

Ratting out one's fellow students was a regular part of Ambassador life. The faculty called it "showing love for one's brother," but most often it was nothing more than tattling. This, of course, gave the faculty "insider" information so they could call us in and set us straight at any infraction of the rules. Often those who were tattling were also in campus leadership positions. Turning informant under the guise of "helping in love" was also encouraged in the local congregation. There always were those who hoped for some advantage from the minister by squealing on a fellow member. Instead of rebuking the snitch, pastors often commended them for "loyalty" and "loving concern." This spy mentality brings with it an atmosphere of distrust and anxiety, which has characterized the past WCG fellowship. Many members were reluctant to speak their minds lest they be reported to the minister or a supervisor at Pasadena headquarters. I have taken the pastorate of a couple congregations where this "police state" mentality was the rule of the day. Members mysteriously would appear minutes before the beginning of worship services and at the last amen would vanish just as quickly, like rabbits scampering away on the first day of hunting season. They were afraid to say much at services for fear they would be reported to the ministry. To change such an atmosphere, I taught publicly and privately that I do not look kindly on telling tales. Further, I encouraged members to follow the principle of Matthew 18 and go to one's brother when there is an offense that needs to be addressed. When members came to me with some inside scoop, I would ask politely if they had discussed the matter with the other party. If the answer was no, as it usually was, I would tell them to take the step that Christ had instructed and go first to their brother. Within months, the atmosphere would change. People would come to church earlier, stay longer, and fellowship openly because trust had been established.

The rest of the senior trip went off without a hitch. Now I just needed to know what would happen to me after graduation. For those who wonder why I was concerned, it's difficult to fully comprehend what it is like to be in a totally controlled and controlling environment. By my senior year, I fully believed that God would lead the faculty, who were mostly ministers, to decide what I would be doing. I was committed to the "Work of God" and to God's apostle, Herbert Armstrong. Students were like pawns in the hands of the master chessman, who would ponder our next move. Faculty members convened weekly during the spring semester in what were termed "manpower meetings." During these meetings, each student was discussed and suitability for employment by the church was determined. As a student, I was on pins and needles. Despite the honors that had been showered on me, I was convinced that I was unworthy for a full-time position in the church. We all wanted to enter full-time work for the church, regardless of the position. We had been told that even changing light bulbs for the church was a wonderful and honorable opportunity for service. So if a man were offered a position in the mailing department to read mail or even to sack mail, at least he was in the "Work."

Along with the rest of the senior men, I awaited word from on high regarding my future. One evening at tea, the business manager entered the dining hall and asked for quiet so he could make an announcement. We knew that the manpower meetings had been in session, so we expected that something would be said regarding our fate. The first announcement was about my friend Robert. He was being sent to Dayton, Ohio, to serve as a ministerial assistant. We cheered for Robert, whom everybody liked. Two more names were mentioned, followed by cheers as their assignments were announced: one to the "field" (a local church assignment) and the other to a job in Radlett (near Bricket Wood) at the church printing facility. Then I heard my name. Immediately my mind went into high alert and a kind of euphoric haze as I heard the announcement that I was being sent to Asheville, North Carolina, as a ministerial assistant. There were two surprises: first, that I was being hired at all; second, that I was being sent "into the field." Both were the highest honors that could be given to graduating senior men. There also was the bonus of returning to North Carolina, my home state, which I loved. I believed "God had spoken," and now my path was clear.

The next issue to resolve was when Linda and I would marry. For that I would need counsel, which meant another trip to the dean's office, who had become less intimidating. As I settled into my familiar place across from his large wooden desk, I asked what

I should do regarding marriage. Most Ambassador students married immediately after graduation. In fact, in the early years of Ambassador College, the need in the local churches was so great that some men graduated, were ordained, got married, took delivery of their fleet car (a new car provided by the church), and were off to their first assignment within days. By 1971, things in the local congregations were far more established, so it was rare when someone was ordained immediately after graduation. When it did happen, it was usually because the man was older and more experienced, like the doctor who had sold his practice in South Africa and come to England for Ambassador training. The rest of us were in our early 20s and needed some seasoning before being turned loose on the congregations. The normal route was to be sent to a local church area as a ministerial assistant (M.A.), where we would work for one or two years before being ordained. If someone was not ordained within two years, that meant that he had not been deemed suitable for the ministry. This determination was quite subjective and generally was made by the pastor with whom one was serving. So if one managed to get along well with the guy, chances were good that he would be ordained. If the two clashed, in all likelihood he would be let go.

The dean, who had become friendly in the last year, gave me a fatherly smile and said, "You know, I would advise you to wait the summer out before you marry Linda. If it is true love, it will wait one summer. This will give you time to get settled before taking on the great responsibility of marriage." Now that was good advice! Linda thought so, too, and we determined to part for the summer. She would remain in England and work at the college, and I would go on to North Carolina to begin my assignment as a ministerial trainee.

As was his custom, Mr. Armstrong came to England for graduation. There was a sumptuous senior banquet and a senior graduation dance. Dancing was one thing that I did not do well—and still do not do well. However, if I were going to make the proper impression on my sweetheart, I knew I had to improve. I asked a couple female friends, Sherry and Candy, to teach me some dance moves before the big event. They agreed, which meant private sessions in the gymnasium. I learned the mysteries of the waltz, the fox trot, and the cha-cha. The sessions were a lot of fun and paid off on the big evening when I held Linda in my arms and dazzled her with my newfound skills!

On the last day of the festivities, Mr. Armstrong stood on the field in front of the men's dorm for a photo with all the graduating students. Another pleasant surprise was the appearance of Frank, the regional director from Germany. He came to England periodically and had flown over to be present for the graduation ceremonies and to meet with Mr. Armstrong. During one of those rare lulls in the hectic graduation week schedule, he said, "Tom, I am happy for you. I hope one day you can come to Germany to work. We'll stay in touch." A seed was planted that would blossom a few years later. The prospect of working for the church in Germany was exciting, but his comments were open-ended and held no commitment. It became something I mused about for several years, wondering if anything would ever happen. The conversation faded as other activities competed for my attention. I was not to see my German mentor for three more years.

Then graduation was over. In a flash the adventure that had begun four years earlier with a Greyhound bus trip from Richmond, Virginia, to Big Sandy, Texas, ended thousands of miles away on an English lawn at Ambassador's Bricket Wood campus. We said our good-byes to one another as most of us left for our home countries: Canada, Australia, New Zealand, South Africa, Germany, France, and the United States. After two years away, I was anxious to return. We were trained "ambassadors," ready to "go into all the world" to spread the Gospel. The problem, of course, was that we did not really understand the Gospel nor anything much about pastoral care or church administration. We were innocents being sent on a mission to teach a message that brought men into the shadows cast by Mt. Sinai, not into the light emanating from the risen Christ at Calvary. But we were convinced of the correctness of our beliefs and were willing, regardless of personal costs, to spend and be spent for the "Work."

Chapter 5

Lifestyles of the Rich and Not-So-Famous

Who dares to say that he alone has found the truth?—
Henry Wadsworth Longfellow (*John Endicott*, act 2, scene 3)

The manner in which members of the Worldwide Church of God view Christ's message to the seven churches in Revelation has influenced significantly the church's worldview. In Revelation, St. John records Jesus' words to the churches in Asia Minor (modern Turkey). Mr. Armstrong, echoing traditional dispensational theology, believed and taught that the history of the true church is represented by these seven churches of Revelation 2 and 3. Each church represents a particular period in history, which the church passes through. Beginning with Christ's words to the church at Ephesus, the history of the true church is played out chronologically. Armstrong believed that Ephesus represented the first-century era of the church, which thrived until after the death of the apostle John. Then the church began to lose its love for Christ, which paved the way for the development of the apostate church of Rome and Simon Magus, the wicked heretic of Acts 8. Gibbon's *Decline and Fall of the Roman Empire* was often quoted by Herbert Armstrong, both in his writing and in his preaching, to demonstrate that by the second century the church was split in two. The false church was different from the original church because it had lost much of its apostolic truth, thus the true church had to break away. A growing apostasy began pushing the smaller true church ever more to the fringes of the empire. This view of church history that Armstrong taught was also erroneous. Apostasy in the church really did not take place until the advent of Constantine in the fourth century. The second-century church was still a persecuted church and was still an outlaw religion that was banned by the Roman Empire. In fact, Mr. Armstrong taught that by A.D. 50 or so, around the time St. Paul wrote the epistle to the Galatians, the true Gospel was no longer preached. Armstrong further proclaimed that God had raised him up 1,900 years later to again proclaim the truth. At the same time, however, Armstrong taught that the true church lived on through the centuries, preserving the truth. This obvious contradiction was overlooked by many. We had learned to live with such cognitive dissonance. One more contradictory claim fit into the WCG pattern of holding simultaneously two opposing views on the same subject.

Another contradiction was that Armstrong claimed not to be a prophet, yet he saw himself as fulfilling the role of Ezekiel—the watchman over Israel—and even the prophesied return of Elijah, who would prepare the way for Christ's return. These were audacious claims, but for members of the WCG, God's end-time apostle was obviously a kind of prophet because God had given him prophetic insight that no other minister or church on earth seemed to possess. Armstrong was the one who unraveled for us the mystery of the true church, laying out the church's history, tracing its roots to the beginning of his own ministry in Oregon in the early 1930s. Many cults do the same thing. Mormons, Jehovah's Witnesses, and others attempt to substantiate their existence by finding legitimacy and precedent in the early church. Joseph Smith, founder of the Mormon faith, taught that God had revealed the true Gospel to him in the early 1800s. Like Armstrong would almost a century later, Smith claimed to be restoring the truth that had been lost for centuries.

With the ready assistance of WCG's own historians, the entire past was chronicled to demonstrate how the true church became the persecuted outcasts who had to flee to the outer limits of the Roman Empire to seek refuge in the Swiss and French Alps. The WCG claimed that Peter Waldo was an ancestor of the true church. Waldo founded the Waldensian movement and boldly proclaimed Sabbath-keeping in medieval Europe. But many other sects throughout the history of the church have laid claim to Waldo as well. Over the years, several WCG members have trekked to Europe to visit followers of Waldo and inquire about their Sabbath-keeping tradition. Much to the surprise of these WCG faithful, the Waldensians informed them that they have never claimed to have been Sabbath-keepers!

We also saw our spiritual forefathers in other groups—the Paulicians, the Albigenses, etc.—branded by the official church at Rome as heretics. As far as I know, however, we never were able to establish with any certainty that members of any of these groups were Saturday Sabbath observers. But for us, observing the Sabbath was the mark of true Christianity. Later we discovered that in our zeal to trace our church's history through these groups, we accepted the term "Sabbath-keeper" at face value, only to find that what most groups meant by Sabbath was actually Sunday observance. Mr. Armstrong believed that a conspiracy existed to obscure the truth about God's work among His people, so with the active support of his in-house "scholars," Armstrong sought to reconstruct history. I have been told by top executives of the WCG that our early historians were diligent about searching the Bible and history, but they did so only *after* being biased by Mr. Armstrong's views. By accepting his presuppositions before conducting their investigations, they literally saw history through the eyeglasses of Herbert W. Armstrong. Rather than interpreting Armstrong's history in the light of their research, they interpreted their research in the light of Mr. Armstrong's historical assumptions. Furthermore, despite many embarrassing discoveries of historical inaccuracies in Armstrong's work, these men continued to enjoy respect among WCG membership. Over the years, I gradually lost all confidence in their ability to discern with any accuracy the truth of ancient history.

Returning to the seven church eras, Peter Waldo was said to have been the founder of the Thyatiran era (the Middle Ages) of the church, which gradually died out and was succeeded by the Sardis era. The Sardis era allegedly began sometime in England and worked its way to the New World in the late 1600s. The Sardis era, which St. John recorded as a church that fell asleep spiritually or became spiritually dead, was represented by the Church of God (Seventh Day). This was the church out of which Mr. Armstrong would emerge after it had refused to adopt as official doctrine his view of the United States and the British Commonwealth in prophecy (or after he refused to send local congregational tithes to church headquarters, depending on the story you believe). I often heard Armstrong refer to the Church of God (Seventh Day) as "a spiritually dead church" that had lost its zeal for God's truth. It is interesting to note that beginning with the administration of Joseph Tkach Sr., official contact was made with the leaders of the Church of God (Seventh Day). Joe Tkach Jr. has officially and publicly apologized to the leadership and membership of the Church of God for the WCG's less than Christian remarks about its doctrine and practice. For its part, Church of God leadership has graciously accepted the WCG apology. For a while, a close friendship was forged with the WCG leadership, including attendance at each other's conferences and regular phone conversations. Although the contact between the two groups today is minimal, it is positive to note the judgmentalism that had characterized the former relationship has ceased. Because of the close relationship that the Church of God (Seventh Day) had with the WCG, it may find it necessary to grapple with some of the same issues the WCG has studied in the past several years, especially the matter of the Sabbath.

The events in the Worldwide Church of God serve as a catalyst for discussion, review, and consideration, not only among the fellowship of the Church of God (Seventh Day), but also in the membership of the many splinter groups of the WCG. It seems that much of what the WCG splinter groups say and preach is a reaction to the actions taken by the Worldwide Church of God, rather than a positive reflection of their individual positions in light of objective biblical criticism. Realistically I don't expect much theological introspection or debate among such groups. The key to their survival is the preservation of the Armstrong legacy, not the identification of truth. This is the case with most individuals as well. For many, truth is too uncomfortable because of the assault on one's personal philosophical/theological equilibrium. Jesus said, "You will know the truth, and the truth will set you free" (John 8:32). Before we are free, we will be made uncomfortable as we discover that many of our cherished views are erroneous. For many, that would be too much to bear. Ignorance is preferred.

The one church mentioned in Revelation 2 and 3 that receives no rebuke from Christ is Philadelphia—the church of brotherly love. Guess which church era the Worldwide Church of God resided in, according to Mr. Armstrong? You guessed it, Philadelphia! With the conviction that we were in the Philadelphian era of God's one and only true church, our zeal to support the modern Ezekiel (Herbert Armstrong) in trumpeting God's warning message to Israel was strengthened. Our greatest fear was that we would lose our zeal and become the Laodicean church era (the last of the seven churches), which is chided by Christ for its lukewarm spiritual condition. When speculating about the Laodicean church, we would ask one another who we thought this church might be or how it would come to be. There were many theories, but the most common was that a "great falling away" would occur within the church, sifting the wheat from the chaff. Those who remained loyal and supportive of Mr. Armstrong would be counted among the zealous Philadelphians. Those who deserted him would become the Laodiceans. They would have to endure the horrors of the Great Tribulation, which would cast its dark shadow over the earth for the three-and-a-half years prior to Christ's return. Most of the Laodiceans would repent and suffer martyrdom, thus gaining eternal life. Meanwhile the faithful Philadelphians would be safely hidden by God in Petra, thus supernaturally protecting them from the death camps, war, and plagues. These views are well articulated in modern dispensational theology. Armstrong was describing a pre-millennial mid-tribulation rapture theory. If you listen carefully to the rhetoric of some WCG splinter groups, you will hear them refer to the Philadelphian and Laodicean era of God's church. Usually they will claim to be Philadelphian (who would want to be Laodicean?) while assigning WCG to the role of the Laodicean flag bearer.

The Worldwide Church of God no longer subscribes to the church era theory of Revelation 2 and 3. Instead, it sees this passage in Revelation as a message to the church of Christ as a whole in which the various attitudes of God's people are described. One effect of rejecting the church era theory is that many members felt as though a part of their identity had been taken away. Perhaps many in the WCG fellowship have yet to come to grips with the issue of identity. Unique teachings such as the identity of nations, the Ezekiel commission to serve as a watchman to warn the modern descendants of Israel of coming national calamity, and being the Philadelphian era of God's true church were important components of the WCG identity. Now that these teachings have been rejected as unbiblical, many in the WCG have struggled with an identity crisis: *Who are we? What makes us different?* These are valid questions that Mr. Tkach Jr. addressed by responding that our identity is in Christ, not in novel doctrines. This is a foreign concept for many and will take time and the grace of God to embrace fully. There are, of course, many who grasp the importance of the centrality of Christ and welcome this truth wholeheartedly. There is a proclivity in each Christian denomination to maintain something distinctive that is used not only to identify, but to exalt the group among other Christians. Yes, vanity is alive and well in the Christian church and leads to no end of bickering and division. This does not mean a denomination should forsake its unique perspectives, but we should not use them as clubs to beat up on others in the Christian faith. A better use of these various perspectives would be as springboards for discussion so, with the guidance of the Holy Spirit, we could study Scripture together and seek the mind of God.

As I winged my way home from England after my final two years of Ambassador College training, I considered the momentous and important time in which I believed I was living. It was June 1971 and according to our prophetic calculations, January 1972 would signal the beginning of the end. It was then that the two 19-year cycles would have been completed since the beginning of the Philadelphian era of God's church. Mr. Armstrong had taught that every 19 years the sun, moon, and some planets came into a unique alignment. In January 1934, the media work of the WCG was launched, and 19 years later, in January 1953, *The World Tomorrow* was aired over Radio Luxembourg in Europe, which marked the beginning of the WCG's international work. This premise of the 19-year cycles, coupled with some rather interesting mathematical calculations extruded from certain Old Testament prophecies, gave us the clear conviction that January 1972 would be a watershed year for fulfilled prophecy. As a sophomore in Texas, I had asked the dean how much time we had left until the "end." He replied that he expected that my class of 1971 would be the last graduating class from Ambassador College. So as I sat on the plane pondering my future ministry, I knew it would be short. However, I rejoiced in the conviction that I was among the blessed few called to understand these wonderful truths of God that had been hidden for centuries. But my faithfulness to God in keeping His commandments and loyally supporting His end-time apostle, Herbert W. Armstrong, meant I had it made. There would be a place for me in Petra and a wonderful future in the millennium as king of several cities—maybe even a country, if I really got it together. But our focus in the WCG was not on winning souls for Christ, rather it was on preparing ourselves to rule in the glory of His kingdom on earth. What a contrast to the servant leadership Jesus modeled through His willingness to humble Himself even to the cross to save undeserving sinners.

As January 1972 approached, I remember that tension mounted within the WCG. Mr. Armstrong hedged his bets by stating publicly that he never had set dates. I thought he was being circumspect, but in his heart he really believed that "in

1972 we'd be through." As the date approached, I began to have my doubts, but I dared not voice them lest I be counted by God among the unfaithful. January came and went, but the only thing that changed was the fact that it was now February 1972. Mr. Armstrong reminded us again that he never had set dates, but the end was not too far off. He would use terms such as "we are now in the gun lap." Rumor had it that Armstrong's jet was fueled and ready to go on January 1, 1972, presumably to head to Petra. Whether this was true, it was not long after that many WCG ministers saw 1981 as a new watershed year for us to anticipate. Because of the 1972 setback, there was much less dogmatic conviction than before, and we were not filled with the apocalyptic excitement or anticipation that we had shared in 1972. Consequently, when 1981 came and went, we were not all that surprised or disappointed. Despite these colossal prophetic mishaps, we trusted Mr. Armstrong and believed that before he died, Christ would return. Many even believed firmly that Armstrong would not die before the visible cataclysmic intervention of Jesus Christ in world affairs. In my mind, Armstrong's advanced age and weakening health became somewhat of a benchmark heralding the nearness of the return of our Lord. In reality we could not face facts—Armstrong blew it! Instead, I was in the forefront, "holding up the hands" of God's end-time apostle. To this day some WCG splinter groups revere Mr. Armstrong as a prophet and deride the current WCG for distancing itself from his teachings and his prophetic legacy. This end-time fiasco reminds one of the Great Disappointment of the Millerites, who waited in vain on March 21 and again on October 22, 1844, for Christ's return. Regardless of human effort, Christ said we would not know the time of His return (Matthew 24:36), despite our efforts to calculate it.

My friend Robert also was on the flight to Richmond because he had grown up there as well. Unlike me, Robert had grown up in a WCG family. As we waited for our connecting flight in Dulles Airport, seeing the big cars, brightly colored clothing worn by men and women (in comparison to the drab colors of English fashion), and enjoying the warm, moist summer air reminded us we had been gone for two years. In Richmond, we parted company to visit our parents and our childhood homes. I had corresponded regularly with my parents while in England, and they were happy to have me back after my two-year odyssey abroad. They were especially pleased that I would be moving to Asheville, North Carolina, somewhere they could visit occasionally. We spoke of my plans to marry, and I don't recall any objections. Maybe they felt opposition would be useless. They promised to attend the wedding once the date was set.

After a couple weeks at home, I was scheduled to be picked up by the pastor under whose tutelage I was to serve. We had spoken briefly on the phone and made arrangements to meet at an interstate rest stop. The pastor and his wife were returning from a district conference just north of Richmond. On the appointed day, I dressed in my English wool suit complete with smartly starched shirt and tie. My dad drove me to the rendezvous spot and I waited in the sweltering June heat for the minister and his wife. Finally, he arrived in his Plymouth Fury III, warmly greeted my father and me, and loaded my sparse gear into his car. Off we went, headed for the mountains of North Carolina.

I assumed from my training at Bricket Wood that the relationship with the pastor and his wife would be formal and distant. To expect a personal friendship seemed beyond the realm of possibility. We chatted politely and I respectfully called them "Mr. and Mrs." Interestingly, they were dressed in jeans, short sleeve shirts, and tennis shoes, which made a striking contrast to the chic and formally attired ministerial assistant! After a few minutes of polite small talk and bantering, the pastor looked at his wife, she looked at him, and they both looked at me. He said with a pleasant smile, "Just call me Wayne and my wife, Joanne." That was a surprise my college instructors had not prepared me for, but with a sigh of relief, I began to relax and enjoy the trip "home" with my new friends.

Wayne and Joanne graciously put me up in their home until I could locate an apartment. Joanne was a sweet woman who displayed a high degree of concern for my comfort and well being. Wayne, Joanne, and their daughter, Heather, lived in a nice tri-level home in the suburbs of Asheville. In those days, WCG ministers were paid well enough to live a little better than the average member. Mr. Armstrong considered the ministers to be modernday "Levites." Using biblical principles, Armstrong instructed how WCG ministers were to be treated. For example, because Levites had been paid better than the average Israelite, WCG ministers should be better compensated as well. However, the Levites had no inheritance, which translated into a better than average, but not exorbitant, salary for ministers. At the time, WCG ministers officially were discouraged from owning a home. To buy a home broke from this Levite tradition and was tantamount to putting too much emphasis on the material world instead of the spiritual calling of the ministry. Ministers were provided top-of-the-line cars. This was not bad because we virtually lived in the car, driving 40,000 to 50,000 miles a year as we visited members and prospective members. Ministers had to avoid marrying a divorced woman and could not consume any alcoholic beverages while on duty. We also received firstfruits from members' gardens, as did the Levites of old. Ministers lived well and had sufficient funds for the normal expenses of clothing, furnishings, etc. We were exempted from paying second and third tithes (second tithe for the celebration of the annual festivals; third tithe given twice in a seven-year cycle for the poor). For the short term, we were better off than many WCG members. For the long term, we were worse off because we had no provision for the future, no retirement fund, no equity in property, and no social security because the majority of us took advantage of a tax law that allowed ministers to opt out of the program.

Almost 30 years later, this situation has worsened. There is still no retirement fund. And in the last years, WCG ministers have suffered continual financial setbacks: salaries have been slow to rise, several years may go by without an increase, church-provided cars are gone, mileage reimbursement has been lowered, health costs have increased as benefits have been trimmed, and housing allowances are reduced. The financial realities have forced many pastors' wives to return to the work force, which makes her unable to participate fully in her husband's ministry.

Some WCG ministers have told me of their sometimes-desperate financial situation, which has a negative impact on their morale. Eventually those of us in the ministry recognized we were not to be compared to the Old Testament Levites, and the entire concept is now no longer taught or practiced in the WCG. Ministers in the WCG now realize that, like most social professionals, ministers are not paid as well as other professionals. In the early 1970s, WCG ministers were doing fairly well financially, which allowed the men to afford certain niceties that the general membership could not. Because times have changed, it has been difficult for some to adjust to much harsher realities. The average pastor in any given denomination is undercompensated, and many pastors struggle financially because of misguided thinking by the laity that the pastor should not live too well. Part of the fallout of such thinking is a shortage of men who are willing to become pastors because they know it will mean economic privation for themselves and their families. In the end, such an attitude makes the entire Body of Christ suffer.

Current circumstances are in stark contrast to our lifestyle in the early 1970s. During my year with Wayne, I learned what some of those niceties were. First, pastors could afford to rent a home in a nice part of town. Second, there was the game room that featured a refrigerator converted to hold a beer keg (not every minister had one of these, but for the men I was around, several did or were striving to get one). Third, there were the latest men's suits available at steep discounts through a minister in our district who was a wheeler-dealer with such merchandise. Finally, several men could afford big motorcycles (particularly popular among some of the ministers in our district).

I also noticed that several of the ministers' wives did not seem as well off as their husbands. In those days, it was a man's world in the WCG. The wives were taught to be submissive to their husbands and support him as a "helpmeet." This translated into living with less and liking it, which was a strange attitude when God's Word speaks of a man's wife as being his own flesh. This attitude toward WCG pastors' wives has changed, and they are afforded much more respect and support. Historically, the

WCG gave lip service to the role of the minister's wife as his helper in ministry, and there have been and still are precious few concrete rewards for a minister's wife.

Everything I just described did not apply to the ministerial assistant. We were not well paid, and we had to learn to get by with considerably less than the pastor. I did not find that out of line because I was a trainee and brought little experience to the job. I was an apprentice and did not expect to be well paid. In fact, for the first six weeks, I was not paid at all. Because of poor communication between Ambassador College in England and the Pasadena headquarters, I was not even listed as an employee! I lived off my savings and money Wayne gave me from the church's emergency account.

After a couple weeks with Wayne and Joanne, I found a two-room basement apartment in a pleasant part of town. It rented for $100 a month, including utilities. It was a nice, furnished apartment with a private entrance. I was happy with my apartment and content with my new lot in life. We had been taught at Ambassador not to complain, but to accept life as it comes, thanking God for the trials as well as the blessings. This was not such bad advice.

What did a ministerial trainee do? Whatever the pastor wanted him to do, which varied from pastor to pastor. There were no formal training guidelines for ministerial assistants or assistant pastors. Each pastor trained the man under him as he saw fit. There also were no standardized norms for evaluating a man's performance to determine his suitability for advancement or the advisability of dismissing him. This is gradually changing for those in the WCG field ministry. While serving as an executive at WCG headquarters, I experienced the same lack of formality in job training and evaluation. There were no standards for evaluating job performance and usually no performance evaluations were given. As a result, mediocrity enjoyed reward while excellence was stifled. After a while, it became clear that you were to do your job but not knock yourself out. If you performed poorly or well, the pay or reward was the same. Advancement was not based on achievement against standards; rather, it was based on "good attitude," loyalty, and maintaining a good relationship with the right people. Skill was important, but it was not always the determining factor for advancement. The best jobs at the middle and top of the WCG were given by appointment of the pastor general or his assistant. The top jobs were not publicized throughout the fellowship or ministry of the WCG, so all who were qualified were not permitted to apply. This "closed system" kept out new blood, delayed the rise of younger people to positions of greater responsibility, and effectively stymied the entry of those who could perhaps challenge the way things were done at the upper levels. What resulted was a good number of men in middle- and upper-level management who have learned to or feel compelled to say yes to superiors without challenging the wisdom of decisions or instructions. Thus, the WCG had many men in their pastorates and in management positions around the world whose visionary strengths were not encouraged. This was the WCG tradition of leadership when I began in the ministry in the 1970s, and it remained so until my departure in 1996.

Wayne had his own system of training: I went with him everywhere. We visited members together, and he talked while I listened. He answered their questions and gave counsel; I listened. He gave Bible studies on Wednesday nights; I listened. He gave sermons on Saturday; I did get to give 12-minute sermonettes fairly regularly. When the grass at his house needed mowing, I mowed it. When the car needed to be washed and filled up, I took care of that. When Prince, his German shepherd, needed a trip to the vet, I took him. When the dry cleaning needed to be picked up, I did it. When Joanne needed help getting someplace or doing something, I helped her. You probably think this sounds as though I was a valet or servant, but I was convinced I was involved in the very work of God, being trained by one of His ministers so I could one day take on greater responsibility. After all, I began my Ambassador College career scrubbing toilets, so it was clear to me that this was part of a greater plan to prepare me for the future. This seemed great until I ran into a few of my buddies who were also ministerial trainees. They were conducting Bible studies, visiting on their own, counseling members, and not doing any of the personal butler work I was doing. My conclusion was not that Wayne was taking advantage of me; rather, I determined that I was not as spiritually advanced as my friends and needed more humbling before God could use me in the same way He was using my friends. In the Worldwide Church of God, I became skilled at denial. Regardless of how impossible something seemed or sounded, I knew it was not so. I believed God was always in the background, leading and guiding so out of every apparent defeat a certain victory would come. That was all part of having a "good attitude" and being a man of faith, which sooner or later crashes into the hard wall of reality. And reality was that Wayne had no idea how to train an assistant, so I became his personal servant so I would stay busy. And if I would have questioned Wayne about my training, it would have been regarded as insubordination to God's true servant.

Not long after arriving in Asheville, I drove down somewhere in South Carolina with Wayne and Joanne to participate in a ministerial conference. This was exciting. It was my opportunity to meet the district superintendent. I considered it an honor to meet and speak to a man of such great spiritual influence. The meeting took place at a lakeside resort cabin in the tidewater area of South Carolina. I remember standing on the pier at the lake, talking to someone else, when the district superintendent came over to me. Wanting to be on my best behavior, I extended my hand to greet this man of God and introduce myself. "Hello, sir, I'm Tom Lapacka," I said. That seemed innocent and straightforward. How could a guy go wrong with an introduction like that? He accepted my extended hand and replied, "Oh, you're the guy who stole Ken's girl." After that warm welcome, he turned and walked off. I got the feeling that life as a trainee was about to get a bit tougher.

Most of the pastors and wives at the conference were either neutral or cool toward me. I had no idea why. There were a few exceptions to the aloof reception I was receiving. Two among the group who treated me more kindly were Joel, who is still with the WCG, and Larry, who served as Wayne's associate pastor at the other end of our circuit, which was Greenville, South Carolina.

Larry and his wife, Anita, were friendly and welcomed me warmly. However, the gentleman who could get the merchandise "deals" was extremely arrogant in his interaction with me and not particularly kind. After Linda and I married in September 1971 and attended the Feast of Tabernacles at Jekyll Island, this pastor commented at one of my infamous personal evaluation sessions that Linda and I acted like "Mr. and Mrs. America." We were newlyweds and had just returned from our honeymoon, so our amorous attention to each other probably did needle him a bit. But I was angered at his callous comment and considered him to be a jerk. For the second time in my experience with the WCG, I had a bad taste in my mouth for a minister of God. It wouldn't be the last time.

My first summer working as a ministerial assistant raced by, and it was not long before Linda flew in from London for a brief visit on her way to see her parents, who had moved to Jonesboro, Arkansas. Wayne loaned me his brand-new Ford LTD (the Plymouth Fury had logged too many miles and had to be sold) to pick her up at the airport. On my salary I could afford only a 1961 Ford Galaxy 500, which I had bought for $300 from a member who was a local used-car dealer. The Galaxy was beat up and made a strange clanging noise when I drove it, so I was not keen on driving Linda around in a clunker. I had spent the morning of Linda's arrival at the lake water-skiing, so I rushed home to shower, then drove to the airport to meet Linda. It was wonderful to see her after nearly two months. She would be in town only a few days, so this would be the moment of truth. I planned to propose immediately. Following the principles of quality and class that Mr. Armstrong had taught us at Ambassador College, I took Linda to a fine hotel restaurant on the outskirts of Asheville. The restaurant overlooked a golf course in the foothills of the Blue Ridge Mountains. After a delightful dinner, I invited Linda to walk with me in the rose garden behind the hotel. On the veranda a live band was playing romantic music as patrons dined. We walked through the garden to a gazebo from which we had a breathtaking panoramic view of the valley. The sun had set, the stars were out, and in the distance we could see the twinkling lights of some homes. You could not ask for a more peaceful and romantic environment. Standing together with Linda in the gazebo, I held her hand and uttered the words that I had rehearsed in my mind so many times. "Linda, I love you with my whole heart. Will you marry me?"

Without any hesitation, Linda fell into my arms, saying, "Yes, Thomas, I will." We embraced and kissed, after which I gave her the ring we had picked out in London months before—a beautiful 18-karat gold ring with lovely settings of small diamonds and sapphires. We held each other again, silently enjoying the romance of the moment. After a few days in Asheville, Linda flew to Arkansas to spend a few weeks with her parents and prepare for the wedding.

I asked Wayne to perform the wedding, and he consented. In late August, Linda returned, and her parents arrived a little later for the wedding, as did mine. Friends from Tennessee came to help organize the wedding party, and our good friend, Sam, traveled from Europe to be my best man. Some WCG members who had a business connection with the Grandfather Mountain Country Club near Boone, North Carolina, arranged a cheap rate for us to stay in a millionaire's condo on the golf course just below Grandfather Mountain.

From all that I had heard preached, all that I had read in WCG literature, and everything I had studied at Ambassador College, it was clear the WCG treated marriage seriously. For Linda and me, our vows were to be for life, and the pre-marriage counseling we participated in made this commitment clear. For years, few, if any, WCG married couples divorced. It happened occasionally, but it was always the exception. Because we taught and admonished people to uphold the sanctity of marriage does not mean there were no marital problems. There were, and we dealt with them as best we could. Unfortunately most WCG ministers were not then, nor are they now, trained to handle marital conflicts in a manner similar to their colleagues in other denominations. Over the years a few pastors have sought additional training or degrees in the area of marriage and family counseling. Those aware of their deficiencies often team up with Christian counselors to offer referrals to members. Before the 1990s, marriage counseling was the domain of the local pastor, who did the best he could. Sadly, the divorce rate among WCG members has climbed as the church gradually had relaxed its strict rules.

Linda and I married on September 5, 1971, and only a few weeks later we were packing for our first Feast of Tabernacles as a married couple. Our assigned festival site was Jekyll Island, Georgia. In those days, each church area was assigned to a festival site. This allowed members to interact with people from their general geographic area and establish friendships. As the years went by, the church allowed each member to attend the feast site of his or her choice. For too many members, however, the Feast of Tabernacles became a big travel holiday and lost its spiritual character. In recent years, members would rave about this festival site or another not for the inspiring sermons, but because of weather, shopping, attractions, food, or lodging. Looking back, the festival experience of the past decades was more of an exercise in legalism that did not bring us the grace of God in Christ. Instead, it served to enforce the works-righteousness mentality that characterized the WCG.

Wayne and his family and Linda and I went to Greenville to spend a few days with Larry and Anita before driving to Jekyll Island for the feast. The others drove ahead and left Linda and me to follow the next day. We wanted to take our time getting to the festival site, so we had dinner in town and enjoyed another relaxing night together before loading the Galaxy for the journey. As we drove out of Greenville, I lost the tread on my recapped tire—the only type of tire I could afford, but in hot weather, the treads tended to come loose. My tire was in shreds, so we stopped at a Firestone dealership to buy another retread. I was low on cash because I had not worked long enough to save much second tithe for the festival. Ministerial assistants in my situation were told to pick up financial assistance at the festival site's business office. But here we were in Greenville, spending our money on dinner, then experiencing an unexpected road emergency, which almost wiped us out. The tank was full when we left Greenville, and we did have a few dollars for gas, but when we crossed the Georgia state line the fuel gauge was not looking too encouraging and we had only about 17 cents between us. I had no credit cards and no checks, so if we ran out of gas, our goose was cooked. We stopped and prayed, asking God to have mercy on us and keep the car going, though it looked like we would not make it to the festival site. That big red machine kept going with the fuel gauge not moving at all. We came to a toll bridge, which cost 25 cents, but we didn't have enough money! We had to drive the long way, but thanks to our merciful Lord, we rolled into Jekyll Island on fumes. That was only one example of the ways our dear Lord intervened to help us in even incalculable ways. Many may think that God did not answer the prayers of WCG members because we were a cult and taught non-biblical doctrines. But such thinking limits the love and mercy of our Lord, who looks on the heart, not the head. We trusted God for help and guidance in scores of ways, and He performed many private miracles as well as public ones. To Him is the glory for His mercy, which He showers on all who with sincere hearts call on Him.

I do not recall much from that Feast of Tabernacles except that we met under a large tent near the beach. It was hot at times, but the sea breezes cooled us. There must have been six to eight thousand people present for the eight-day Feast of Tabernacles. In those days, either Herbert or Garner Ted Armstrong would visit each U.S. feast site because there were not many places to visit. My only other memory is the tremendous business we did with the liquor stores on the island. We constantly were admonished to use moderation in our alcohol consumption so we would not offend others. It is rather difficult in a place such as Jekyll Island, Georgia, however, not to be noticed for one's inclination toward a cold brew. WCG members enjoyed the freedom to consume strong drink, and at the Feast of Tabernacles we usually had plenty on hand. Although I believe the Bible does not prohibit the Christian to drink alcoholic beverages, we must take care not to offend others with our liberty. In general, I believe WCG members set a good example, though we would be criticized by some Christian groups for our liberty.

Linda and I received some money after we reached Jekyll Island, and we enjoyed the stay. After the Feast of Tabernacles, we returned to North Carolina and our normal routine. A large part of that routine was visiting church members. WCG membership tended to be scattered as opposed to residing mainly in the city where the church was located. This required a tremendous amount of driving for the ministry. In those days, ministers had strict quotas for visiting. We were supposed to make at least 17 visits each week. After each call, we had to fill out a visit card, which was sent to Pasadena. At headquarters, some dedicated soul was supposed to read everything we wrote. I doubt, however, that anyone actually read the visit cards. A minister I knew left the North Carolina area to assume a position in the Church Administration Department (CAD) in Pasadena. He reported finding stacks of boxes filled with visit cards in them—unread visit cards. Our duty was not to reason why, but to obey, and obey we did. The members were used to the routine. Sometimes we lined up visits in advance; other times we dropped in on families. No one dared to tell us to buzz off because we had interrupted their plans. They politely would invite us to sit and talk, which illustrates the control WCG ministers exercised in members' lives— yet another characteristic of a cult mentality. Today I am careful to respect a member's privacy and would be reluctant to drop in uninvited.

Creativity was often necessary to meet the weekly quota, so we would fish, hunt, golf, or whatever with a member and count it as a visit. It wasn't a lie because we did visit. Maybe this was not what the Church Administration Department had in mind, but as a forest ranger told me once when complaining about silly reports his superiors made him fill out, "The guy with the pencil always wins." As a trainee, I usually visited with the pastor. The days were long, and I returned home late at night. Because I rode with the pastor in his car, Linda could use our Ford during the day. She accepted our lifestyle as normal. Later Linda and I were allowed to call on members by ourselves, and she willingly participated in my work, doing what she had been taught to do. Linda became my assistant, helping me to better understand and deal with members' daily struggles.

My average week went like this: Sunday was usually a day for church activities of some kind, such as ball games, picnics, or special group meetings. As a trainee, I spent Monday morning in the office in the minister's home, filling out reports, updating maps/directions to members' homes, and transferring vital information from visit cards to the permanent member file. If I had preached on the previous Saturday, I was evaluated. Wayne was encouraging and provided an ideal role model when it came to public speaking and administrative skills. Monday, Wednesday, and Friday mornings at about 10:00 A.M., we went to the YMCA and played pick up basketball. On Mondays and Wednesdays, we showered, dressed, and left from there to make visits, normally not returning before 11 P.M. On Fridays, we generally spent the afternoon working on sermons or, in my case, sermonettes.

After I married Linda, Wayne gave me more free time and reduced my "valet" duties. If I was not preaching, I received the rest of Friday off. On Saturday, we started early in the morning, arriving at the rented hall, which belonged to a Greek Orthodox Church, about 9:30 A.M. Services started at 10 A.M. and lasted two full hours, after which we visited with the members for about 30 minutes before rushing to Wayne's car to head to South Carolina. A group of church ladies took turns making the four of us and Heather sack lunches so we could drive straight through without stopping for a meal. We drove through the mountains at breakneck speeds and would arrive in Andersen, South Carolina, sometimes a little green around the gills, about five or 10 minutes before worship services began. Another two-hour service was followed by nearly an hour of visiting with members. Finally, we went to Larry's home in Greenville, had dinner, played cards, had a beer, and often spent the night. If we didn't stay over, sometime around midnight we would pile back in the car and make the 90-minute drive back to Asheville. On Sunday the cycle began again. Was it boring? Not on your life! It was the most exciting time of my life. Something always was happening. Church social life included meetings, clubs, sports, and more. There was never a dull moment.

The visits were interesting as well. Members would open up to us and pour out their hearts when discussing their struggles. We took everything seriously and worked hard to help members through their trials. Life as a Christian is tough enough, but add to that WCG requirements regarding tithing, Sabbath keeping, holy days, and the strict performance of Christian disciplines and you have a real struggle. Members were struggling under the great burden of Law that we had laid on them (and on ourselves). We didn't understand Christ's words in Matthew 11:28, where He invited all who are weary and burdened to come to Him and receive rest. In the WCG mind-set, rest would come in the "world tomorrow." Now we had to work out our salvation, build godly character, and qualify for God's kingdom. Our spiritual lives were burdensome, and though we rejoiced in one another's fellowship, fellowship with God was a struggle. I cannot tell you the joy WCG members feel now that they have grasped Christ's invitation to rest. They rest in the Lord, understanding that they are accepted, justified, and sanctified by the work of Jesus and the indwelling of the Holy Spirit and not by their own work. For WCG members who have understood the Gospel message of grace, it is indeed *good news*.

During a visit, we often asked members about their prayer and Bible study life. This was intended as an encouraging prod to keep everyone on their knees and noses (in the Bible). But it actually was a "policing" of members' spiritual lives. Ministers felt the weight of responsibility for members' spiritual welfare, and we desired that they draw close to God. However, we were admittedly too zealous and controlling. When members were not performing as they should (the 30/30/30 method was a yardstick against which to gauge performance), they often became defensive, apologetic, and discouraged. We did not stress the grace and forgiveness of God through His Son, Jesus. Instead, we focused on the need to perform to please God. We did not know it is not *our* performance that wins God's favor, but it is our faith in *Christ's* performance. He is the one who measures up to God's standard of perfection. He is the one who is perfect in obedience. It is our faith in Christ's perfect obedience on our behalf that moves God to grant us forgiveness and impute righteousness to us.

For WCG members, accepting such "policing" methods by the minister was part of church life. Pastors were God's "true servants" and the guardians of their spiritual welfare, thus WCG members understood ministers who dropped by on short notice were to be welcomed. The minister became the focal point of congregational life. What he said was "law." His advice was tantamount to God's advice. When a minister gave counsel or admonishment, it was to be followed or one would be regarded as faithless or rebellious. In some cases, members would seek ministerial advice on car purchases, personal grooming, travel plans, business decisions, etc. Some ministers conducted themselves as "lord of the manor," expecting special treatment and deference from members, including the best table at a picnic, personal service from the members, or special deals on merchandise. Of course, not all WCG ministers acted in this way; some were humble and unassuming. In the WCG of today, if a minister uses his office for personal exaltation, it will come to the attention of the administration in Pasadena and remedial action will be taken quickly. During the administration of Mr. Tkach Sr., ministers whom he called "sheriffs" were reeducated. I believe he was fairly successful in communicating that ministers were servants and not overlords and in enforcing this position. The irony is that he gave them a dose of their own medicine as he used the same methods to correct those "sheriffs" whom he was opposing. Currently, WCG ministers are dedicated, humble servants of God who are truly spending and being spent for God's people.

The Lord has brought the ministry of the WCG a long way from where it was in the 1960s and 1970s when pastors were viewed as omnicompetent. Because WCG ministers were the only true servants of God among the false prophets of mainline traditional Christianity—and the WCG was the only true church in a deceived world—we were viewed as "experts" in almost every aspect of life. At Ambassador College we had been trained to recapture "true values." Therefore, it was no wonder that members would look to us for answers and guidance in almost every facet of life. Today, WCG ministers are far more modest in their self-assessment and are more likely to decline to offer advice in areas outside their calling and training. They are far less reluctant about referring WCG members to experts who are trained to give appropriate help.

One area the WCG did not emphasize 30 years ago was group prayer. We prayed faithfully and regularly in private, but as a rule, ministers would not pray alone with members or in groups. This practice resulted from a misunderstanding of Christ's admonition to pray in private. I remember visiting in the early 1980s with an elderly Swiss widow. I spent more than an hour answering her biblical questions. After having coffee and cake, she asked if I would say a prayer with her before I left. It was an awkward moment, but I wanted to be true to our understanding of Scripture, so I said, "I'm sorry, we don't do that in our church." She was stunned and asked why not. I turned to the passage quoting Christ's direction to "go into your room, close the door and pray to your Father, who is unseen" (Matthew 6:6). What could she say? She had confidence in me as one who understood Scripture, so she accepted the answer. What a great misunderstanding of Scripture we espoused, how many thousands may have benefited from our prayers, and what a loss for WCG ministers who would have been strengthened to hear members praying for them. Today WCG ministers understand Christ was giving a contrast in Matthew 6 to the self-aggrandizing public prayers of the hypocrites who "love to pray standing in the synagogues and on the street corners to be seen by men" (Matthew 6:5). Jesus was not forbidding public or group prayer among Christians. In recent years, WCG ministry has made great strides in motivating the membership to small-group intercessory prayer. This is another positive Spirit-led and rejuvenating change in the fellowship of the Worldwide Church of God.

When discussing visitations, I shouldn't neglect to mention the prospective member, the individual who expressed interest in becoming a member of the WCG. There were two broad areas of contact that led people to seek membership in the WCG. One was through its media efforts (*The Plain Truth, The World Tomorrow,* or one the WCG's dozens of published booklets). The second method of contact was via a friend or relative already in the church. An interested individual would write or call Pasadena, expressing the desire to join the WCG. Many would ask for the address of a WCG congregation nearest their home. Such requests were forwarded to the local pastor, who would send a letter offering an in-home visit rather than an invitation to church services. If the interested party was a friend or relative, we would ask the WCG member to inform the prospect that a minister would need to visit in the home before he or she could attend worship services.

Many people found this screening process puzzling. *What church demands that the minister visit with you before allowing you to attend worship? Why?* The official answer was that we did not want anyone coming to services who would hear the truth of God and treat it lightly. We felt that once a person heard the truth, he or she was held accountable by God. If people did not accept the truth, they were jeopardizing their eternal well being. Therefore, unless one was ready to accept and act on this truth, it was better that they did not even hear it. We taught that their day for salvation would come in the Second Resurrection (Revelation 20:5; Ezekiel 37) after the millennium (a mere 1,000-year delay!). Upon reflection, it seems to be an excellent method of screening out possible "dissidents" who might bring "false doctrines" or cause division. Ultimately, a cult is about control.

Once we were in your home (in most cases, we came in "twos," following Christ's admonition), we introduced ourselves as "representatives of Ambassador College," not as ministers of the Worldwide Church of God. I've never heard an official reason for this introduction. Undoubtedly, it presented a more respectable image because the church was sensitive to those who called it a cult. After initial introductions, we asked how the individual had learned about WCG literature. We asked about family members, occupation, religious background, and what information had been gleaned from our literature. Once we knew what you had read, we had a good idea what you did and did not know.

Invariably the prospect would ask about attending the local congregation. Most often we would avoid an invitation on the first visit, explaining the need for someone to "prove all things" before making such a step. We would encourage a person to think about baptism by WCG ministers because unless the prospect either was baptized or nearly ready for baptism by us, he or she would not be invited to worship. To be ready for baptism meant the prospect had to accept certain key doctrines of the WCG—tithing, Sabbath and holy day observance, abstinence from smoking and unclean meats, acceptance of the WCG as the one true church, and a willingness to be rebaptized (if one had been baptized already in a "false" church). To help the prospect along the path to "truth," we would leave with them or recommend they write for additional literature. This meant the next visit often had to wait at least a month. If the prospect did as recommended, we would return to continue our discussion, which would lead to a decision regarding baptism. It was not unusual for new people to attend worship services for the first time only after being baptized as members or for them to be baptized soon after their first attendance at services.

How did the Worldwide Church of God grow? It's not really that surprising that the WCG grew. I think there is a quirk of human nature that places greater value on something that is difficult to attain or expensive. Low standards for acceptance make membership in the club—or church—less desirable. Joining and remaining a member of the WCG was anything but easy. Therefore, those who were determined to become members and undergo the membership process demonstrated a high level of commitment. Today, there is an increasing loss of commitment. One reason may be how easy it is to become and remain a member of the current WCG. This acculturation process is similar in other denominations, so declining membership and a growing lack of commitment is no surprise.

In the 1960s, 1970s, and into the 1980s, the WCG continued to grow. Armstrong's message was compelling, the world situation looked frightening, and he claimed to have the answers, bold, audacious claims that brought a continual flow of new people into the ranks. Membership grew to nearly 100,000 baptized members in some 120 countries around the world. (Our peak for the fall Feast of Tabernacles attendance was nearly 150,000 world-wide.) In recent years, these numbers have dropped off consider-ably, leveling out in the late 1990s at around 60,000 members—30,000 in the United States and another 30,000 scattered throughout the world.

When a prospect was baptized, it was usually done in pri-vate. We would find a swimming pool, lake, river, or even a bath-tub. Some ministers had portable baptismal tanks that could be set up in a member's garage. This tank had a metal tubular frame around which a heavy-grade plastic sheet was configured. It was practical and served well in the absence of a baptistry. Many of the baptisms I performed in North Carolina were conducted in members' garages, which was not the most inspiring setting, but no one complained. By the time prospects reached the decision to be baptized, they were just thankful God had called them to His "one true church." Who cared that power tools, lawn mow-ers, used cars, and general garage junk served as the backdrop to this momentous event? I believe the environment for a baptism should be more reflective of the solemnity of the occasion than a garage. However, without our own worship facilities, we had to do the best with what was available. While still a WCG executive, I suggested to the director of facilities that when constructing our own church building, we should plan a baptistry in the sanctuary so this sacrament could be witnessed by the entire congregation.

After one year of service as a ministerial assistant, I had yet to be ordained. Wayne and Joanne were transferred to another church area, and a very different pastor arrived. He asked what kind of work I had been doing. When I told him about my mod-est duties of landscaping, auto maintenance, and valet chores, he said those days were behind me. From now on, I was going to "get my butt to work!" This sounded good to me, and I soon saw that he meant it. He began sending Linda and me on visits by our-selves, allowing me to conduct Bible studies, and even giving me sermon opportunities. That was the positive side of the new administration. The negative side was that he was not a gracious man toward Linda or me. During my Monday morning evaluation, he would go beyond job performance and speaking skills to comment on my character and spiritual condition. On a less-frequent basis, Linda was called in for similar uninvited "spiritual insights" into her person and character. We both began to feel miserable about ourselves and developed an unhealthy antipathy for him. I am sure this pastor meant well, and most likely he was only doing for (or to) us what had been done to him. Since that time, I have determined not to let anyone pontificate about my spiritual condition without my permission nor will I allow anyone to evaluate the spirituality of my wife. Such experiences are absurd, hurtful, and not in the least edifying. They bore no positive fruit in our lives. Our working relationship became unbearable at times, and we felt like the Israelites under the heavy hand of the Pharaoh, praying for deliverance. And deliverance finally came.

When I was at this pastor's home, either doing office work or between meetings, he would invite me to a game of bumper pool. He needed a partner and to refuse would have been unthinkable. One day while playing, the pastor asked if I felt ready to be ordained as an elder. Almost two years had passed since my assignment to this local church. Most of my friends, who had been sent to congregations at the same time, had long since been ordained as elders. I was at the point of personal despair, so I said rather glibly, "Either I'm ready or the church should let me go." I must have been ready because shortly after that conversation, on Pentecost 1973 during the lunch break between services, I was ordained. On that particular feast day, we met in a Moose Lodge in a rural setting outside town. For some reason, the pastor decided to ordain me privately in the presence of the elders and wives in the kitchen. We were having a potluck meal, so we stood in a small circle, heads bowed and eyes closed, as the pastor prayed over me amid the smell of fried chicken and other assorted aromas. The pastor and the other elders laid hands on me and asked God to place me into the ministry of Jesus Christ as a local elder. When the afternoon service began, the pastor announced my ordination and the people applauded.

Admittedly, I am saddened by the "private" ordination, which was not unlike my baptism—somewhat alone and isolated from the congregation. Today and for most of the WCG's history, however, it has been the practice to ordain a man in the presence of the congregation. Why I was ordained amid the pots and pans of the Moose Lodge kitchen, I do not know.

How did a man become ordained as an elder or deacon? Did the WCG ordain women? First, the WCG does follow the biblical example in Acts 6 and ordain both men and women to the office of deacon and deaconess. They understand the office of deacon or deaconess to be one given to the physical service of the congregation. Deacons and deaconesses are responsible for overseeing the hall, including such things as setup, cleanup, ushering, greeting, caring for the physical needs of members, and congregational activities (picnics, sporting activities, etc.). These dedicated men and women are to a large degree the backbone of the local congregation. Generally, they have lived in an area for a long time and are well known and respected among the members.

Current WCG practice is not to ordain women to the office of pastor. Despite no movement on the part of WCG leadership to change this position, some female members of the WCG would like to see women ordained as elders and/or pastors. The WCG is no different from many evangelical churches that have experienced the pressure to clear a path to the pulpit for aspiring women. Thus far the WCG has resisted the temptation to change its stance on the question of ordaining women to the pastorate. I hope they will continue to uphold this biblical teaching and the tradition of orthodox Christianity.

The ordination of men to the office of elder followed a set pattern. The local pastor observed a given man as he served in the congregation and prayerfully considered whether this person should be recommended for ordination. The pastor may well seek advice from other local church elders or deacons regarding the possible ordination. Again, there are no other criteria to follow except those given by Paul to Timothy (1 Timothy; Titus 1). The pastor looks for a man who has a good marriage, is an able teacher of God's Word, is meek in spirit, and has a heart for God's people. When the pastor believed these criteria were present in a man's life, he would pray, then speak to the man about the possibility of ordination. After hearing their pastor speak of ordination, some men declined, feeling this was not what God would have them do. Some, however, did accept the recommendation for ordination. After receiving a favorable response from the candidate, the pastor filled out a form requesting ordination and sent it to WCG headquarters for approval. Generally, the director of church administration would grant the request. (Men and women could be ordained as deacons and deaconesses without permission from a superior). The administration would run a "tithe" check on the candidate before granting permission for ordination to any church office. A quick computer check determined whether the individual was donating on a regular basis—the check was for frequency, not amount. If a man was not faithfully giving to the church, he would not be ordained. Although there is logic in this statement, I failed to see scriptural justification for the tithe check. In my final years with WCG, I came to view this practice as a repugnant invasion of privacy, as well as a not-so-veiled consequence of legalism. The tithe check was not far removed from the demand that WCG employees tithe to the church as a condition of employment. This policy was instituted by Joseph Tkach Jr. soon after he assumed leadership of the WCG in 1995. On one hand, the church taught that giving is a voluntary matter of the heart; on the other it seemed to deny this by mandating giving among certain members—namely employees. I hope this distressing issue has since been addressed.

By the time that I joined the WCG in 1967, Armstrong had a clearly established hierarchy in the ministry. The lowest ordained position was that of deacon/deaconess. Then came the office of local elder. There were two classes of local elders—those employed by the church and those not employed by the church. Those on the church's payroll were called local elders; those not on the payroll were referred to as local church elders. Both were equal in rank, but there was a tendency to give preference to the employed elder in the area of local church leadership. This practice caused some friction. The next rank was that of the preaching elder. One had to be a preaching elder in the WCG before he could pastor a church. Preaching elders did most of the preaching in the congregation and directed the pastoral administration of the local church. Generally a man would have been a local elder or local church elder for several years before being ordained to the rank of preaching elder. Some exceptions were made to this scenario, which happened more commonly when the church was growing rapidly and the need for pastors was acute. It was possible for a man to remain in the office of preaching elder for the duration of his ministry, but some were ordained to the next rank of pastor. The concept of "pastor" in the WCG was a bit fuzzy. It was the highest rank I held in the WCG, but I cannot honestly tell you what it meant. "Pastors" did not have more competency to perform ministerial duties, but it did mean a greater measure of respect among the ministry and membership, as well as an automatic pay raise. Generally, ministers who served in greater administrative capacities carried the title of pastor. An example of such administrative roles would be a regional pastor, who is responsible to minister to and supervise eight to 10 ministers who serve 20 or more congregations. WCG regional directors, who administer the church's work in foreign countries, were all pastors or evangelists, which was the next rank. Like the function of pastor, the evangelist rank was a bit fuzzy. In the mid-1990s, there were less than a dozen men worldwide who held the rank of evangelist. I know of no guidelines that spelled out the qualifications for promotion to evangelist. It seemed those pastors who had been around a long time, had greater administrative responsibilities, and were well liked by the administration were ordained into this small club. The rank of evangelist had nothing to do with ability to preach, pastor, teach, or grow churches; rather, it was administrative in nature. The current administration was less than happy with the rank system it inherited from Mr. Armstrong. The system has since been changed to reflect what one finds in mainstream evangelical churches.

One example of how the ordination process worked is illustrated by a telephone call I received while working in Pasadena.

An evangelist in church administration called to ask my opinion about raising an employee in rank from local elder to preaching elder. Because I was pastor of the Pasadena headquarters church, the evangelist wanted my input on the proposal of holding the ordination during a Sabbath worship service. The individual in question was a department head and regularly interacted with our ministers in the local congregations. "Why do you want to ordain him?" I asked.

"Well, he works a lot with our church pastors and this would give him more respect in the ministry in carrying out his duties," was the response.

I could not believe my ears because I thought by 1994 we were beyond such reasoning, but I was wrong. "If you want to ordain him, that's your business," I said. "However, as pastor of the Pasadena church, I don't need another preaching elder. In fact, I don't need another elder at all. I think the people in the congregation would find it odd that we ordain a guy to preaching elder without any obvious reason. It would be without a context."

The evangelist said he saw my point and concluded, "Well, maybe we should just ordain him in another venue." I didn't agree with this response either, but as I had learned over the years at the church's headquarters, to offer an unsolicited opinion was seldom appreciated, so I let it slide.

After my ordination as a local elder in the spring of 1973, life quickly became better for Linda and me. Our church circuit had changed when Wayne and Joanne were transferred to another area. We gave up our South Carolina congregation and started a new congregation in Lenoir, North Carolina, a town north of Ashville. Linda and I were told to relocate near Lenoir. Because we were renting and not buying a home, the housing prospects were more limited. We ended up in Hickory, North Carolina. We found a house to rent, and the pastor said he wanted to check its suitability. That hit me the wrong way because I thought our living arrangements were a personal decision. But he was the pastor, and I concluded he had the right to investigate such matters. Somehow we managed to distract him, so he never made it to inspect our new home. I remember telling Linda's uncle of the incident. He advised me to tell the guy that when he paid the rent, he could inspect our house. Until then, he had no business meddling. However right Linda's uncle may have been, to speak to God's minister in such a way was not proper. So we never said anything.

Life in Hickory was good. We were given a brand-new car by the church and a rather generous raise. Our days were filled with visiting members and prospective members, conducting Bible studies, and leading Sabbath services. All was going well until a major doctrinal crisis struck the church in 1974. The question arose about the day on which Pentecost was to be observed. It had been our practice to observe Pentecost on a Monday. This was based on counting 50 days from the Sabbath that falls during the days of Unleavened Bread. The way Herbert Armstrong interpreted Scripture located Pentecost on Monday. In 1974, a WCG scholar had presented a paper that stated the correct day for Pentecost was Sunday. This caused no small stir in our fellowship because the *day* of worship was critical. We had observed Pentecost on Monday for decades and the thought of being wrong was disturbing. Mr. Armstrong announced he would restudy the subject and make a determination before Pentecost.

There were other tensions building in the WCG as well. At issue was authority in the church. There were those who were subtly calling into question Mr. Armstrong's ability to lead in the wake of his dealing with his son, Garner Ted. Ted had been removed from office in the early 1970s for undisclosed reasons. Rumors of immoral conduct were rampant, but Mr. Armstrong would say nothing more than that his son was in "the bonds of Satan." After some time away from active duty, Ted was restored months later to his executive responsibilities. Undoubetdly, there were some men who were not happy with Herbert's newfound grace extended to his wayward son. I have since learned that Ted faced challenges of his own in Pasadena with men who sought to drive a wedge between him and his father. My sideline observations in the Armstrong vs. Armstrong affair was that these other church leaders were successful in fanning the flames of discord between father and son.

Shortly before Pentecost, I was visiting my parents in Richmond and decided to worship at the local WCG congregation on the Sabbath. The minister gave a not-too-veiled sermon about taking care that we not allow ourselves to be "deceived by lies." One did not have to be a rocket scientist to determine he was making veiled allusions to Mr. Armstrong's leadership in Pasadena. This pastor concluded his sermon by announcing a special study paper on the subject of Pentecost would be made available to all members immediately after the service. I was alarmed. Mr. Armstrong had written the entire ministry stating that he would make the decision regarding the correct day of Pentecost worship shortly before the feast. Up to that point, nothing had been sent from Pasadena. *What was this guy doing,* I wondered. Immediately after the worship service, the ministerial assistant began passing out the study paper from the WCG scholar who had submitted the same to Mr. Armstrong, claiming that the correct day for Pentecost was Sunday and not Monday. I asked the pastor by whose authority he was passing out this paper. Didn't he know Mr. Armstrong was going to give us an official document before Pentecost?

"I don't need anyone's authority to do this," came the response.

"What about your district superintendent?" I asked. "Does he know what you are doing?"

"Yes, he does, but I don't need his authority either," the pastor replied.

There it was plain as day—open rebellion. Linda and I began our drive back to North Carolina in a state of shock. Along the way, we stopped to call our pastor to tell him of the mutiny in Richmond. Unbeknownst to me, the minister in Richmond had called to tell my pastor that I was a troublemaker and should be fired.

I discovered later that approximately 40 pastors along the eastern seaboard were working together to form their own church, which they called the Associated Churches of God. Word got back to Pasadena that a rebellion was in the making, which got the wheels turning. It was rumored that the opposition was planning to announce its break from Pasadena the next week at Sabbath services. Mr. Armstrong's response was swift. He canceled Sabbath services. It was a controversial move that some maintained he had no right to do. The reply was that Mr. Armstrong was the head of the church under Jesus Christ and had all the authority necessary to cancel a weekend service, if he so desired. And he did so desire, so the word came from headquarters to cancel all Sabbath services for the next weekend. For most Christians such authority exercised by one man over an entire church body is unimaginable. Yet it was so with Armstrong and those like him who arrogate to themselves illegitimate authority in the church.

Armstrong's tactic was a good move because the next week the rebels' hands were forced, and they made their stand, refusing to vacate their pulpits. They called for normal services, and many members who attended services that week made the break from the WCG. It was a horrific time. From South Carolina to New England, the WCG lost about 40 ministers and about 5,000 members. Entire congregations were lost or reduced to a few dozen people. I remember a couple congregations that had numbered into the hundreds reduced to a group small enough to meet in someone's living room. It was a terrible time for me personally because I spent days on the road, visiting members who had left the church. They were angry and often hostile, wanting nothing more to do with the WCG. My pain was increased when I learned Wayne and Joanne had joined those who had jumped ship. The whole affair was so upsetting that my stomach felt as though it were tied up in knots, and I became physically ill for several days.

Like so many of the splinter groups of the WCG, the Associated Churches of God soon withered and virtually disappeared. But the lessons of this experience often go unheeded, and others have split off from the WCG over the years to start first this and then that "Church of God . . ." I believe there have been more than 100 splits since Mr. Armstrong founded the Radio Church of God in 1934. Each splinter group vies for legitimacy by claiming a greater orthodoxy to Armstrong's teaching. What a picture! Theologically challenged and spiritually deluded men arguing among themselves, each claiming to have a more certain lock on the "truth," which in reality is no truth at all but a duke's mixture of error and heresy.

In the aftermath of this uprising, we asked ourselves if this was the "great falling away" of which the Bible spoke. We wondered if this was the sign that the end was about to come. This was not the case. As time went on, we saw more uprisings as members became disillusioned with the WCG leadership and sought to find their own path with a new leader—while still carrying much of the same doctrinal baggage.

Mr. Armstrong was as good as his word. Just before the Pentecost celebration, he announced he had been in error regarding the day of the observance. It was to be kept on Sunday and not on Monday as we had so faithfully observed for decades. Armstrong wrote that the mistake lay in his misunderstanding of the Hebrew word for *from* as used in Leviticus 23:15, the passage in which the Israelites were instructed to count 50 days from the Sabbath during the Days of Unleavened Bread. Previously, he had thought the word should be interpreted "away from," that is, not including the day on which the count began. After consulting with a Hebrew scholar in Israel, Mr. Armstrong was made to understand that in Hebrew the word used in that verse means "inclusive counting." That is, the count begins with and includes the day after the weekly Sabbath. This is a short synopsis of the entire argument, which required many written pages to communicate.

Suffice it to say, Armstrong admitted his error and changed the day of celebration. Ministers and members alike rejoiced about this "new truth" and reasoned that God had not been upset with us about the wrong day because things in the "Work" were generally going so well. No one wondered why Armstrong had been in error for so long because we believed in progressive revelation, that God was restoring lost truth gradually to His church through His apostle, Herbert Armstrong. Of course, there is no progressive revelation because the truth was revealed in Christ once and for all. This orthodox faith of the first century received by Christians was preserved through the centuries and passed to us with the call to hold it fast (Jude 3).

Armstrong's measure of the church's health was in large part determined by its financial statement. In the early 1960s, the WCG experienced an almost 30 percent increase in income per year for several years. What greater proof could one ask for that would demonstrate God truly was blessing us? When I arrived at Ambassador College in 1967, the 30 percent annual increase was beginning to weaken, so the faculty and ministry urged us to pray that God would send the funds to continue "the Work." But as time progressed, the financial growth continued to erode. Mr. Armstrong would tell us it had to do with deficiencies in our personal spiritual lives, so along with most of the membership, I would fast and pray, examining myself before God to see what it was in my life that might be causing Him to withhold His heavenly blessings. This often did the job for members and those we called "co-workers" (those who contributed regularly) because they would rally to Armstrong's call and send cash.

In the late 1970s, Armstrong asked members to take out personal loans to send money to headquarters. A number of people did! By that time, I had had enough and would not mortgage my family's financial security. That was another brick coming loose in my dedication to Armstrong and his mission. On several more occasions, Armstrong appealed for additional financial sacrifice, and I could not bring myself to participate. Today this concept of the "health and wealth" gospel is not playing so well. Armstrong associated financial well being directly with contributions to him. "Give faithfully, and God will reward you financially." Having rejected his doctrines and embraced many truths of Christianity, the WCG has paid dearly in terms of lost revenue. In recent years, the WCG has spoken in terms of deficit rather than surplus. Since Mr. Armstrong's death in 1986, the WCG has experienced a steady decline in income. But Christians should avoid *quid pro quo* when giving. Yes, God does bless those who give, but for Christians, giving is motivated by love, not driven by law or, worse, a mercenary motive for gain. Financial exploitation is common not only in cults, but also in many law-driven Christian churches that would seek to measure a member's faith and trust in Christ by the size and frequency of financial contributions. Guilt-evoking (and income generating!) statements are made, such as "If you really trust God, you will give generously" or "Your financial woes are directly related to your lack of faithful tithing." Such a psychological or sociological ploy is another effort to control members.

In 1974 another major event in my life sent me abroad. Probably during a ministerial conference in Pasadena, I ran into Frank, the regional director of the WCG's German office. At the time, I was an elder and had received training as a field minister, which was precisely what Frank needed in Germany. He asked if I would be willing to come to Germany to help. Linda was pregnant with our first son, Rhett, and we were expecting a transfer to another assignment in the United States. But our hearts were committed to serving God as He would lead us, and we felt that He was calling us to Europe. We talked to our district superintendent, and he encouraged us to consider our choice prayerfully. For us, the choice was obvious. I spoke some German, the German Work needed me, so it became apparent that we should go. I didn't realize that a certain streak of "glory hound" in my soul also drove me to accept the offer. This opportunity fit into my long-range personal plans for ministry, and it appeared to be a "call from God." So Linda and I, Bible in hand, set off on an adventure that would make a lasting mark on our lives.

Chapter 6

Back on Track

The deeds we do, the words we say, Into still air they seem
to fleet, We count them ever past; But they shall last,— In
the dread judgment they And we shall meet. —John Keble
(*The Effect of Example*)

In the summer of 1974, I felt as though my career were in high
gear as I flew to Germany with my pregnant wife, Linda. I had
fond memories of Germany—the land, culture, and people. Now
it was going to be my home—until the end. You see, Frank, the
German regional director felt that once someone was called to the
German Work, that person was always called to the German
Work. This was to be a lifetime commitment to serve until the end
came, which was okay because we did not think we had much
time before the end anyway.

The way we understood prophecy meant Linda and I would
soon be in the middle of earth-shattering world events. Mr.
Armstrong taught that the dictatorial leader of the United States
of Europe would emerge from Germany. In fact, Armstrong spec-
ulated that this pan-European German leader would be none
other than Franz Joseph Strauss (the now-deceased governor of
Bavaria). "Why, you could see the power in the man's eyes,"
Armstrong said, and he knew Strauss was destined to be the

prophetic beast. Herr Strauss even accepted an invitation to visit Mr. Armstrong in his private residence in Pasadena. Afterward, Armstrong related that in a private moment, he had put his hands on Strauss's broad shoulders and told him he would have great power one day and must remember to use it wisely. Undoubtedly, Herr Strauss was thinking of winning the race for German chancellor and was totally oblivious to Armstrong's hidden meaning. But Strauss died in the 1980s, and his death ushered in a new round of speculation regarding the identity of the coming "beast." It was not long before we located him—an Austrian heir to the Habsburg throne, Otto von Habsburg. Habsburg also never fulfilled his prophetic role, so with Armstrong's death in 1986, we eventually quit trying to figure out the identity of the "beast."

There we were in the land of the "beast," excited about being on the front lines of prophetic developments. Frank, the German regional director, was a Teutonic version of Herbert Armstrong. He lived, breathed, and ate "the Work" and kept all the members in the German-speaking areas on constant alert for the "end time," just as did Mr. Armstrong. I felt privileged and thrilled to share this incredible prophetic journey with him and others in the German-speaking church.

There weren't many members of the Worldwide Church of God in Germany. In fact, we didn't call ourselves the Worldwide Church of God; instead, we used the name "Ambassador College," which later became "Stiftung Ambassador College" (Ambassador College Foundation). The name had an air of respectability that allowed us to conduct business more easily. Our German leaders correctly surmised it would make our work hard to use the name WCG. But the problem with the *Stiftung* (Foundation) title was that it obscured who we were for the uninitiated and clouded our identity in our own minds. Were we a church or a foundation? I think the arguments put forth to justify the name "Ambassador College" were weak. The WCG in Germany, Austria, and Switzerland never numbered more than about 1,100 men, women, and children. Meanwhile another group viewed as a cult, the Mormons, publicly used their church name in Germany. Today they have more than 45,000 members. Playing the name game did not help us in the long run.

Linda and I learned within our first months in Europe that the WCG had no concept about how to deal with expatriots. Most international firms know that extra effort and expense is involved in keeping Americans happy and effective in foreign posts. Things such as special schools for children, American-style housing, a social network, frequent furloughs home, and pre-move language and cultural training are some common forms of assistance. The WCG did not provide much of this for its American citizens living abroad. We were mostly on our own and were expected to adapt and function at top effectiveness in a foreign and often unhelpful culture. Even with the aid of the Holy Spirit, we were still human beings susceptible to all the weaknesses of those who are placed in such circumstances.

Linda and I were pre-wired for failure from the start. The WCG machine needed people who would sacrifice without complaint, do their job, suffer, and ask for more. If you stumbled, you were out. Young, inexperienced, unprepared, and pregnant was a combination of circumstances that caused us to stumble.

Frank determined that Linda and I would need to move to Hannover in northern Germany to pastor the congregations in Hannover, Hamburg, and Berlin. Naturally, the director was concerned that everything would go well. To prepare us for the assignment, we were told to live in Düsseldorf (the WCG German home office) so we could spend time at a language school. We were given an apartment in which to live.

I cannot fully express the shock and disappointment Linda and I experienced when we moved into the apartment. Visiting a foreign country is one thing, but living there is an entirely different matter. We were not prepared for what we were about face. No one had told us what German apartments are like. No one had told us what to bring from America and what to leave behind. Unfortunately we were not insightful enough to inquire. We didn't know that our American electrical appliances would not work because the current is 220V instead of 110V. When we walked into the sixth-floor apartment on a busy city street, we were greeted by a long, narrow room. It was dark, noisy, and almost devoid of the expected basics. Other than toilets, sinks, a stove, and an overhead light bulb or two, there wasn't much else. There were no cabinets, no closets, and no rugs. The church provided some sparse furnishings, including a bed, a table and chairs, and some dishes and pots and pans. There was no air conditioning or fan, so when a hot day rolled around (and we did have some hot days), we suffered. In all fairness, this was intended to be transitional housing, so we grinned and bore it, knowing that things would get better—we hoped.

I went with the director to visit several schools, and together we selected Bènèdict Language Schools, a local German chain of language institutions. Frank enrolled me in an intensive program of five or six weeks of five hours each day of one-on-one language training. Linda enrolled in a class with mostly Polish-speaking Germans. Her class met for a few hours each day for several weeks. I guess the director figured giving Linda the same language training that I received was not worth the expense. As a result, it took her longer to grasp the language, thereby making her adjustment to Germany more difficult. After completing my course, I had a good grasp of the language and felt ready for my first assignment. Now I needed the practical daily experience of using the language in real-life situations.

Linda and I took our church-provided car—a new silver Audi 80—on a house-hunting trip to Hannover. The director wanted us to live near the airport, presumably so it would be more convenient for him when he visited. We were not keen about living near the airport because of the noise, so we decided to look elsewhere. After checking the papers and driving around a lot, we found a nice three-bedroom apartment in Hämmlerwald, a village east of Hannover. It was a peaceful place that was not yet part of Hannover's urban sprawl. The brand-new apartment was situated on the first floor and was virtually stripped, which was standard for German apartments. It was equipped with the bare essentials—a stove, kitchen sink, toilets, bathtub, bathroom sink with one light, and a broom closet. But it had beautiful wood parquet floors and a balcony off the living room.

We were excited about getting set up in our new home. Our furniture arrived from the States in a large metal container. Everything fit nicely, and we bought a few things such as clothes closets, a washer and dryer, a refrigerator, and some kitchen cabinets. This was as much as we could do because money became a problem within a short period of time. It must have had something to do with the Watergate scandal, which had broken in the summer of 1974. The dollar plummeted against the deutsche mark, and it was not long before this devaluation cost us one-third of our income, which was paid in U.S. dollars. I had hoped that our businesspeople in Pasadena would be aware of what was going on and move to make up the difference. But no help was forthcoming. They were not aware of the situation because they had not been told to look out for the ministers serving in international areas. Paychecks were automatically cut in U.S. dollars—period.

Things became so bad for Linda and me financially that we had difficulty buying shoes. Thankfully, my parents sent care packages to keep us going. We kept in contact with our parents but did not share our plight with them. Finally, after much prayer and with some trepidation, I mustered the courage to lay out the entire financial picture for the director. We sat together on a couch in his home in Düsseldorf as I explained and presented our situation mathematically. After searching my eyes with his penetrating gaze, he expressed surprise and agreed that something should be done. He lived quite well in a single-family home (at that time, this was a sign of upperclass status). It had a manicured lawn and a garden with a swimming pool. Staff members from the office took care of the garden property, so the director and his wife could devote themselves full time to the "Work." Both he and his wife were salaried employees. In those days, Mr. Armstrong did not allow ministers' wives to work because he wanted them available to help their husbands in the ministry. The exception was the ministers' wives in the international offices and at Pasadena. These men generally earned more than their counterparts in local congregations. Their salaries, combined with what their wives earned, yielded a comfortable living.

Perhaps this is why the director could be losing money to the exchange rate and not have felt its impact in the same way Linda and I had felt it. In the year that we were in Germany, nothing was done to compensate for the loss of money in exchange.

One year? Yes, we lasted only one year. Several things worked against us, which, when taken together, made the situation unbearable. First, the financial dilemma hung over our heads like a black cloud. Then our first son, Rhett, was born. In those days, the WCG discouraged the use of medical doctors and many WCG women sought to have their babies naturally with the assistance of a midwife. Linda and I were convinced this was the way to go, so we found a midwife for her prenatal care. We also thought it wise to visit a doctor so he could be available in case of an emergency. (This may not have been consistent with our beliefs, but consistency was never a strong point of the WCG.) When the birth pangs began, Linda was home, and we called the midwife. We quickly realized something was wrong because the baby's heartbeat was irregular. The midwife advised us to go the hospital, so I packed Linda into our Audi and we flew down the Autobahn to Peine, the neighboring town to the east.

Once in the hospital, a nightmare began for Linda. Her German was not proficient yet because we had been in the country for less than six months. The personnel were not particularly friendly nor were they particularly helpful, especially when they realized that two crazy Americans wanted to have natural childbirth, which definitely was not the rage in Germany at the time. The birth was painful and Linda lost much blood in the delivery. It was a good thing that we were in the hospital because Rhett's umbilical cord was wrapped around his neck. This could have proven fatal without expert medical help. (That experience with these "pagan doctors" did register as a little yellow warning light in my mind, noting that maybe they were not quite as evil as I had thought). After the birth, Linda was extremely weak and was required to remain in the hospital for 10 long days. The staff was unfriendly and gruff, which is the last thing you need after such an ordeal. Of course, we weren't fully cooperative either, especially when it came to giving Rhett some shots. I declined and watched them closely to make sure they did not give him one against my wishes. (It was not until a few years ago, at age 21, that Rhett received his first shots courtesy of the United States Coast Guard.) I told the hospital personnel that I wanted Rhett circumcised, which was something they did not do normally. However, I insisted and demanded that it be done on the eighth day (just as God commanded in the Old Testament). About this time I imagine the staff must have thought we were aliens from another planet. They relented and referred us to a Persian doctor who circumcised our eight-day-old son. Now he bore on his flesh the mark of the covenant with Abraham, which marked the beginning of a childhood steeped in Judeo-Christian teaching. Finally, Linda came home, and we enjoyed the presence of Rhett Thomas Lapacka in our lives. As was the custom in the church and in keeping with the Old Testament covenant, we gave an extra financial offering as a thankoffering for our firstborn son. In fact, Mr. Armstrong taught that we were *between* covenants, neither under the old nor the new, but somewhere in between. This was a bizarre teaching that caused no end of difficulty when it came to determining what had to be observed from the Law of Moses and what was obviated by Christ. It seemed as though all the laws regarding the tithe conveniently were taught as binding.

I spent much time on the road in Germany, trying to keep up with three small congregations. The distances between Hannover, Hamburg, and Berlin are enormous. It was usually a two-hour trip from Hannover to Hamburg. Traveling to Berlin was a tortuous six hours. And getting into Berlin was no easy matter. In the early 1970s, the Communists had firm control of East Germany. Once you came to the border between East and West Germany, you were subjected to long waits in your car, questioning, and searches. After making it past the dour, threatening border guards, you were confronted with a poor road system and ever-changing speed limits. There was no grace given on the speed limit. If you were over by a kilometer or two, it was grounds to be stopped and fined—and you had to pay on the spot. Once I was stopped for driving in the left lane of a four-lane autobahn (two lanes in either direction) and had to pay a 20 deutsche mark fine to the police officer. To leave the main road made you subject to arrest. Thus the twice-monthly trips to Berlin were not among my most-coveted duties, but I made the trip. Richard, a deacon in Hannover, volunteered many times to keep me company on those long weekend trips. We often traveled to Berlin together and became close friends and remain so to this day. I nicknamed him "Lucas" after St. Paul's travel companion, the good doctor, Luke.

In February 1975, Linda, baby Rhett, and I drove through East Germany to southern Poland. We were looking for Victor, a man who had requested a visit and baptism. By the time we arrived in his little Polish village, it was dark, late, and snowing. The street lighting was poor to nonexistent. The signs also were poor to nonexistent. Linda became worried; so did I. Our visa stated that we were tourists. The Polish officials were less strict about Communism than most other nations behind the Iron Curtain. A Catholic majority still was convinced that the power of the church would one day overcome the Communists, which in fact happened. But our situation on that particular night was precarious.

We were concerned that the state police would pick us up if we continued to wander around lost. There were no Holiday Inns to pop into for the night. This was a country village. I prayed, "Dear God, please help us find this guy soon." Finally, I said, "Honey, I see some lights in that apartment complex over there. I'll go over and ask if someone knows Victor." Don't forget that people spoke Polish, not English. Only occasionally could you find an older Pole who spoke German. By this time, I was fairly proficient at German. My Spanish was passable. I could struggle through enough French to figure out what was going on, and I could work a little with Italian. Polish, however, was like a language from Mars—and I'm even half-Polish and had heard my Dad and relatives speak it around the house. I parked the car, stepped into the snow and cold, and approached the apartment.

I spied a teenage girl and called to her. She came toward me. Out came German. No response. Then English. No response. Using German again, I said, "Do you know Victor P.?" She nodded enthusiastically when she heard the name and motioned that she would ride with us to take us to him. She rattled on a bit in Polish as we drove through the night, but the conversation was definitely one-sided. Within minutes, we were at Victor's house. He warmly greeted us and told us the girl was his niece and this had been her first time in a Western car. Linda and I thanked our dear God for the obvious help provided us in time of need.

The visit with Victor went well. He was proficient in German, so there was no communication problem. We spent several days discussing the Bible and answering his questions. On the Sabbath, we drove to the city of Katowice, where Linda and I took a hotel room in a four-star hotel. In those days a four-star hotel in Poland was like a Best Western, but it sure beat the primitive conditions in which Victor lived (by Polish standards, Victor was not doing badly because he owned his own house with an outdoor toilet and an indoor bathtub). Victor took his tithe in Polish Zlotys that he had been saving and paid for our stay in Katowice. There in our hotel room I baptized Victor as our first Polish WCG member. (Victor is still a faithful member of the WCG more than 20 years later. I had the pleasure of seeing him several years ago at the Feast of Tabernacles in the Black Forest, Germany.) Since that February day when I baptized Victor, a few other Poles found their way into the WCG, but all have since left the fellowship.

In Hämmlerwald, I would take a daily jog through the woods to stay in shape. It was on the jogs that I would think and pray about our situation in Germany. The financial pressure, the homesickness, and especially the loneliness were overwhelming. At this time in Pasadena, the church was entering the human potential movement. WCG had a few gurus on campus who spoke often on the subject and even prepared audiocassettes for the ministry. It was at this time that Mr. Armstrong got involved in a venture founding a magazine known as *Quest*. It appeared to be a noble project because it would accentuate the best in human ability and spirit. Armstrong hired an outside editor who set up an editorial team in New York City. *Quest* was a paid subscription magazine that targeted the upscale market in the United States and abroad. Large sums of church money were spent on staffing and promotion to get *Quest* off the ground. The first issue looked great and included paid advertising. I was not intimately involved with this magazine venture, but I recall being told that Armstrong and the editor got into an argument one day. Mr. Armstrong wanted more editorial control, and the editor balked, resigning his position. The publication collapsed, and the church lost a considerable sum of money on an enterprise that had nothing to do with the church's purpose. But those were the days when money was flowing freely and Armstong could afford to dabble. Besides, there was no clear business plan that Armstrong followed. He was an opportunist entrepreneur with a keen sense for what would work and what wouldn't. Most projects he undertook ended with success. A few did not, so he would bite the bullet, cut his losses, and write a letter to the membership to drum up more money.

The human potential audiocassettes that I listened to while driving around the German countryside posed disturbing questions for me to which I could find no clear answers. One series had to do with midlife crisis and the uncertainty that can occur regarding one's choice of profession. I was especially vulnerable to that line of questioning. We were on the eastern frontier of the "Work" in Europe and felt isolated and uncertain about our choice. Realizing that we had signed on to this location forever— or until Christ returned—provided no immediate relief. After several months of desperate prayer, I told Linda I felt we should leave the ministry and return to the states where I could get a job. Linda obediently agreed, but since that time has learned that agreeing with her husband is not always the most helpful thing to do. She has become a wonderful partner in life, helping me through thoughtful dialogue to work through difficult issues.

Shortly after our conversation, the director came for a visit. I took advantage of the opportunity to tell him that we did not like it in Germany and wanted to return home where I could seek another line of work. He was stunned by this announcement but kept his composure. After the discussion, he said he would make arrangements for our return to the United States and would get back to me in several weeks. In two weeks, he returned to Hannover. He and I went out to lunch after Sabbath services. During those two weeks, I had had a change of heart about ministry. I had determined I really wanted to remain a minister, but I couldn't take anymore of Germany. I told Frank about my change of heart, and again he said he would take care of everything. I thanked him profusely and was grateful to have such a wonderful man in our corner who understood our situation and would help us smooth things over with the executives in Pasadena.

In May 1975, we said our good-byes in Germany and flew directly to Pasadena. Robert, our good friend from Bricket Wood, was now pastoring a church not far from Pasadena. He had a travel trailer in his front yard and offered it to Linda, Rhett, and me while we waited for reassignment. I called for an appointment with the international director of church administration. Because he was the next level up from the regional director in Germany, I knew I had to start with him. He was a friendly man with black wavy hair and a deep booming voice. His manner was casual and rather nonchalant, which I appreciated. I thought he would welcome me back, express understanding for our difficult situation in Germany, and work toward our reassignment in the States. He asked me to tell him why we wanted to return to the States after such a short stay in Europe. I explained everything. When I came to the part about the financial pressure because of the falling dollar, he said, "Tom, we have to learn to sacrifice."

That sounded philosophical and maybe even spiritual, but I happened to know a little about his own circumstances. He lived in a large, nicely furnished home on fashionable Orange Grove Boulevard that was provided by the church. He drove a beautiful late-model luxury car. And he had time in his busy schedule to pursue oil painting. Somehow, knowing that about his lifestyle made his advice ring a bit hollow. At the conclusion of the meeting, he told me he was uncertain about my future, but we would talk again.

I left the meeting perplexed. Hadn't the German director pled my case with Pasadena? Next, I called on one of the assistants to the international director of church administration. This man was a high-ranking minister in the church and closer to my age. He was cool and distant toward me as we talked. After a brief warmup, he asked, "Why did you desert your post in Germany?"

"What? I didn't desert my post," I replied. "Another minister moved in to replace me."

The minister glowered at me and almost shouted, "Bulls—! Are you calling the German director a liar?!"

That was like a slap in the face and a bucket of cold water at the same time. The German director obviously had not pled my case. In fact, the opposite had happened. He had either painted me as a deserter or at least given that impression. I knew my next response had to be measured or I would be in much worse trouble. Slowly and carefully I answered, "I'm not calling anyone a liar. I'm saying that I didn't desert my post." I added that I had worked through my internal struggles and still desired to be in the full-time ministry of the Worldwide Church of God.

"You just want this job because of the money," the minister said.

That remark from this "man of God" was like a bullet aimed at the heart. Never in my wildest dreams had I thought of ministry as a way to make a living. This made me angry on two counts. First, the open accusation that I was only in this for the money (and heaven knows we were not exactly in Fat City while in Germany) and, second, he implied that I could not make it in life unless I worked for the church. But I controlled my anger and excused myself from his office, all the while telling myself that this guy was not what I would expect of a high-ranking minister.

Now our personal situation was looking bleak. On the next Sabbath, I ran into the German director, who had come to Pasadena on busines. "They think I deserted my post," I told him. I hoped that when he heard this, he would respond with assurances that he would take care of the situation.

His response, however, led me to believe that he already had "taken care" of everything. Without one sign of compassion or warmth in his face, the director looked at me and said, "You did." With that he turned and walked away. It was the last I saw of him for five years.

I realized it was possible I would be fired, so I put together a résumé and started checking the *Pasadena Star News* for jobs. Not all avenues were exhausted, however, so I called for an appointment with the minister in charge of the human potential program. Surely he would help. He was warm, friendly, and encouraging and said he would do what he could. Then I went to another top minister at headquarters and asked if he would vouch for me to be granted a sabbatical in Pasadena. (At that time the WCG had a sabbatical program whereby selected ministers were brought in for a year of Ambassador College classes. I discovered later that many of these men were brought in for disciplinary reasons and the sabbatical program was nothing more than a euphemism for what was derisively called a "retreading" by many field pastors. To be on sabbatical meant something was wrong with you. The sabbatical was not especially designed for the ministry; instead, pastors were tossed in the classroom with the undergraduates. I did not know all this at the time, believing the church propaganda to be true. After a few years in the WCG ministry, one learned to read between the lines, distinguishing what was said officially from what was meant.) The minister was encouraging and said he would speak to my superiors on my behalf.

Weeks passed and nothing happened. No one said anything, and I was left to hang around, waiting for the phone to ring. I decided to go to the director of church administration and ask either for reassignment to a local congregation or permission to be put on the sabbatical program. This man was an evangelist with whitish-blonde hair. Once ushered into his office and seated, he asked me to tell him what happened in Germany. I told my story. To my surprise, he looked out the window as I spoke and seemed to pay me little heed. Undeterred, I completed my story. He looked at his watch, stared out the window, and said, "I have a luncheon with Ted [Armstrong]. It's apparent you never really wanted to be a minister. It would probably be best for you to go get a job and if you want to come back into the ministry in a year or so the door will be open."

He excused himself, and I left the office angry and went home thinking, "He's a jerk!"

By now the picture was clear—I was on the way out. No one in Pasadena was sympathetic to my case. I considered going to see Garner Ted Armstrong, but I was so disillusioned that I did not think I could bear the possibility that Ted would treat me in the same way. Frankly, I think that subconsciously I was seeking to protect myself from the possibility that Ted would be as insensitive as the other men I had dealt with to this point.

I discussed my situation with Robert, who said he thought I was getting ram-rodded. He encouraged me to see Ted, but I could not bring myself to do it. To Robert's credit, he went to see the international director of church administration and declared they were making a mistake. That could have cost Robert his job. Despite that possibility, he went to bat for a friend in need. I am forever indebted to Robert for his courageous loyalty in defending me at great risk to himself. After Robert's valiant defense, which yielded no results, I decided to make one last appeal to the director in charge of the international ministry. I met him in his office with his two assistants. We spoke for a long time, but it was obvious we were at an impasse. They were not going to recommend that I be hired back into the U.S. ministry nor were they going to recommend that I be given a sabbatical. Finally, the international director said, "Tom, we don't know what to do with you. Either you are going to quit on your own or we are going to let you go."

I was prepared for such an ultimatum. I had interviewed for a few jobs and been offered a position as a moving consultant for a local Allied Van Lines franchise. There was no way I was going to be thrown out in disgrace, so I offered my resignation and left.

That was a sad day for me. I was struggling with all kinds of emotions, including bewilderment, shock, anger, and bitterness. Despite what was rather shallow treatment of a man in distress, I determined that I would prove myself to my church superiors on two fronts—financially and in service. I vowed to myself that I would never return to work for the church until I was earning more money than they could pay me. Then I would prove my ministry by serving in the local congregation at no cost to the church. Robert agreed with my resolution and encouraged me to begin my service in the local Pasadena congregation. In my prayers, I bitterly repented before God of any and all sins that I could think of, especially for having "let Him down" in Germany. I asked Him to help me deal with the bitterness and anger I felt gripping my heart.

In 1975 there were four large WCG congregations in Pasadena, each consisting of 500 to 900 members. They met on the church's property. I decided to attend the congregation that met in the Imperial School's gymnasium under the pastorship of a minister who had formerly been a chiropractor. Robert suggested I talk to this pastor's assistant, a local elder named Joe Tkach. On a bright Sabbath day, Linda and I went to the Imperial School's gymnasium with the hopes of beginning a new career of service. I asked where I could find Joe Tkach, and someone pointed him out to me. He was a gregarious man who wore a large smile as he greeted me. After a brief introduction, I told him that I would like to attend that congregation and would be available to help in any way I could. He responded that there was more than enough to do and welcomed me heartily. He said he would speak to the pastor and set up a meeting. I thanked him and felt good about finding a niche in one of the headquarters' congregations so I could, in effect, do penance.

A few days later, I went to the pastor's office to meet with him and Joe. Again I briefly told my story to the pastor and added that I desired to help in the local congregation. After hearing this, he replied, "Well, there's not that much here for you to do. Maybe you could help out in another congregation." Joe was silent, and the meeting was over. (I didn't speak to Joe Tkach again until years later when he had become director of church administration.)

I left the pastor's office with a deep hurt in my soul. It became painfully obvious that I was being blackballed. How could such a warm welcome and promise of service suddenly turn into a "no help needed" sign? That meeting almost took the heart out of me. I told Robert of the meeting, and he said he would love to have me help in his congregation. Again Robert reached out to help a brother who was down and out. Had Robert not offered that visible help, I do not know what I would have done.

One illness that plagues cults and Christian congregations and indicates a church has gotten off track is that the goal becomes more important than the individual. In one sense, it is not far removed from what I saw in Communism—the state was supreme; the individual exists only to serve the needs of the state. This is the way we were treated in Armstrong's church. He often remarked to the membership that ministers were there to "hold up his hands." So, what happened when someone faltered in his duty to support "God's anointed"? Such an individual was dismissed, demoted, disgraced, or excommunicated. In his place would step another bright-eyed eager soul, prepared to give everything for the cause while having his own soul impoverished.

Does such callousness in dealing with people's lives and spiritual welfare occur in Christian congregations? Sadly, it does when the leadership is so driven by its goal that people are seen as means to an end, rather than the end itself. These goals are masked in pious-sounding phrases such as "seeking and saving the lost," but all the while, God's precious lambs are used to gratify the leader's ego. As new people enter through the front door, streams of disillusioned, wounded, and hurting souls exit through the church's back door. When the leadership is made aware of the exodus, phrases such as "God is pruning" or "spiritual immaturity" are used to justify the destructiveness and poverty of their own ministry.

What a contrast to Jesus, the Good Shepherd of our souls, who leaves the 99 to seek the one who is lost. How opposite to Jesus, who comforts, consoles, forgives, and strengthens His precious sheep. How unlike the charge Jesus gave Peter to "feed My sheep." May God bring such misguided leaders in His church to their senses so they may tenderly shepherd the souls Christ has commended to their care.

After two months in Pasadena, our furniture arrived from Germany, and we moved into a townhouse apartment around the corner from Robert. I began my new job with the moving company and my volunteer ministry in Robert's congregation. The normal person would have washed his hands of the whole thing and moved on, but I was not normal. I was convinced the WCG was God's only true church and that in being dismissed from the ministry I had failed God. It was clear that I had to make amends and again become involved full time in "God's Work." Only years later did I see that God's "Work" according to Armstrong used a person until he or she had a problem, then solved the problem by getting rid of the person. This was the cold steel side of the "Philadelphian era"—the church of brotherly love—that cut the bone and heart of many people who failed to live up to the exacting demands of perfection. The "work of God" rolled onward and over the lives of the people who served and stumbled while in service. The mission was too great and the time too short to care for the wounded. Blind to this, I hung around Pasadena, hoping that the sales job would pan out and somehow lead to a new opening with the church. But the sales job was not going well; the business was hard. Only a couple members of the sales staff even reached quota, and once it was reached, it was raised the next month. This was not particularly motivating.

Within three months, I knew my time with the moving company was over. I determined to give the owner plenty of notice, then look for another job. I had seen how other salespeople would just walk in, lay their keys on the desk, and say, "I quit." That didn't seem right, so I decided to give the boss 30-days notice. After an early Monday morning sales meeting at the country club in Pasadena, I offered my notice. He smiled and said, "That's okay, you can go today."

Welcome to the real world. Leaving the dining room, I called Linda and told her I had just lost my job and was on my way home. We were not worried; we trusted that the Lord would provide for us. After talking about what steps we should take, I said, "You know, if we are going to starve, let's at least go where it's pleasant." So we asked my dad for a loan of $500 and moved north to Sacramento, California, where Linda's parents had settled.

I was still dealing with my hurt and bitterness over what had happened to us in the wake of Germany. I prayed regularly that God would show me what I needed to learn and take all bitterness from my heart. The great difficulty was dealing with reality, which was that the church I had served and for which I had sacrificed had tossed me aside. It was difficult even caring about a career that did not involve the church. This mental turmoil lasted about two years until I finally concluded that I would never return to the full-time ministry. I had had my chance and blown it, now I had to get on with my life.

In Sacramento I learned that my friend from South Carolina, Joel, and his wife, Pat, were serving in the pastorate. Joel was supportive, treating us like close friends and allowing me to assist with ministry in the local congregation. Hal and Bob, two local church elders, also were encouraging and offered us their friendship. Sacramento became our home.

We moved into an apartment with enough money for two months' rent, a car payment, and a few groceries. I immediately started looking for a job and landed one as a sales representative with a secretarial school. It provided a straight commission, and I worked off leads generated by television ads. It was a tough business, but I was making a little money. Initially, we were tight financially, so I applied for food stamps, which was a great blow to my pride. But I remembered my dad telling me to do whatever it took to take care of my family, as long as it was honest. We were awarded food stamps for a month or so until I could get on my feet. Linda's parents also fed us from their huge vegetable garden. We had a large sack of wheat we had brought from Germany, which I ground by hand so Linda could make breads and cereals. We were never hungry, but we were not exactly putting on weight.

What little income we had, I faithfully tithed the first and saved the second tithe. My rationale was simple. I believed God commanded tithing, and we were prepared to trust Him for our daily bread, believing He would provide. And provide He did. We did not live like kings, but we always had something to eat. King David said, "I was young and now I am old, yet I have never seen the righteous forsaken or their children begging bread" (Psalm 37:25). Our dear Lord always mercifully has provided for my family in times of need. We lived by this simple faith, and God in His mercy answered us. To this day I thank God for every morsel of bread we receive and all the material gifts He provides. It is by His gracious hand that such blessings come. I praise Him for His faithfulness and loving care.

Within six months, I was blessed with an excellent job with Kellogg's (the cereal company). Kellogg's was an outstanding employer and showed great concern and appreciation for its employees—something I had not experienced with the WCG. We were treated well and given opportunity to advance. In fact, within one year as a local salesman, I was offered a job in Battle Creek, Michigan, as international advertising coordinator. I would work directly with the vice president for international advertising. We were happy to take the job because it offered a clear career path and greater stability. I was still heavily involved with the local WCG congregation, but my desire to be back in the full-time ministry had waned.

By 1977, things in the WCG were changing. It was becoming much more liberal. Herbert Armstrong was often gone on his trips to visit dignitaries, and Garner Ted Armstrong was minding the store. Ted's ways were less rigid than his father's, and he was moving the church into an attitude that was more open to the world around us. Under his direction, a staff team at Pasadena developed the infamous *Systematic Theology Project* (STP). This was an effort to write down in a systematic fashion the beliefs of the WCG. With a three-ring binder in hand, a pastor or WCG member could turn to any given section and read and study the church's teaching on various theological subjects. Ted said his father had seen and approved the project, so it was distributed to the ministry in 1977 or 1978. The STP caused some turmoil because several theological positions had been modified or changed. One such modification occurred in the teachings on medical help. The STP taught that members could avail themselves of medical assistance and not be guilty of a lack of faith. The STP project coincided with a general liberal trend in the church. I do not remember many specifics, but there seemed to be an air of materialism, probably a result of the disappointment over the failed 1972 and 1975 prophecies.

When we moved to Battle Creek, Michigan, to work at Kellogg's international headquarters, I discovered that the student who had befriended me during my first Sabbath brunch in Big Sandy was the local WCG pastor. Ken (not to be confused with the man to whom Linda had been romantically tied) had married a young woman, Nancy, who was not an Ambassador graduate. This was not commonly done among WCG ministers. As Linda and I got to know her, we became convinced she was one of the finest people we had ever met. We became close friends with this wonderful couple, who continue to dedicate their lives to the ministry of the Worldwide Church of God. Ken and the pastors in the surrounding areas were not liberal. They held to the old line and steadfastly supported Herbert Armstrong. This came as a great relief to Linda and me because we were beginning to believe the entire ministry was becoming liberal.

Meanwhile, things apparently were not going well in Pasadena in Herbert Armstrong's absence. He was constantly in the air in his Gulfstream III, visiting heads of state all over the world. Armstrong believed that time was running out, so he wanted to take his warning message to the heads of state. He reasoned that if he reached the head of a nation with the warning, then the whole nation was warned. Because the head of state is responsible for his people, if he accepted the truth, they would accept it, and if he rejected the truth, they would reject it too. This sounded great at the time, but this reasoning is completely unfounded because few people look to political leaders for direction in spiritual questions. Mr. Armstrong knew a Japanese entrepreneur who had contacts all over the world and used his influence to gain audiences with dignitaries such as Ferdinand Marcos (former president of the Philippines), King Hussein of Jordan, the prince of Japan, the king and queen of Thailand, the former emperor of Ethiopia, and several Japanese Diet members, among others. Herbert Armstrong always took a piece of Steuben crystal as a gift to these leaders, then delivered his message. He tailored what he had to say to fit the audience: He spoke of the great God of the universe and the two ways of life—give and get. By leading the give way of life, one was fulfilling the will of this great God of the universe. Numerous WCG members felt Armstrong was watering down the gospel. They wanted to see him blast these government leaders for their sin and proclaim the soon-coming great tribulation, which would be followed by Christ's return. This irritated Armstrong, and he addressed it often when he spoke, chastising those who would presume to accuse him of watering down the "true gospel." I think history will agree that Herbert Armstrong accomplished nothing on these trips except the expenditure of a lot of money, giving us the illusion that something magnificent was being accomplished. Besides, Armstrong's theology was completely man- and works-centered. He did not stress what God has accomplished for us in Christ, rather what we must do to please God. Notice St. Paul's message in 2 Corinthians 5:17–21:

> Therefore, if anyone is in Christ, he is a new creation; the old has gone, the new has come! All this is from God, who reconciled us to Himself through Christ and gave us the ministry of reconciliation: that God was reconciling the world to Himself in Christ, not counting men's sins against them. And He has committed to us the message of reconciliation. We are therefore Christ's ambassadors, as though God were making His appeal through us. We implore you on Christ's behalf: Be reconciled to God. God made Him who had no sin to be sin for us, so that in Him we might become the righteousness of God.

Paul is not stressing a life of giving; he is stressing what God has given to us—reconciliation to Him through Christ's sacrifice. Paul's appeal is not to pursue a different philosophy of life. It is that each person should believe and have faith in God's work through Christ so one may become personally reconciled to Him.

When I was in Manila several years ago, I spoke to the WCG regional director in the Philippines about Armstrong's massive public campaigns in that city. He flew into town and packed the large civic auditorium. The mother of President Marcos attended. Those back home thought Armstrong was knocking them dead in the Philippines. This director confided in me that Armstrong's front men had arranged to pay the citizens of Manila $5 each to attend the meeting. This amount for an evening in an air-conditioned and comfortable auditorium was a good deal, regardless of who was speaking. I do not know whether Mr. Armstrong knew of the monetary incentive that was offered to bring in the crowds. He left town, the people went home, Marcos got his gift, we thought the "gospel" had been preached in power, and everybody was happy.

Herbert Armstrong's decision to remarry delivered another shock in the late 1970s. His first wife, Loma, had died in the spring of 1967. He now was an old man in his 80s, and we thought he would remain single, given his advanced years. I am told that Loma had not liked to travel, so Armstrong had limited himself to few trips while she lived. Once she died, he increased his travel schedule until, by the late 1970s, he was away from Pasadena most of the time. Somewhere he met a divorced church-woman much younger than himself and married her. Many leading ministers in the WCG strenuously opposed Armstrong's marital plans, as did other leading churchmen in Pasadena. I was shocked because Herbert was marrying a divorced woman and I had believed that as "spiritual" Levites, ministers were prohibited from doing such a thing. But he was God's apostle and knew the Bible better than I, so what he did must be okay. I would understand it in time. We had such high regard for ministers that we would never second-guess them. What they did had to be right. Their example became the model by which we cast our own lives. When they did something that was questionable, we found ways to justify it. This worked well for Armstrong because we were ready to believe and accept most anything he did.

By the late 1970s, there were many voices bemoaning a slide into liberalism. We waited for Herbert Armstrong to put a stop to this slide. Rumors began to circulate again about Ted's lifestyle. I refused to believe them because Ted was an evangelist, Herbert Armstrong's son, and certainly a man of God. However, things changed with Ted in a hurry. Herbert Armstrong received a copy of the *Systematic Theology Project* (STP) and was incensed. We had been told that he had read it before publication, but he denied that, claiming it was published without his knowledge and contained grievous doctrinal errors. Word went out from Pasadena that the STP was recalled and every minister, whether full-time pastor or local church elder (which I was at the time), was to send his copy of the document back to Pasadena. Ted Armstrong was relieved of his office and disfellowshiped from the Worldwide Church of God on grounds that his conduct was unbecoming that of a minister of God. Many accused Ted of leading a double life: one of the righteous man of God and the other of the playboy. He left Pasadena under a dark cloud and moved to East Texas. He founded his own church, the Church of God (International). Since that time, Ted Armstrong has reappeared in the headlines as the subject of further improprieties.

Even after the rumors and the bad press, many of us hoped that once again Ted and Herbert Armstrong would be reconciled so Ted could resume his broadcasting responsibilities. The reconciliation never happened. I was told by some who were close to the events that Ted tried several times to call his father, but his calls were intercepted by a select few on Herbert Armstrong's staff. Whatever happened, one thing is clear: When Ted was disfellowshiped in 1978, it stuck. He never had anything more to do with the Worldwide Church of God and continues to this day with his involvement in his own church.

By 1979, I had left Kellogg's. Linda and I had moved from Michigan to Lubbock, Texas, where I went to work for Johnson Wax as a manufacturer's representative in the West Texas area. I continued in my responsibilities as a local church elder, which I enjoyed. My contact with Pasadena was limited to receiving the biweekly ministerial letter *The Bulletin,* as well as the regular member letters sent out by Armstrong. Linda and I were enjoying the best time of our lives. We loved life in West Texas and felt very much a part of the Lubbock, Texas, congregation of the Worldwide Church of God.

Herbert Armstrong was now spending more time in Pasadena and, in his own words, "putting the church back on track." Those of us with a conservative bent, who were in the majority, saw this as an answer to prayer. Finally the slide into liberalism was being halted. As proof that the church was "back on track," I read one day in *The Bulletin* about a major doctrinal reversal. It had to do with makeup. In the early days of the church, this had been a contentious issue among the membership, which had forced Armstrong to make a ruling. He searched the Scriptures and came up with a few passages in which women of ill repute—such as Jezebel—apparently used makeup as part of their evil plotting. In addition, Armstrong claimed that in the early part of this century only women of the street wore makeup. Therefore, his conclusion and his binding decision on WCG women was that makeup was sinful. A true woman of God would not be permitted to wear it. By the 1970s, this ruling had been reversed and WCG women made normal use of cosmetics. However, human nature being what it is, the issue came up again and another study was launched. This time Armstrong said that makeup was associated with spiritual vanity. He would rant and rave about this "dirt" on women's faces and decry its sinfulness. At this time Linda was a budding Mary Kaye distributor. I read the decision in *The Bulletin* and said to Linda, "Hey, honey, read this. I think you might find it interesting."

My own reaction to the reversal was that Armstrong was making a big deal out of a tiny issue. However, I was impressed with Linda's response. She read the article, said she would comply, and gave up her cosmetics business. Once again, off came the makeup from the faces of WCG women (at least in church and at church activities). I believe most women complied with the ruling, even if they did not fully agree. It is interesting to note that one of the first "doctrinal" changes that Joseph Tkach Sr. issued after succeeding Herbert Armstrong was to drop the makeup restriction. He rightly said that makeup is a non-issue and that the church would make no ruling other than to state that it is up to the individual Christian woman to make her own determination. No woman is more or less righteous with or without makeup. One may be surprised to note that the church even bothered with such a trivial issue, but as time progressed the membership gradually began to look to Mr. Armstrong for God's view on many such non-issues. So the church spoke on these issues, giving what it thought to be the biblical view. Today, the WCG wisely sticks to those issues that are addressed clearly in the Bible, either directly or by principle. Otherwise, its policy is not to speak when the Bible is silent.

Sometime in 1979, another major crisis struck the Worldwide Church of God. This time it was not small potatoes but a life-threatening situation. Some disgruntled ex-members of the WCG had brought legal charges against the church, accusing its leadership of illegally siphoning funds and dumping church property at below-market prices. This came to the attention of the attorney general of California, who swiftly installed a receiver to manage the church's financial affairs. I was in Texas at the time and not employed by the church, so I received much of my information from people who were in Pasadena during this crisis, as well as what I read in the church's publications. Herbert was counseled by his in-house lawyer to relocate to Tucson, Arizona, where he had purchased a home. The WCG's chief attorney, who had become a member and been ordained to the rank of evangelist by Herbert Armstrong, was Mr. Stanley Rader. While Mr. Armstrong was in Tucson, Mr. Rader ran the ship in Pasadena. Word went out to the membership to begin sending all donations to an address in Tucson instead of to Pasadena. This was a successful effort to deny the state-appointed receiver control over corporate funds. Mr. Armstrong was counseled to remain in Tucson and away from the California legal system. Meanwhile, Mr. Rader launched a brilliant effort to combat the state, rallying many churches as friends to support the WCG position. If the state were allowed to maintain its authoritative position to oversee the affairs of the Worldwide Church of God by declaring the church to be a charity, then it would only be a matter of time before other churches would fall under the state's control. At issue was a basic constitutional point of the separation of church and state.

At one juncture in this assault by the state of California, an attempt was made by the state police to take control of the WCG's main administrative building. Armstrong dwelt safely in

Arizona, and those left in charge in Pasadena were uncertain about what to do. One evangelist encouraged Joe Tkach—at this time a local elder—to stage an around-the-clock church service in the administrative building. Men, women, and children were asked to come to the building to participate in this form of passive resistance. Some 80 armed officers were stationed at the Rose Bowl, not far from the WCG campus, prepared to take the building by force, but the sight of innocent people in a worship service caused them to back down. Within a short time, they withdrew. The courts eventually ruled the state's action to be illegal and the case was dismissed. Joseph Tkach Sr. was heralded as a hero for his bold action in resisting the state and protecting the integrity of the church. Not long after, Mr. Tkach was raised from the rank of local elder to evangelist (skipping all the ranks between) and promoted to director of church administration with authority over the worldwide ministry. His predecessor, the man I had in anger characterized as a "jerk," allegedly had collaborated with the state in its action against the church and was dismissed.

With that crisis behind us, we were ready for the next one. Things were going poorly for Herbert Armstrong and his new wife. There were rumors of a conspiracy involving top executives in Pasadena who allegedly planned to trap Mr. Armstrong in his home in Tucson and have him legally declared incompetent, thus gaining control of the church. As the story goes, some Armstrong loyalists got wind of the plot and managed to get him out of the Tucson house on the evening that the trap was to be sprung. (No one pressed charges and no complete story was ever told; I have heard only bits and pieces from those who were around at the time.) Mr. Armstrong returned to Pasadena and soon accepted Mr. Rader's public offer to resign once the legal battle for the church was concluded. Mr. Rader was rewarded with an exceedingly generous severance package, including retirement benefits.

This whole affair with the state served to strengthen Herbert Armstrong's leadership over the church, as well as firmly establish Joseph Tkach Sr. as the number two man in the organization. Mr. Tkach was loyal to Mr. Armstrong and could be counted on to keep him up to date on what was happening in the church. Mr.

Armstrong's marriage eventually broke up, ending in a nasty divorce trial that lasted for some time. There was no official report made to the membership of the settlement, but again rumors were rampant.

Once the divorce was final, Armstrong's daughter Beverly would join him on trips around the world. She was not a member of the church, yet she lived in a home provided by the church in an upscale community not far from Pasadena. This seems a rather strange arrangement, but Mr. Armstrong was the "one true end-time apostle" and could do no wrong. God had vindicated him against the state of California, and we believed that God would deal with him if he got out of line. There was no man in the WCG who could hold Armstrong accountable for anything, so he did what he pleased and quickly silenced internal criticism. His daughter has since passed away, and her home eventually was sold with the proceeds going to the church.

By 1979, an evangelist who was serving in a West Texas congregation recommended that I be rehired into the full-time ministry. My career was going well, but I had switched from Johnson Wax to a local distributor in Lubbock, which caused my regional boss for Johnson Wax to try to get me fired from my new job, claiming I was a religious fanatic. Bobby, my new boss, stood his ground and told the man to drop the issue or get his products out of his warehouse. At the prospect of losing a good client, my former boss left me alone.

Bobby did ask about my religious beliefs. But I had been in sales long enough to know that the bottom line was performance, not belief systems. So I looked at Bobby and Jay, the sales manager, and said, "You know I can sell, and that's what counts here." They nodded in agreement and that was that. I am still indebted to Bobby for defending me, much as Robert had done several years earlier in Pasadena. Over the years I have maintained contact with Bobby. It turned out years later to be a friendship that would again offer me support in an hour of need.

When the request went to headquarters that I be rehired, the evangelist reported that no file had been found on me. Not surprising, I guess, because in the years that I had been out of the employ of the church, I had been a *persona non grata* in the ministry. When Linda and I went to the Feast of Tabernacles, we were regularly left out of ministerial functions and basically shunned by the full-time ministry. This hurt deeply because I felt that these men were my spiritual brothers, yet they often dealt with me as though I were nonexistent. Years later, when I assumed high-profile responsibilities in Pasadena, many of these same men were quick to pump my hand, slap me on the back, and treat me like a long-lost brother. As a result of that experience, I lost trust in many WCG ministers as dependable friends. There were exceptions, of course, and these were men who proved faithful friends when I was a "non-person."

What happened to my personnel file in Pasadena? I have no idea, but I imagine it was fortuitous because whatever was written about my German experience, if anything, was lost. Those men who had been involved in the affair were either gone or were themselves no longer in positions to effect me. At the time of the request, I wanted to return to full-time ministry. I was just as content, however, to remain in my sales vocation. "Let God lead" was my motto.

As we approached the 1980s, the church seemed to be in good shape. Membership was expanding. Money was flowing. The circulation of *The Plain Truth* was growing toward eight million copies a month. It was published in seven languages. The Ambassador International Cultural Foundation (AICF) was going great guns in Pasadena, putting on a star-studded yearly program of concerts. Mr. Armstrong had founded the AICF in the mid-1970s with the intent of promoting the good in the human spirit in the area of arts. He loved the arts and was a faithful patron through the auspices of the AICF until his death. The AICF also provided Armstrong with a nice calling card when visiting heads of state because it was much easier to gain an audience as the president of a foundation than as pastor general of the Worldwide Church of God. Again, some members questioned the use of church funds for the concert series, as well as the fact that Armstrong did not travel under the name of the WCG. However, Mr. Armstrong deftly dealt with such criticism by producing photos and sometimes even videotapes of his international visits. These were hailed as proof of his effectiveness and tended to silence criticism.

As we sailed into the 1980s, the church was "back on track." Although Mr. Armstrong was approaching 90 years of age, many felt he would not die until the Lord returned. One traveling evangelist would make statements to that effect during his colorfully prophetic sermons. I looked at the state of the church, the uncertainty of the world's geo-political situation, and Mr. Armstrong's old age as sure signs that the end was closing in on us. And I longed to again be a full-time member of the team involved in this end-time crusade to warn the world and prepare the way for Christ's imminent return. The opportunity to devote myself and my family once again to the "Work" was about to knock on my door.

Chapter 7

The Storm Clouds Gather

Justice is truth in action.—Joseph Jourbert (*Pensèes*)

Life in West Texas was good to Linda and me. We found our place in the local congregation of the Worldwide Church of God. We were among friends with whom we shared our spiritual journey. Linda and I also were blessed with our second son, Dustin, who was born in July 1979. I should have been satisfied to let things be, but there was an uneasiness that beat in my heart. Although I felt resigned to live my life in Texas as a salesman, there was still the hope that God would open the way for me to again serve full-time in ministry. The evangelist who had tried to get the WCG to rehire me moved to Pasadena, so it seemed my life would continue as it was.

A year passed and as I reflected on the time Linda and I had spent in Germany and the disappointment we had caused, I felt the right thing to do would be to write the German director and thank him for the opportunities he had provided. Yes, he had let me drop when I really needed support, but I bore him no ill will. Besides, I felt that God is our judge and would take care of each of us in His own time and way. So I wrote the German director a letter of thanks. I said I was not looking for a job (which was true), but if he ever needed help, he should let me know. With the posting of the letter, I felt I had finally closed that chapter in my life so I could move on. To my utter surprise, a couple weeks later the phone rang, and it was the director. He wondered if I would be interested in returning to Europe and serving in Switzerland. The offer took me by surprise, so I told him I would need to discuss this with Linda. We talked about it and prayed about it. We concluded that God was again returning us to His service. I called the director and told him we would be willing to return. He was delighted and told me that once he received approval from Mr. Armstrong, Linda and I could come over. The approval came within a couple weeks, and the director suggested that I come over first, in time for the spring holy days, after which I could find a place to live. Linda and the boys could follow. This suggestion made sense, so within a month, I was again winging my way to Germany.

It had been five years since we had left Germany, so my return made me apprehensive. A little voice of fear in my heart was saying there was a good chance I would fail again. I raised fervent prayers that God would strengthen me with the will to serve Him and His people—no matter the cost. I asked that He would help me with the language and grant me love for the German people. The spring holy days in Hannover and Hamburg went well, though my language skills had deteriorated somewhat. Once I concluded the worship services, I traveled to southern Germany, near the Swiss border, to visit with the local pastor who was being reassigned further north. The area was beautiful with lush green hills surrounded by the dark evergreen Black Forest. I loved it.

With the help of the local pastor, I searched for a place to live. My time was limited, and the available housing was equally limited. Finally, it seemed the best option was to take over the pastor's apartment in Laufenburg on the Rhein. From his living room window, I could look over wheat fields that extended to the Rhine River and into Switzerland. It seemed perfect, and I knew Linda would love it. When she arrived in Germany a few weeks later, my great enthusiasm was met by tears. She found the apartment so horrible that she sat down and cried. The apartment was old, poorly heated, displayed water pipes—in short, it was "bare bones," just as it had been five years earlier, but this time, the owner, who lived just below us, was an overbearing older gentleman. This was not a great start to our second tour of duty. I did learn one important lesson through that experience, never—and I mean, never—choose a place to live unless your wife has seen it and is happy with it. But Linda was a trooper and soon overcame her disappointment, making the best of the situation.

Upon my return to Germany, I again enrolled in a language school to brush up on my skills. This time I went to Basel in Switzerland, about an hour's drive away, and took private lessons at the Orsini School of Language. This was not the five-hour each day routine, but a more relaxed pace of three hours each day for several days a week stretched over several months. Linda had two young boys to keep up with (our youngest son, Dustin, was born only months before in Lubbock), so she was tied to the apartment and relearned her German by watching television and visiting with WCG members.

My church circuit was Zürich and Basel, congregations consisting of about 75 and 35 members respectively. My area included virtually all of Switzerland (except the French-speaking cantons), the Black Forest in Germany, Alsace-Lorraine in France, Liechtenstein, and a small section of western Austria. The scenery was breathtaking, the weather was better than in northern Germany, and the people were reasonably friendly.

My introduction to the Swiss congregations was memorable. I believe it was Pentecost and the combined congregations of Zürich and Basel were meeting in a small hall in a park in Zürich. The German director gave the first sermon in the morning and opened his message by asking if the members had any questions about the "Work." A few hands went up, and he fielded all the questions in a friendly and enthusiastic manner. Then one Swiss member began to criticize the director for the way he was running things. Such a public challenge from a member during the service was unheard of in the WCG! The atmosphere became tense. Most of us were in a state of shock. The challenger continued his assault until Frank interrupted and tried to answer the man's questions. The member countered every answer with another charge, visibly frustrating the director, who finally asked him to take his seat. But the member was on a roll and was not inclined to obey. He did not relinquish the floor. His onslaught continued. The director interrupted the man's diatribe and asked him to leave the hall. The man shot back, "You have no authority to tell me to leave. Only the people here in this hall can make me go."

Not a bad answer, I thought. How would the unflappable Frank deal with that comeback? Without a moment's hesitation, the director directed his words to the audience, "How many wish that this man leave the hall? Please raise your hands."

This was another shock! The members were never asked to express an opinion by a show of hands. The majority of the members quickly raised their hands, indicating they wanted the rebel to hit the road. Those who remained motionless later told me they were so overwhelmed by the entire affair that they were immobilized. Once the malcontent saw his fellow members give him the boot, he shut up, picked up his things, and left. Thus, peace returned to our little community.

This would not be the last time I would see such actions, though perhaps they occurred in more subtle ways. When a member voiced dissent, whether in a public fashion or among friends, word eventually filtered to the ever-alert minister. It was his unspoken duty to squelch dissent, which, as Armstrong taught, was the work of the devil. It was the spirit of rebellion after the likes of Korah of Old Testament infamy. Korah, his family, and sympathizers had opposed Moses in the Israelite camp, but they met their fate when the earth swallowed them by the judgment of God. Disagreement was rebellion—and rebellion had to be rooted out. And it was! As a WCG member, one must come to see the error and sin of his or her ways or be excommunicated. To be excommunicated equaled being cast out of the kingdom of God. Members sought to avoid such a fate at all costs. When rebellion was remedied, we often spoke of the peace that had returned to our fellowship.

What actually happened was somewhat analogous to Wyatt Earp bringing peace at the O.K. Corral. Once the "bad guys" are either shot or run out of town licking their wounds, the decent folks can go about their business. Whatever issues dissenting members may have had were not generally addressed. Dissenting members became the problem by raising the issue, thus disturbing the peace. Such a breach of the law in "Tombstone" was not allowed, so a shootout inevitably followed. When the dust settled, peace graced us once again. I have seen similar behavior in Christian congregations in which members have taken issue with questionable practices of those in spiritual offices. Dissenters are "gunned down at high noon" or "driven out of Dodge" while the "sheriff" proclaims how God has brought peace to His congregation through divine pruning. This is a sad aberration of the way the body of Christ should treat its members.

As was the custom in the Worldwide Church of God until recent years, we held two services on holy days. The morning service was followed by a potluck and a second service in the afternoon. It made for a long day, but that was our tradition and few people complained. In the afternoon, the regional director introduced me as the new pastor. At the proper time, I stood to deliver my sermon. Things went well except for some extremely noisy children, who seemed invisible to their parents as they roamed around the hall, making a general nuisance of themselves. Even the director became fed up. He got up during my sermon and personally chased down some of the wild bunch to send them to their parents. This was embarrassing. As I was trying to comprehend the day's experiences, Frank said, "This church is unruly, Tom. I want you to bring order here." That was no easy task. Nevertheless I was determined to do as he requested. I made some mistakes and upset a few people, but within a few months, church services were respectfully quiet. The children also underwent an amazing transformation as their parents responded to the pressure I put on them to train and discipline their little ones.

One of my first duties in this new assignment was to seek and obtain legal permission from the Swiss authorities to move into and work in Switzerland. This was no easy feat because so many people from all over the world are eager to enjoy the high standard of living, security, and stability that Switzerland affords. Each canton (like an American state) has its own rules and quotas for foreign visitors. Permission to live, for example, in Canton Zürich does not extend to other cantons. Because our larger congregation was in Zürich, I began my work to seek legal admission into the country by finding a lawyer in that canton who knew the laws intimately and was well-connected politically. Through the help of a church member who was a manager for Swiss Air, a lawyer was located. After 13 months and several refusals, we were granted permission to move to Zürich.

Life looked a lot better on the Swiss side of the border. The Swiss enjoy a living standard similar to the United States, which was immediately noticeable in the apartments. This time Linda and I worked together and found a beautiful tri-level apartment, which was at the foot of a vineyard on the river Limmat in a lovely area of Zürich called Höngg. What a welcome improvement from the German apartment. This place had a built-in kitchen, light fixtures, a fireplace, and a patio that opened to a community (shared) lawn. It was typical by U.S. standards, but for someone accustomed to German standards, it was really nice. As an added bonus, we had amicable English-speaking neighbors with whom we visited often.

I was not in Europe long before the director told me I was responsible for expanding readership of the German edition of *The Plain Truth* (*Klar & Wahr*) in Switzerland and Austria. Through the office manager in Bonn, he instructed me to visit kiosks and determine what types of magazines were offered. Then I was to develop an advertising plan to promote our publication. My experiences with Kellogg's had given me some insight into the mysteries of print advertising, so one thing I knew for certain was that we needed an agency. There was no way a novice new to a country could, in such a short period, survey the available magazines, determine their editorial direction and demographics, and plan an advertising campaign. Besides, we were not talking about buying space to advertise chocolate or tissue, but a religious magazine. In fact, many people believed this magazine was supported by a cult. When trying to secure advertising space with a publication, being turned down can prove fatal. Once turned down, it can take years before a no is converted to a yes. Such was the case for the WCG and the North American publication of *Reader's Digest*. The magazine's corporate office in New York had refused WCG ads, thus making *Reader's Digest* inaccessible to the worldwide church for advertising placement. I knew of the long-standing ban by *Reader's Digest* and did not want to be banned by Swiss publications.

I called my friend at Swiss Air and asked for a recommendation of an advertising agency. He referred me to Hermann & Schneider, an agency in Zürich. I learned the agency was a partnership between two men—one the copywriter and strategist and the other the graphic artist. Herr Hermann and Herr Schneider were likable men who accepted our account even though the advertising budget was far below their minimum. Hermann said he accepted the job because it presented a challenge; however, he did set one condition. We were not to solicit the readership for contributions. That was absolutely no problem, I assured him, because the stated policy of the church was never to solicit the public for donations. (This was based on Mr. Armstrong's misunderstanding of the statement Jesus made to His apostles before sending them on a training mission, "Freely you have received, freely give" [Matthew 10:8].)

Hermann came up with a well-conceived advertising campaign for Switzerland and Austria that included a new design for the ad. I liked it, as did many of the members. But Frank, in Bonn, did not like it and wanted to kill it. He had been successful in Germany with a design of his own and wanted the same one used in my area. I politely countered that he had given me the job and I wanted to run the new ad. Frank reluctantly agreed. The ad met the targeted projections, but for some reason Frank had expected greater response and dubbed our Swiss ad a failure. After that we had to use his design. This experience is typical of the management style I came to know in the WCG. Micromanagement was especially common in the WCG administration immediately after Mr. Armstrong's death. Under Mr. Tkach Sr., virtually every decision of any consequence was made by him—hires, layoffs, purchases, *Plain Truth* covers, ad layouts, days off, transfers, etc. He had a need to feel in control. Mr. Tkach Jr., the current pastor general, demonstrates an opposite style, delegating responsibility at least one level down. As a result of micromanagement, employees do not feel empowered to do their jobs and shy away from decision-making.

Another snag with the advertising campaigns in Switzerland and Austria developed a few months later. It had to do with commitment and budget. The director wanted a plan presented first, then he would determine a budget. I told him this was not how things worked. He would have to give me a budget, then I could provide a plan. He relented and gave a figure. Hermann and Schneider developed a plan. With media plan in hand, I asked for the release of funds to do the job. I was told that we could not get the promised money because of other priorities, so I returned sheepishly to the advertising men to tell them the budget had been trimmed. They continued to work with me, and as a result of our efforts, circulation of *Klar & Wahr* grew from around 1,500 readers each in Switzerland and Austria to some 10,000 in Switzerland and 7,000 in Austria.

This advertising adventure took place in the early 1980s. Frank was sinking a lot of money into advertising, trying to boost the circulation of *Klar & Wahr* through the roof. And he was succeeding. In the early 1980s, Frank felt the end was near, so he was putting a big push on the magazine to get the warning message out while there was still time. By this time I was not so sure about end-time claims, but who was I to argue with the boss? We felt God was blessing our efforts as thousands of new readers joined the list. Of course, the ads were written so the subscriber did not know he was getting a religious magazine. Once *Klar & Wahr* arrived, the reader got a big surprise. Most people let the subscription continue because it was free. The renewal rates for the advertisements were fairly low, so each year we poured additional huge sums of money into advertising to keep the readership at an artificially high level. As the list expanded, the membership rejoiced, believing the "gospel" was going to the world. But the true gospel was not being preached; instead, we were promoting Armstrong's distorted prophetic message. The ever-increasing subscriber list was a function of spending, not necessarily the magazine's appeal. The more we spent, the greater the number of readers, especially when the publication is free. Of course dumping millions of dollars into the promotion of a free magazine will result in an amazingly large list of subscribers. However, the number of people on the list is not a reflection of how many actually read the material. Further, on average only 50 percent or less would renew our *free* magazine after repeated renewal letters. At one time we even stopped sending renewal letters to keep the larger subscriber base. In retrospect, this was a classic case of self-delusion. Such ventures in self-delusion are not confined to the WCG past or present, but are engaged in by many religious organizations that want to believe their own claims rather than face reality, which is often contradictory.

Today *The Plain Truth* is promoted as a religious magazine, so any potential subscriber knows to expect an evangelical message. And the magazine now carries a subscription price, which breaks with more than 50 years of tradition established by Herbert Armstrong. Both the change in editorial content and the addition of a subscription price have caused the list to shrink from more than 8 million subscribers worldwide in the 1980s to around 60,000 paid subscribers in the United States alone.

Things were going well with our Swiss advertising agency when someone in the Pasadena editorial office thought it would be a great idea to run a lead article on the subject of tithing under Mr. Armstrong's name. The material was taken from an article that had appeared in *The Good News*, a magazine intended primarily for WCG members and financial supporters. Because additional income was needed, someone thought such an article from Mr. Armstrong would do the trick. Undoubtedly, such content was an effort to motivate *The Plain Truth* readers to give a little instead of only taking from the church.

Once the issue hit the desk of Hermann & Schneider, I received a call from Hermann. "Tom, we have a problem. In the latest issue of *Klar & Wahr,* there is a direct appeal for money. You said this was not done. How do you explain this?"

I stuttered and stammered, then told him I would read the article myself and get back to him as soon as possible. After reading the offending editorial, I called the director and presented him with the problem. He, too, was upset, but his hands were tied. No one other than Mr. Armstrong told editorial in Pasadena what to do. Frank assured me that he would take the matter to Mr. Armstrong personally to ensure that this would not happen again. I gave this assurance to Hermann, but I could tell he was not convinced.

After meeting with Hermann and discussing the matter, I knew it was only a matter of time before Hermann & Schneider would drop our account. If the agency fired the client, I knew our name was mud in Zürich, so I spoke to Frank, suggesting that, in light of the shrinking budget (he had put a major drain on the German bank account because of his advertising campaign in that country), we should break off the relationship with Hermann & Schneider. He agreed, and I carried out my unpleasant duty. At lunch on the banks of Lake Zürich, I suggested to Hermann that we end the business relationship. He did not protest. Everyone saved a little face; however, I think the church went away with a black-eye from that affair.

After we lost Hermann & Schneider, our advertising in Switzerland was limited to *Reader's Digest* (the ban on WCG advertising having been lifted), which I booked directly with the publication. After dealing with the director's continual waffling and reversals on budget for several years, I was relieved when a bright young man came to Bonn and took over the advertising job. I gladly turned over the reigns to him and washed my hands of the advertising business in Switzerland. Gradually, because of overspending and the tremendous losses of readership through unpaid renewals, the subscription list dropped drastically. When all was said and done, one wonders if there was any lasting value. I would conclude that our efforts were mainly an exercise in self-delusion, which made little lasting impact other than attracting a few people to the Worldwide Church of God.

For many years, we attended the Feast of Tabernacles in Europe—six times in Bonndorf in the Black Forest and two times in Czechoslovakia. After my first two years in Germany, the director asked me to become festival coordinator of our German-speaking site in the Black Forest. My predecessor had performed the job for a number of years and needed a break. The job was time-consuming because I had to plan all the details of an eight-day convention for about 1,100 people, several hundred of whom came from other countries. It took the help of some talented people to turn Bonndorf into one of the most desirable locations for WCG international festival visitors. And once Mr. Armstrong allowed members to transfer to any feast site they desired, our international sites became very popular.

The church administration in Pasadena historically determined which festival site would receive a VIP visitor from Pasadena. In the first couple years I was in Bonndorf, we got no one. Apparently the German-speaking church did not rate consideration for such a blessing. But once Bonndorf began to offer first-rate activities, not only did hundreds of members from other countries flock to the Black Forest, but so did our Pasadena VIPs. It was not until I moved to Pasadena that I understood how it was decided who went where. There were a few factors that figured into the decision. Did the members have a particular need? How long had it been since a visit? Who was available? There was a short list of top evangelists who were on the "must send" list. They were not sent to a site because they were particularly gifted speakers, knew the language or culture, or had been requested. They were sent because they were senior evangelists who were "entitled" and were given the "plums"—Hawaii, Fiji, Bermuda, England, Australia, etc. We had better speakers who were not high-ranking, so either they were not sent or they would be sent to someplace less exciting, such as Hot Springs, Arkansas. This irritated some of us in Pasadena, but nothing could be done because the entitlement system was entrenched. However, Joe Tkach Jr. has effectively killed the entitlement mentality.

By virtue of my job as festival coordinator, I was privileged to work with Peter Folkerts, the mayor of Bonndorf. Peter was a dynamic man about my age. He was always open to new ideas and was extremely enthusiastic about the church having the feast in his town. The festival brought money to the local economy. As our association with Bonndorf continued, Peter told me our members added a positive spiritual dimension to the community as well. Our friendship grew and our families visited regularly. Peter and his wife, Regina, visited us in Zürich, and Linda and I would return the gesture in Bonndorf. One day while Peter and I were having lunch in one of his favorite Bonndorf locales, he said, "Tom, I want to make you an offer."

Peter was a prankster, so I did not know what to expect. "Okay, Peter. What?" I responded.

"I want to offer land here in the city of Bonndorf to Ambassador College for one dollar," he said.

I could not believe my ears. "What? Why would you want to do that? What is your angle, Peter?" I replied.

"I am quite serious about this, Tom. I want to offer Ambassador College land in the city of Bonndorf for one dollar," Peter said. "I have the perfect spot for you. My only requirement is that you must build something permanent."

This really got my attention. I grew excited at the prospect of the church finally having a permanent presence in Germany. Then I thought of the probable objection that would come from Frank, who would quote Herbert Armstrong. Armstrong always wanted our regional offices to be in a major metropolitan area because of the prestige he thought it would give us. But I felt Peter's offer to be a bold initiative that I took seriously because I could see a positive future for the church. With a base in the Black Forest, supported by the local mayor and citizens, the church could begin to legitimize itself in Germany. I had no authority to accept such an offer, so I told Peter that I would take the offer to the director, who would give it serious consideration before taking it to Mr. Armstrong. When I presented the offer to the director and explained the potential, he listened, but there was no serious response. The opportunity passed. A few years ago, Linda and I were in Bonndorf and visited briefly with Regina, Peter's widow (Peter had died in a small aircraft accident a few years earlier while on vacation in Austria). On the spot where the church could have planted its roots stands a community swimming pool. I counted it as a missed opportunity—one of many the WCG looked in the face and passed over. Today, the WCG has virtually no presence anywhere in Germany. This state of affairs is largely because of Mr. Armstrong's aversion to buying real estate except in Pasadena. This leaves the vast majority of WCG congregations and most of its international offices without much local presence or permanent roots. In the last few years, the church has secured permanent facilities in Manila, Cape Town, and in Burleigh Heads, Queensland, Australia.

After Peter's offer, Frank decided to open an office in Zürich. He asked me to look for a prestigious address near the airport. This venture came while the advertising campaigns for *Klar & Wahr* were causing the subscriber list to soar, even in Switzerland. I asked about office personnel, but the director said that initially we would receive the mail and forward it to Bonn for processing. After inquiring in Zürich, I found we could hire an international secretarial service that would provide an answering service in three or more languages, receive and forward mail, and provide office space as needed by appointment. This seemed the most practical thing to do because we were not planning to hire any staff. I suggested this to Frank, but he declined, stating that we could not trust a service to handle calls and mail discreetly, especially when some of our mail contained donations. Eventually I found an office in a modern building near the airport, which delighted the director. He signed a five-year lease for a reasonable monthly rent, and we were in business, which meant I bought office furniture and went in once a week to get the mail. Occasionally, I met at the office with a member or a prospective member for a counseling session.

Within a year, I realized the office was a losing proposition because nothing was happening nor was going to happen there. The church had to subsidize significantly the rent Linda and I paid so we could afford to live in such an expensive city. For the total of the apartment subsidy, the office rent, and the amount Linda and I paid in apartment rent, the church could have bought a large house. The timing was good because real estate was moving slowly and a 95 percent loan would have financed the property. If the church had a large house, several birds could be killed with one stone. Presence, parsonage, and office could be rolled into one. The director was open to the idea, so Linda and I scoured the countryside for the right place (near the airport, of course). Soon we found the right place—only 15 minutes from Kloten airport in a quiet valley with a view of a vineyard. The builder was having a hard time selling the property and was willing to sell it at cost. It was not cheap (nothing in Switzerland is cheap!), going for around $500,000 (U.S. dollars). Although this was a lot of money, it could be had for only a $25,000 to $30,000 down payment, which meant monthly payments would be no more than our current payments for apartment and office space. In addition, the down payment would be only a fraction of what had been spent on our Swiss advertising campaign. Frank visited, inspected the house, and liked it—and that was it. Like the offer Peter had made, the prospect of buying the house died a quick death. The house still nestles in that quiet Swiss valley. By a local WCG member's estimate, the property is now worth more than $830,000 in U.S. dollars. I do not know why Frank got cold feet, but several WCG executives could tell similar stories of missed opportunities. Why? One reason is the WCG was never much for planning. WCG leadership zigged and zagged over the years, taking some opportunities and rejecting others, but never according to a predetermined plan. Another reason for not responding at a local level has been the absolute rigid focus on the international headquarters in Pasadena. Thus, many local areas have mortgaged their future to follow obediently the dictates of the Pasadena administration. The current WCG administration plans gradually to change the focus of the church from its headquarters to the local congregation, a change most should welcome.

In the fall of 1985, word arrived in Switzerland that the 93-year-old Herbert Armstrong was weakening, though he still continued to produce a syndicated television program. His vision was poor and he was having difficulty getting around. But he pushed himself through each day. Herbert Armstrong was part of the generation that did not believe in retirement. He made it plain that a true minister of God would not retire; therefore, there was no retirement plan for the ministry or other WCG employees. Nor was Armstrong a great fan of vacations, so there was no real vacation policy. It was not until around the time of his death that we were allowed more than "time off." In fact, the benefits afforded by the WCG under the administration of Herbert Armstrong were virtually nonexistent—no medical, no dental, and no vision insurance. I believe there was life insurance, which was about it. We lived for each day, trusting God to provide for us. Later Mr. Tkach Sr. changed everything by instituting a vacation policy, as well as by providing generous medical and life insurance benefits.

Just before the Feast of Tabernacles in 1985, Armstrong weakened to the point that he could no longer do a telecast and he stayed home most of the time. I believed that God would raise him up "on the wings of an eagle," as Armstrong himself often said. Mr. Armstrong appointed Joseph Tkach Sr. as the deputy pastor general to continue in his stead should he die. This appointment had to be approved by the Council of Elders. With a little arm twisting, Armstrong got everyone to sign a document unanimously pledging support to Mr. Tkach. I had little experience with Joseph Tkach Sr. other than my brief encounter when he was an elder in the Pasadena congregation, but I believed God was leading Armstrong, therefore, I would support whomever he appointed to the position.

To my utter amazement an announcement came in January 1986 that God's apostle, the man we thought would lead us to the place of safety and live to see Christ's return, had died quietly in his favorite sitting chair at his church-owned home in Pasadena. I wept as I read the announcement and again as I read it before the congregations in Switzerland. It seemed to me like the passing of King Josiah of ancient Judah, yet I had the absolute confidence that God would lead Mr. Tkach Sr.

There is no doubt that Herbert Armstrong was an exceptionally gifted man, skilled in public oratory and possessing great powers of persuasion. He also was an entrepreneurial visionary who saw tremendous future possibilities for "the Work" and had the uncompromising fortitude to see the vision through to reality. At a time when many Christians were lax in obeying God, Armstrong called for a recommitment to the Law of God and warned of God's judgment for continued disobedience. When the world teetered on the brink of self-destruction during the dark years of World War II and throughout the Cold War, Herbert Armstrong offered the hope of Christ's glorious return to save errant humankind.

For those of us in the WCG at the time, Armstrong was bigger than life, God's end-time apostle, the modern-day Elijah who was heralding the coming of our Savior. Now, he was gone. His failed prophecies of Christ's return in 1972, 1975, and 1982 were like ghosts haunting us. Didn't we believe that Christ would return soon? Didn't we know that Herbert W. Armstrong would lead us to meet Christ in His glorious kingdom? In the fall of 1986, the questions remained unanswered. How would we, how could we, possibly go on? In fact, Armstrong had publicly mused about an eventual "falling away" in the WCG if and when he died. We were faced with an uncertain future.

A few extremists believed God would raise Herbert Armstrong back to life on the anniversary of his death, but I can assure you Herbert Armstrong's grave in Altadena, California, still holds his remains and those of his first wife, Loma. Most members at the time were as shocked as I was. Many wept as I did. They looked to their pastors for answers, leadership, and direction. As always, we looked to Pasadena. Armstrong had been wise to name his successor publicly, so the "Armstrong machine" in Pasadena quickly moved to instill confidence in the membership so the Work would continue.

In the messages that came from Pasadena, Armstrong's passing was compared to that of Moses, who had anointed Joshua to take his place. How fitting when you consider that Moses was the man God had used to give Israel the Law and who had presided over a theocracy governed by the letter of this Law. Herbert Armstrong had been our Moses, leading God's elect to our Promised Land, a millennial reign with Christ as gods over the nations. Mr. Tkach Sr. was compared to Joshua, who had been told to be of good courage because the Lord would be with him. He was expected to follow in Armstrong's footsteps as Joshua had followed Moses. Joseph Tkach Sr. had proven himself loyal to Mr. Armstrong, though he had displayed moments of respectful disagreement with the apostle, thus winning Armstrong's trust and admiration.

One traveling evangelist sought to rally support for Mr. Tkach by relating all kinds of life stories about the new pastor general, unwittingly trying to make him into a living legend. He told how tough Tkach had been while growing up in Chicago. He described Tkach's exploits in the Navy during World War II. He said Tkach's name meant *weaver* in Russian and that he was going to weave the church together, just as God had planned. This sounded perfect, though during the next few years I felt this evangelist was trying too hard to make our pastor general into something more than he was. Finally, Mr. Tkach put the clamps on the man, giving him a script to read from on his trips. The script left out much of this hyperbole. He made only one or two trips after Armstrong's death before the Pasadena church administration offered him retirement, which he took. Later, this man left the WCG and joined one of the many splinter groups.

For his part, Mr. Tkach Sr. did not assign himself any great prophetic role. He told me on several occasions that he saw himself as a simple man suddenly placed into an important position. He had not strived for this position. He was a servant of God called to lead the WCG, whether he wanted to or not. I believe that Mr. Tkach Sr. felt uncomfortable in the position of pastor general, but he had a strong sense of duty and service, as well as a love for the people of God. Therefore, he was committed to giving the job his best. He made mistakes, but his mistakes do not diminish the role he played as a man of God who gave his utmost while leading the Worldwide Church of God into the light of biblical truth and out of the shadows of legalism. Mr. Tkach Sr. also discontinued the practice of claiming to be an apostle, though initially after assuming office, some continued to refer to him as such.

By 1986, our time in Europe was drawing to a close. After one year in Germany, Linda developed a bad cough that persisted for all seven years we were there. We tried one natural remedy after another, but nothing worked. Finally, we visited a lung specialist in Zürich. He diagnosed chronic bronchitis and advised Linda to leave the damp European climate and move to a warm dry environment. Concurrent with her health problems, we noticed that Rhett was losing the ability to express himself clearly in English. Although we spoke only English in the home, while he was in school or playing with friends, he spoke only German—in this case, fluent Swiss German. To combat this, we taught Rhett and our younger son, Dustin, at home through correspondence courses from the United States. Their English skills began to improve immediately and their German did not suffer too much. As they grew older, however, we were aware of our own limitations in home-schooling and the need to expose them to American culture. Friends in similar circumstances had raised their children in a foreign country and educated them in the particular foreign language. Upon repatriation to the United States, these children had difficulty fitting in. By 1984, we knew we would return to the United States, and we desired that our sons not be linguistically or culturally disadvantaged. Once Linda's health problem became a pressing issue, even overshadowing the educational question for the boys, we knew our time in Europe was limited.

Here we go again, I thought. The director still believed that once you were part of the German "Work," you remained in the German "Work." For one solid year, Linda and I prayed that God would show us His will. Should we ask for reassignment to the United States or wait for God to move those over us to suggest it themselves? Linda believed we should wait on God to move our superiors to notice and respond to our need. I agreed with her, but I noted we already had alluded to Linda's health condition on several occasions, as well as the boys' educational needs, with nothing forthcoming from Frank. Gradually I came to believe it was my responsibility as head of the house to ask for the transfer and let God work His will. Linda agreed. During a routine telephone conversation with the director in late winter of 1986, while he was discussing his plans for the German "Work" and how I fit in, I told him I had a problem that needed his attention. He cautiously asked about the problem, to which I responded with the story of Linda's health and the boys' educational needs.

Frank responded in measured tones, yet betrayed a shock. He assured me that Linda's health was of primary concern. He asked that I submit a written request, stating clearly the issues of concern. Knowing that I needed proof of my claim regarding Linda's health, I asked the lung specialist to write a confirmation of his findings along with his recommendation. This was sent with my request to Frank in Bonn. He read it and forwarded it to the director of church administration in Pasadena, who had been a student at Ambassador College in Big Sandy while I was there. (The previous director of international church administration had assumed the presidency of Ambassador College in Texas). With this new man, I knew I would be treated with respect and given the benefit of the doubt. Linda was chronically ill and needed to get out of the country, period.

Soon after the request was submitted to the German director and forwarded to Pasadena for review and action, Frank and his wife came for a visit. I believed the purpose of the visit was an "attitude check" to see if we were okay spiritually and whether there were hidden issues that required exploration. Upon his request, I found a restaurant where the four of us could share an evening together. Linda and I were apprehensive, expecting the third degree. To our surprise and dismay, not a word was spoken about our request. It was as though nothing had transpired. *I can live with that,* I thought to myself. *If he does not wish to talk about it right now, that's fine.*

After six years in the Swiss region, Frank and I had gotten along together quite well. He trusted me completely, and I valued that trust. I was honest and kept him up to date on everything in the church. I sought his advice when difficult issues arose. He was generous in his praise and gave me great latitude to do what needed to be done. He never questioned the wisdom of my actions, though he did not always act according to my recommendations. Under his empowering administration, I blossomed and enjoyed success, doubling the size of the congregations by adding new members, increasing the readership of *Klar & Wahr*, and making the Black Forest festival site a world-class destination that routinely had to turn away applicants. My only criticism of his administration—until this incident with our family—was that he lacked staying power when it came to budgetary commitments. Overall, his treatment of me and my family had been generous during this second tour of duty.

Now that we were expressing a need to return to the United States, Frank was in a real bind. The WCG was heavily dependant on foreign leadership to man the pastorates, which was not the healthiest situation and has proven to be a major flaw in WCG's long-range planning. Frank liked me, needed me, and told me so. Soon the subject of departure came up every time we were together. One time he offered me trips to Spain's dry climate as often as I needed them to heal Linda's bronchitis. But I could not accept this generous offer on two grounds. First, once Linda returned to the wet climate, she would become ill again. Second, I was sure somebody in Pasadena would raise a stink about such preferential treatment. I turned him down. He reminded me how God had prepared me for the German Work and that God would continue to provide for us. That was real pressure that almost caused me to relent. I talked it over with my friend John, the office manager, and he suggested I stay the course and let God lead matters. I determined to stick to my request and ride it out to the end.

Six months after sending the request for transfer, no word had come from Pasadena. We had not even received an acknowledgement that the request had been received. That was disconcerting because it would be obvious to anyone reading the letter that Linda's need was real. What had happened? Frank assured me the request had reached the desk of the international director. Upon my suggestion, Frank allowed me to call Pasadena to speak to the man personally. So I called the international director and respectfully asked if he had had an opportunity to review our situation. He was, as I had expected, warm and affable, replying that he had studied our request carefully and there was no question in his mind that we needed to come home. His problem was finding a replacement. We talked a month or so later, and he informed me that a replacement had been found. He asked if I would like to pastor the Dallas-West congregation. That sounded fantastic, especially because Texas was Linda's home state, and it would put us close to her family. I responded that the offer was excellent and accepted the assignment, expecting the congregation to be around 250 people. When I called the local pastor, I was shocked to hear that there were nearly 600 members in the Dallas-West congregation and at least 500 more members in the Dallas-East church. Combined, the Dallas congregations had as many members as the entire German-speaking church! I was overwhelmed at the trust demonstrated in offering me such a large congregation. I looked forward to this new challenge.

Again we were faced with a major move, pulling up roots, and saying good-bye to dear friends. Although we needed to go, wanted to go, and were excited to go, we had grown to love the WCG members deeply. Had it not been for Linda's health, I could easily have stayed in Switzerland, but health and family needs cannot be ignored lest one find oneself alone in ministry. We said our farewells and watched as our earthly belongings were loaded into a metal sea container to be shipped to the United States. When you see a truck drive off with everything you own, you have a sobering realization that life should not be measured by how much we possess, but in how much we contribute to the welfare of others. Materialism affects those in ministry as it does the laity, dulling our spiritual senses and hollowing out our souls. I recall the words of St. Paul, who wrote: "But godliness with contentment is great gain. For we brought nothing into the world, and we can take nothing out of it. But if we have food and clothing, we will be content with that" (1 Timothy 6:6–8).

It is amazing how a few hours in an airplane can radically change your world. One day we were in Zürich, viewing the verdant hills and snow-capped Alps, living amidst the guttural sounds of the Swiss dialect. The next moment we were racing down a concourse at the Dallas-Ft. Worth airport to catch our connecting flight to Amarillo, Texas, where we had planned to spend several weeks with Linda's parents before returning to Dallas to hunt for a house. On the way to that commuter flight, we grabbed a copy of the *Dallas Morning News* to check the real estate section for rental homes. The flight from Dallas to Amarillo took about an hour, which was enough time for us to get an idea of what kind of house we could afford and where we would locate. Our lives seemed settled, and we were thrilled at the prospect of being back in Texas.

Our jet touched down in Amarillo and Linda's mother met us. We laughed, embraced, and cheered one another at the reunion in the small Amarillo terminal. We had barely finished our greeting when Linda's mom said, "David in Pasadena has been trying to reach you by telephone." David was a friend with whom Linda and I had spent two years at Ambassador College in England. After graduation, he had served in various media capacities for the church in several international posts. Finally, he had been recommended to Mr. Armstrong to coordinate the church's international media buying efforts. With Armstrong's passing, David, an ordained evangelist, had become one of four presenters who replaced Mr. Armstrong on *The World Tomorrow*. David, an extremely intelligent and articulate man, had worked well with Mr. Armstrong and enjoyed his trust. After Mr. Armstrong's death, Mr. Tkach Sr., who also had become a good friend of David's, had promoted him to director of communications and public affairs and vice president of the Ambassador Foundation. Over the years, David and I had met or corresponded infrequently, but we had remained friends. When he moved to Pasadena to assume an executive position, Linda and I had visited him and his family when we were in town on church business. We had spent some time together in Europe on one of David's trips abroad. During that time, he had learned of my involvement with media for the church in Switzerland and Austria.

I could not imagine why David wanted to talk to me, other than to urge us to bring Rhett and Dusty with us to Pasadena on a brief visit that had been planned after our visit in Amarillo. His sons and ours always looked forward to being together when we were in Pasadena. Because of the expense, however, Linda and I were planning to leave the boys with relatives in Texas while we visited Pasadena. I called David and received the shock of my life. "How would you like to come to Pasadena and work for me?" he asked.

I was caught so flatfooted, I hardly knew what to say other than to ask what I would be doing.

"I need help with the media buying," he replied. Several emotions swept over me—surprise, delight, a sense of being overwhelmed, excitement. David briefly outlined what he had in mind, which was to assist him in overseeing the time buying operation for *The World Tomorrow* and purchasing advertising space for *The Plain Truth*, which involved an annual budget of more than $20 million dollars. After a brief conference with Linda, I accepted the job. There were two motivating factors. First, I liked and respected David and knew he was overwhelmed with his workload. I also wanted to help a friend. Second, I desired to serve God in whatever capacity He thought best. Additionally, the climate in Pasadena is even drier than that of Dallas. (Within a year of our move to Pasadena, Linda's bronchitis healed and she began to enjoy better health.) But I did not desire to work at headquarters because of the terrible stories I had heard about the in-fighting, back-biting, elbowing, etc. Most local pastors would say to one another that they hoped never to be asked to go there. But here I was being asked and *accepting*! I was assured things were much better in Pasadena than in previous years, and I found that to be true.

Within a few weeks, we were in Pasadena, living in a temporary apartment on the church campus until we could find a more permanent situation in town. The change was enormous. Instead of the erratic hours of the local church pastor, I was working from 8 A.M. to 5 P.M., which was a pleasant adjustment. I had a nice office on the executive fourth floor that adjoined David's suite. On top of that, I had a recent college graduate and two young specialists—one in print media, the other in electronic media—to assist me. I sat with my back to a large window that looked out on the gentle lawn of the luxurious old mansion estate of the late H. C. Merritt, which Mr. Armstrong had bought at auction in the 1950s for the cost of the iron fence that surrounded the property. It was a scene I had viewed in Ambassador College's yearbook, the *Envoy*, and now I had this picture of paradise as a backdrop to my daily work.

One of the first things I asked David was what I could expect my salary to be because I wanted to establish a monthly budget. David was a generous man who paid his staff well and treated us fairly. He had assembled gifted and able people who were dedicated to the mission of the church. We were encouraged to express our opinions, even if they were contrary to his, but he did expect us to defend our position. There was never any retribution for disagreement; instead, we felt a sense of freedom to work in such an open and empowering environment. David gave me a figure for my salary that was generous yet not out of line for my position as assistant director of communications and public affairs.

My first unpleasant experience in Pasadena came when that first paycheck arrived and was noticeably lower than what I had been told. I went to the department responsible for budgetary matters and asked why my expected salary had not materialized. The department head looked up from his desk and said, "Mr. Tkach decided not to give you the full amount so as to encourage you by giving you a raise after six weeks." My jaw almost dropped to the carpeted floor when I heard that. *How was docking my salary for six weeks going to encourage me?* I wanted to ask. What Mr. Tkach probably wanted to do was start me lower than what David had set as a salary, then give me a nice boost after six weeks. That sounded great except I already had received the commitment for a higher amount. I bit my lip and left the office, hoping this incident was an exception to the rule rather than the rule itself. As time went on, however, I found that many such oddities took place in Pasadena.

Working for David was a delight because he trusted me. He taught me the business side of television time buying, as well as how to purchase advertising space in print media. I participated in meetings with him as he met with the executives of the BBDO advertising agency in Los Angeles. As time progressed, I chaired the meetings in his stead and became his chief liaison to the agency. Our working relationship with BBDO was outstanding. Its president was a fine southern gentleman from my home state of North Carolina. He had an easy manner, which helped immensely in working through all the little problems that would arise between agency and client.

It was not long before I was making trips with a BBDO vice president to visit television stations all over the world. We would present *The World Tomorrow* telecast so we could secure airtime or improve time slots. Programs are placed in time slots according to targeted audience goals. The ratings showing the public's like or dislike of a program determine if advertisers will buy spots to promote their products, which is where the money is made. With a religious program, there are no advertisers. Therefore, there must be a sponsor to pay for the airtime. Normally that sponsor will be a church, as was the case with *The World Tomorrow.*

Religious programs receive ratings just like every secular program on television, but the ratings are generally much lower, which means fewer people watch religious television. Good program managers at television stations understand the viewing patterns of people and will schedule religious programs in "the God slot"—generally early Sunday morning. During the two or three years that I was involved in time buying, *The World Tomorrow* ran a close second in numbers of viewers to Robert Schuller's *Hour of Power,* even occasionally beating his program for first place in the religious category.

Mr. Armstrong's death meant the sole personality of the church's TV program was gone. Mr. Tkach no longer wanted to have one man as presenter, which would increase the possibility of creating another personality cult within the ranks of the WCG. He did not feel that it was his calling to be a television presenter, and he had the humility to avoid any pressure exerted on him to do so anyway. Mr. Tkach selected four men, all evangelists, and each with a different audience appeal. The weekly viewership to *The World Tomorrow* climbed to nearly 1.25 million, with as many as 50,000 calling a toll-free number to receive free literature. WCG members were enthusiastic about the program and gladly supported it. The cost for syndicated television is enormous, often running into the millions of dollars. The WCG did not appeal for funds on the air nor in its literature. The tithes and offerings of the dedicated membership of the Worldwide Church of God kept *The World Tomorrow* on the air. Eventually, however, as income began to slip, Mr. Tkach and a few of us on the staff began to question the enormous expense in light of the sparse "back end"—the number of new members it brought into the church. By the early 1990s, the WCG's annual membership growth rate was flat. It also appeared that television was a dinosaur that was eating us out of house and home. Parallel to this realization was the gradual doctrinal shift that was occuring. We began doing fewer programs on prophecy, and when we did, we stayed away from the spectacular claims that had been a hall-mark of Mr. Armstrong's messages. Further, we used to "beat up" on Christmas and Easter, but there was a subtle shift in thinking on these holidays as well, making us less willing to be so judg-mental and condemning.

Many of these changes were painful for those in Pasadena, including David. He began to experience some difficulties with several on Mr. Tkach's immediate staff regarding strategy and administrative matters. Little by little, he lost major responsibili-ties—first went the media buying, including me and my staff. We were transferred to the director of media operations, and I was demoted to supervisor. No one said I had done a poor job; in fact, comments were just the opposite. I was told I had done a fine job, but the demotion held, which was personally painful. I believed that as David's star dimmed, mine would as well. David's strug-gles continued as he lost part of his public relations functions, which were divided between me—I became responsible for church relations—and another Tom at Ambassador University in Texas, who became responsible for the university's public affairs. David still managed the high-profile performing arts series at Ambassador Auditorium in Pasadena. He continued to attempt to move it toward financial independence, but the continuing slide in financial support from the public and the membership forced Joseph Tkach to cancel the series and dissolve the foundation.

This came at about the same time that Mr. Tkach made his 1994 Christmas Eve address in Atlanta and announced that the WCG was no longer between the covenants but now, through Christ, under the New Covenant. The implication of such a doctrinal stand reversed our view on fundamental issues such as the Sabbath, the holy days, clean and unclean meats, as well as our claim to exclusivity. Such a monumental switch was too much for many in the WCG fellowship, including David. He resigned to become president of a newly formed WCG splinter group, the United Church of God. Since that time, David has left that organization, which he helped found, to start yet another WCG splinter group. As with most groups, he remains faithful to the legacy of Herbert W. Armstrong, trapped in false and heretical teachings that keep people in the shadows.

I had been transferred from David to work under Ray, another long-time friend, who directed media operations. This man had left a successful business career to attend Ambassador College in England as a married student. He had enjoyed many high-profile positions in the church over the years, including a period as treasurer. Unfortunately, some past mistakes and some current personality conflicts with members of the new administration were causing his star to wane as well. Within a year after my transfer to his area, he was encouraged to seek employment elsewhere, which he did. He eventually left the WCG as well.

After Ray's departure, I was promoted to manager of television time buying, working directly for Bernie, the director of media operations. Bernie turned out to be a great boss and a personal friend. Our media budget continued to shrink as Mr. Tkach tried to match the expenses of the church with its declining income. We had changed advertising agencies during my stint as supervisor, selecting a smaller Los Angeles company owned and operated by Dick Janik, a dynamic man. Dick had been given the task of managing our down-sizing while increasing our efficiencies in cost and numbers of viewers reached. He and his staff did a marvelous job of lowering our cost per viewer, lowering our total spending, and increasing our audience levels. I reported regularly to Mr. Tkach on the efficiencies being achieved, as well as our increase in audience levels. He always expressed his satisfaction, though there were many times when he seemed distracted. Even during our regular Monday morning meetings, in which we did a post mortem of the previous weekend's episode of *The World Tomorrow,* he would seem preoccupied.

Mr. Tkach's manner was to allow free discussion among the five of us present with him during these meetings, even allowing some sharp disagreements. He would not say much himself; rather, he would listen and ask occasional questions. He seldom made a decision in my presence, preferring to discuss the matter with his son, Joe, and his personal assistant, Mike Feazell. We would learn about any decisions later. He avoided one-on-one confrontation, choosing to express his consternation in a public forum, such as a church service or an all-employee meeting. Saving money was central to his thinking. He saw the income slipping and member support eroding, and he felt the weight of responsibility to keep the church afloat financially. When it came time to cut a program or a project, Mr. Tkach would cut it. The cuts were seldom strategic. Often they came as a reaction to momentary pressures. His willingness to come to grips with the church's economic dilemma caused him to make necessary cutbacks. He steadfastly refused to borrow money or to mortgage property, thereby keeping the church in sound financial order.

The position I enjoyed as manager of media time buying soon began to lose its significance as the budget allocated for media continued to be cut. After much soul searching, Mr. Tkach pulled the plug on the 30-minute weekly television program in the fall of 1993. He moved to one- and two-minute television ads that offered literature via a toll-free number. He hoped we could do one-hour television specials a few times each year and even announced to the membership that we would do them. This never came to fruition because the finances would not permit it. Besides, we knew that the most we could hope for from such an effort was thousands of pieces of literature being sent out with little return in the way of donations or new members. As financial pressures continued to mount, the WCG eventually had to leave television altogether, pulling back to print media and the church's flagship, *The Plain Truth,* which is where the WCG is today. A short while before the church left television, the director of media operations asked me to accept a newly created post as international media operations coordinator. I said yes, realizing that time buying was on its way out and desiring to remain involved in the international arena, which I truly enjoyed. This job meant travel to some of the church's foreign offices to keep the regional directors updated on developments in Pasadena, as well as to assist them with operational questions, especially in the area of budgeting and planning. I enjoyed the job and enjoyed working for Bernie, my boss, who was an excellent manager. We became good friends and comrades as we worked to help the international offices adjust to the changing economic times in the church.

This job was rather short-lived because the work of the international offices came under the complete supervision of the director of church administration international. It was suggested that I consider another newly created post. The new position was manager of evangelism support services, and I was to begin a program of education and implementation of public evangelism in the church. This was exciting because I had been reading extensively on the subject and saw the critical need for our church to attract new members and infuse new life into the membership. I accepted the job and together with a small staff conceptualized a program called Open House.

Open House was a simple but effective idea. Using *The Plain Truth* mailing list, we would mail an invitation to readers in select geographic areas, inviting them to a special series of sermons at a local WCG church. We called it Open House to convey to readers, as well as to our members, that we were coming out of our self-imposed exile and inviting all who wished to worship with us, without any fear of pressure or obligation to join. To ensure the effectiveness of the program, I selected six pastors in the United States to run the pilot program and flew them to Pasadena for a few days of lectures, discussion, and training.

I had difficulty from the beginning of this venture. My new boss, Joe Tkach Jr., who was director of church administration, placed me on the same level as his two assistants who worked specifically with the United States and international churches. I answered to neither of them, but I did seek to work with both of them because my efforts would impact their areas of responsibility. The international assistant said he would like to await results from the American experiment before trying Open House overseas. This was logical and fair.

The assistant in charge of the U.S. ministry repeatedly pledged his support to my efforts, but secretly, he worked to block me. I wanted to select six regional pastors to do the pilot program for Open House, but he said they would be too busy. With his approval, I selected six church pastors. I wanted to train the men in Pasadena. He wanted the training done in the field. (He later relented when I showed him costs for training at headquarters compared to field training.)

Another important part of the mix for a successful Open House was to shorten our two-hour worship service to 90 minutes, as well as to make a few adjustments to the service format. Again, the assistant director of church administration for the United States was skeptical. I began to hear rumors from friends that in private conversations he expressed his uneasiness about the entire venture. But we pushed onward and launched the Open House campaign in Washington, D.C.; Miami; San Francisco; Baltimore; and elsewhere. The results were encouraging as hundreds of new people came to WCG church services and many baptisms occurred. Another positive benefit was the excitement generated among the membership because they were involved in reaching new people and seeing their congregations grow. Those initial six pastors became mentors to train the next group of pastors, which numbered about 20. Again, the results were wonderful as hundreds more visited local congregations and more baptisms were registered. Just as we had hoped, planned, and prayed, enthusiasm spread throughout the ministry and more members clamored for an Open House in their area. My staff and I developed a systematic program that would cover the United States in two years. Meanwhile the Canadians and the British decided to run parallel Open Houses. Mr. Tkach Sr. was delighted with the results and stated in a Friday morning meeting that evangelism support services was the most successful thing the church had going and he did not want to cut its budget. It seemed I had found my niche and God had given me a wonderful opportunity to inject life and enthusiasm into the WCG.

Then one morning several months into the Open House campaign, I was called to Joe Tkach Jr.'s office for a meeting with him and the two assistant directors. I came prepared to give the latest report on the positive growth through Open House, as well as to report on the Second Wave, a small-group concept I had initiated. We sat around the small round table Joe kept in his office for discussions, and he began the meeting by voicing concern that evangelism support services was causing an uneasiness among the regional pastors in the field. I asked why, and he deferred to the assistant in charge of the U.S. ministry. He, too, was vague, unable, or unwilling to cite any specific examples of problems in the field as a result of my efforts. But he was clear enough that I soon figured out what the meeting was really about. They wanted me out of evangelism support services. It was also clear that I could go peacefully or be yanked out. Seeing that no one supported me, I felt that trying to fight was foolish. After a little more verbal sparring, I suggested it might be best for me to step down from evangelism support services in favor of the U.S. ministry assistant. I would concentrate on my managerial duties in the area of media relations. Joe thanked me for making the meeting easy for everyone, and we were done. I felt a deep sense of betrayal because everyone had earlier pledged their support. No one had presented concrete grounds for removing me from this evangelism position nor had any previous warning been given. I was told by another executive more than a year later that the assistant director of church administration in the United States had threatened to resign if I were not removed. This was the same man who had promised me his support and cooperation. This apparent betrayal stung my soul deeply, but with God's help, I bore the pain and tried to help the church where I could. A few years later, when I spoke to Joe Tkach about these events, he assured me there had been no threats of resignation and that he had been led to believe that I wanted out of the position. I don't know the truth, and I suppose at this point in my life the truth would not be particularly helpful. (Once the assistant director assumed responsibility, evangelism soon ran out of steam and the entire program was dropped. This was yet another missed opportunity for the WCG.)

Perhaps the biggest opportunity that Mr. Tkach Sr. missed was the failure to see the vital importance of the strategic planning process he had initiated in 1987. This was an effort he approved to assess the church's organizational strengths and weaknesses in preparing to meet future opportunities and obstacles. It was a planning process that would have given the WCG a clear vision for the future and the track to run on to arrive there. It was a gigantic effort that involved all the international offices and Pasadena headquarters. Plans were to use this strategy to develop a five-year plan. Mr. Tkach would say that if we did not know where we were going, we would likely end up there. Unfortunately, when it came time to commit to the demands of such a project, Mr. Tkach Sr., upon the recommendation of his closest advisors, ordered it to be discontinued. This termination occurred around 1993, which probably accounted for the lack of clear vision and direction in the Worldwide Church of God in the early- and mid-1990s.

Another situation arose during the administration of Joseph Tkach Sr. that later proved detrimental to the church when he sought to prevent the fissure and split that rocked us in 1995. In an effort to correct doctrinal errors that had been in the church for decades under the administration of Mr. Armstrong, there were several in the Tkach administration, including Mr. Tkach himself, who were accused of "Armstrong bashing." Fault was readily found with the way Mr. Armstrong had done things, as well as the obvious errors of his teaching. Many members were driven into defensive postures, however, as they perceived that their years of sacrifice and commitment were now discounted and meaningless. Many held Mr. Armstrong in high esteem and reverence, and to hear him directly or indirectly criticized by the Tkach administration caused resentment among the membership toward "Pasadena"—which was a euphemism for Mr. Tkach and his staff. Joe Tkach Jr. and Mike Feazell often were singled out as especially culpable.

Of course, this is only one side of the story. The other is that Mr. Tkach and his staff were trying to demythologize Herbert Armstrong, as well as correct his obvious non-biblical teachings. It was a no-win situation. The members were highly sensitized regarding anything that smacked of disrespect to Herbert W. Armstrong. And Mr. Tkach and his staff were at times awkward and less than sensitive in trying to deal with the situation. As a result a "we vs. they" mentality developed between headquarters and the field ministry and its congregations. Added to this were perceived contradictory statements made by the Tkach administration. One example was to state that there are true Christians in other church bodies outside the WCG, but still maintaining that we were the one true church of God. (This has since been clarified to state that the WCG forms only part of the visible body of Christ.) The result of such perceived double-speak was distrust and lack of confidence. The administration seemed unaware of the gravity of the situation nor did the leaders seem to know how to deal with it. The problem was ignored, which resulted in further estrangement. This set the backdrop for a terrible split.

In the spring of 1993, I was told to report to a several-day meeting on the campus in Pasadena. All the regional directors and their wives from our international offices, as well as key personnel from headquarters, were to be in attendance. I had no idea what it was about and did not particularly want to go because my duties were quite demanding. The thought of being confined to a room for several days did not sit well. Little did I know, however, that this meeting would be a watershed for a radical change in the course of the Worldwide Church of God. It was at this meeting that the WCG's sole scholar was introduced, Dr. Stavrinides. He addressed us on the nature of God. Here the storm clouds began to gather, and in less than two years, the Worldwide Church of God would suffer its most crippling blow.

As discussed earlier, the WCG had maintained for years that God was a family consisting of the Father and the Son, both separate and distinct beings with form and shape. We understood the Holy Spirit to be the power of God, as well as the essence out of which God consists. The doctrine of the Trinity had been viewed as pagan; therefore, for decades the church had strongly rejected and lampooned it. In this series of meetings with Dr. Stavrinides, we were shocked to learn that our former belief was now officially rejected in favor of a view more closely aligned with traditional trinitarian teaching. The Pasadena leadership was hesitant to use the word "trinity" because it called forth such explosive negative reaction. Thus, the words *triune* or *triad* were used. This caused confusion because ministers and members would ask if we now accepted the doctrine of the trinity, but the reply was carefully worded to avoid an absolute affirmative. There were those who felt the administration was not being forthright in presenting the doctrine.

After several days of meetings that included lively discussion, I was confused. I did not understand, and thus could not agree, with this teaching of the triad God. Until this point, I had been able to work through every doctrinal change the church had undertaken. Now it seemed I had reached an impasse. Word of this new doctrine regarding the nature of God soon spread to the entire ministry and membership. Members had many questions, which the WCG ministry was not prepared to answer. How could they be? They had found out about the change at the same time as the membership. This did little to boost morale because the ministers felt left out of the loop and the members were frustrated that their ministers were not able to answer their questions. This situation is characteristic of the way the WCG administration introduced doctrinal change at that time. An announcement was made and articles were written in the ministerial publication, *The Bulletin* (later *Crossroads*), and in the member publication, *The Worldwide News*. Ministry and membership were on the same playing field, trying to understand at the same time. This produced ill will from both parties.

Now that I found myself in disagreement with the church on the doctrine of God, I felt it only a matter of time before I would have to leave the church's employment. Recently I had been appointed the church's public relations director, but I could hardly represent the church's position when I personally disagreed with such a defining issue. This matter troubled me greatly and drove me to my knees in prayer many times, asking God to reveal His nature to me through Scripture.

It was during that year that the administration conducted regional conferences throughout the United States and other parts of the world. I attended the conferences in the United States where I presented a lecture on personal evangelism. Dr. Stavrinides presented a condensed version of his Pasadena lecture on the nature of God, followed by hours of questions from the ministry. This was the administration's effort to provide the ministers with the understanding they needed to deal with the members' many questions. Having Dr. Stavrinides on hand was positive and negative. It was positive because he thoroughly understood the subject and could explain the teaching in a clear, logical, systematic manner. Unfortunately, most of the American WCG ministers had little experience with a man like Dr. Stavrinides, who as a highly educated Greek European loved debate and logical argumentation. However, the sensitivity the changes brought to the ministry coupled with the mounting lack of trust in the administration meant many ministers found Dr. Stavrinides to be abrupt and rude (which was not a fair characterization). This perception made it difficult for many to understand what he was trying to teach. In time, however, a majority in the ministry understood and accepted the teaching that God is one yet three distinct non-separate Persons, which is the orthodox historical view of the Trinity. After about the seventh regional conference, God was merciful to hear my prayer and grant me this same understanding, which I strongly confess to this day.

The doctrinal crisis surrounding the nature of God passed and we came out pretty much in tact. Members' understanding of the doctrine was still a bit fuzzy, but there was no movement toward a split. Things began to settle down until rumors of trouble on the East Coast came to our attention in Pasadena. One of our well-known ministers was preaching a clear message of grace, which was delighting some and alarming others. The implications of his message were far reaching, and there were those both in the ministry and membership calling for Mr. Tkach Sr. to take action. They wanted him either to voice his approval or to silence the man. Once again clouds began to form on the horizon, this time darker and more menacing than we had seen in a long time. What would soon break over our heads was a violent storm. It would forever change the direction of Armstrong's church.

Chapter 8

The Dawning of a New Day

Grace comes into the soul, as the morning sun into the world; first a dawning; then a light; and at last the sun in his full and excellent brightness.—Thomas Adams

Life as the manager of church relations was not bad. After losing the responsibility for evangelism, my staff shrank from four people to Barbara, my secretary. But Barbara, a woman about my own age who had been on my staff for several years, moved to a better job in the festival department. She had been an exceptional help to me and had become a friend, yet when I saw my star dimming in Pasadena, I encouraged her to look for a better position and not remain tied to someone who may not be able to help her career. She left reluctantly, realizing I was right. Within a year of moving to the festival department, Barbara felt unfulfilled and accepted a job with a Pasadena health care provider.

I advertised in-house for a replacement for Barbara. Perhaps I had a bad reputation because few people applied for the position. Another factor may have been the declining workforce at headquarters. Gradually people were being let go because of budget constraints, so available candidates were diminishing. After interviewing a few people, I hired a young woman from another department who stayed with me for about a year. Then she resigned to pursue a job in Pasadena. She eventually left the WCG to join the same splinter group her in-laws had joined.

As the church relations manager, I was responsible for dealing with the bad press the Worldwide Church of God received. There are numerous cult-watch groups, cult experts, and pseudo-experts, as well as religious authors, who were constantly writing about what they considered worrisome and sometimes dangerous religious organizations. It was my job to buy all the books that mentioned anything about the WCG and seek to get correct, updated information published.

By the time I assumed this responsibility, the church already had made some significant doctrinal strides by accepting orthodox positions on what it means to be born again, the nature of God, and the acknowledgment that we were not the "one true church." In addition to these changes, we were backing off Armstrong's Anglo-Israelism doctrine. The WCG also had softened its views regarding the observances of Christmas and Easter, taking a less judgmental and combative stance. It was important for me to get this message out to the cult-watching groups and the Christian press quickly and clearly.

At that time, the WCG Doctrinal Committee was meeting regularly, reviewing and discussing the doctrines of the Worldwide Church of God. I was not invited to join the committee, nor given reports on the substance of their meetings, so I would ask committee members what was being discussed. Sometimes it was difficult to obtain information because of the charged atmosphere in the church and the reluctance of committee members to speak openly about their discussions.

Unfortunately, there was a growing distrust among those who staffed the field ministry and the general membership toward the leadership in Pasadena. Some felt Joseph Tkach Sr. was being manipulated by Joe Tkach Jr. and Mike Feazell and that he did not know what was happening. This was not true. Mr. Tkach Sr. was a micromanager. He knew exactly what was happening. There were no doctrinal decisions that did not receive his approval. Not that he personally conducted the research, but before anything was published regarding the theology of the

WCG, he saw it and approved any changes. I recall being in his office with a few church executives one day. Mr. Tkach was upset about something regarding doctrine. With red face, he shouted, "I am the one who determines doctrine in this church!" That was true and underscores a problem the Worldwide Church of God has had since its early days—one man determined doctrine for thousands of members.

While still in charge of evangelism support services, I conducted a qualitative telephone survey of church members across the United States. The reason for the survey was to identify the main issues of concern the membership hoped the administration would address. I found the common perception was that Mr. Tkach was not fully aware of the doctrinal decisions being made, which was not the case. Members also wanted clear and complete information regarding doctrinal changes disseminated at one time, rather than piece-meal and containing contradictions. I suggested that we take the survey findings and quantify the magnitude of the perceptions, then develop a plan of action to deal with members' concerns. The results of the survey were read, but no action was taken. The administration felt it knew members' feelings and perceptions and how best to deal with them.

Little was being done to win the confidence and trust of the membership. Rumors would circulate about possible doctrinal changes. There were those who were suspicious that even the Sabbath and holy days would be compromised. The fact that few people knew exactly what was being discussed in the doctrinal committee meetings provided grounds for members to be suspicious and to speculate the worst. Mr. Tkach Sr. denied there was any intention of changing doctrine regarding the Sabbath and holy days, yet rumors persisted and there was a general uneasiness. You cannot imagine the shock in December 1994 (only months later) when Joseph Tkach Sr. announced that the Sabbath command was no longer binding on Christians. The doubts and suspicions of many concerning Mr. Tkach's faithfulness to the fundamental teachings of Herbert Armstrong were confirmed. Many WCG members left as a result of this announcement.

Two young men on staff at Pasadena—one of whom worked for me—studied the results of the member survey further and produced a memo to me in December 1993. It underscored the suspicion held by many members regarding doctrinal changes within the church. These two men noted that such suspicion created an unhealthy spiritual environment in the local congregation, which was impeding the church's work. They suggested reviewing the way doctrinal decisions were made and introduced into the church. Instead of the traditional approach of one man or a few men at the top deciding what 100,000 or more people were to believe, they suggested a more open process that provided the ministry and Ambassador University with more involvement. Further, the memo recommended that the ministry be informed in advance of the announcement to the laity. This would help educate the ministers so they, in turn, could help communicate the changes to the general membership. Many ministers were exasperated when caught flat-footed on doctrinal change. They were expected by the congregation to clearly articulate the church's doctrine, but they often found themselves pressed to the wall, trying to comprehend new teachings themselves while explaining them to the membership. Such an atmosphere fueled doubt, suspicion, and distrust at all levels.

From the perspective of the larger body of the Christian church, the doctrinal change occuring in the WCG was astounding. In what ought to be "unchanging truth" as articulated in Scripture and in traditional orthodoxy, the sheer volume of change was phenomenal. In addition, the notion that doctrine could change was, in itself, a novelty. The changes certainly have been for the better.

The two men who had written the memo to me regarding the release of information about doctrinal change had spent several days in Silver Spring, Maryland, at the headquarters of the Seventh-Day Adventists. Their assignment was to gather information that might be helpful in the area of evangelism. We selected this church body to study because it was the main branch of religious thought out of which grew the WCG, thus we believed our members would be less likely to criticize such a meeting. While these men were in Silver Spring, the subject of how doctrinal change took place in the WCG arose. One Adventist leader commented that he felt our procedure did not follow the model given in Acts 15, which shows a greater level of church involvement in doctrinal decisions. This information was included in their memo, which I passed up the ladder for consideration. It was decided, however, that the best and only way for the WCG to proceed was to continue doing as it had always done. The chief argument for this position was that without continuing the "doctrine by decree" approach, the ministry and membership would not go along with the sweeping doctrinal changes that Mr. Tkach wanted to make. This was probably a correct perception, which put us in a no-win situation. To continue in doctrinal error was unthinkable, but to mandate change, especially in areas of core belief, would alienate a large portion of our members.

It was easy to sit on the sidelines and criticize how things were done, particularly if you were not in the eye of the storm. But what was the atmosphere in which Joe Tkach Sr. and staff found themselves while these startling changes were being implemented? They unwittingly allowed trust and confidence in their leadership to erode, which only exacerbated the difficulties they faced. Yet they were confronted with entrenched heretical teaching that had to be rooted out. To be faithful to God meant taking a stand for truth, even in the face of severe opposition. The opposition was not from outside the church, but from inside and at all levels. Even some who daily ate lunch at Mr. Tkach's table and who had been his close friends opposed biblical truth, preferring to maintain Mr. Armstrong's errant teachings. To gather the ministry for a study and vote on change ran the risk of being defeated. And truth could not be allowed to suffer defeat. Judging by the way many of the WCG's departed ministers refused even to read the information that was sent to them for study, I believe closed minds would have sabotaged the necessary doctrinal reformation. Does the end justify the means? Of course not, but in light of the loss of trust that gradually undermined Mr. Tkach's ability to persuade the ministry in particular and the membership in general, I think he was left with only one option: decree the change in doctrine and let the chips fall where they may. It was not the most elegant solution, but I don't believe he had another viable option.

Naturally, the cult-watching groups were following developments in our church closely. My opinion of the few groups with which I had contact is not positive. I found them to be like hounds of hell, nipping at our heels, always looking for an opening to tear us down, and always doubting what we said. Their attitude was formed in large part by dealing with cults who were not honorable and deserved to be treated with suspicion. Nevertheless, when under attack, you do not generally look to justify your persecutor. For the most part, the cult-watching groups were stumbling blocks that offered no encouragement as we tried to reform. It seemed that no small step in the right direction was good enough. They wanted everything changed immediately and completely, including a public statement denouncing Mr. Armstrong as a false prophet.

Such lack of understanding and graciousness astounded me as I tried to appreciate the position from which these Christians were coming. They certainly had no comprehension of the historic struggle we were facing. It seemed that the fate of the more than 100,000 members of the Worldwide Church of God was of little concern to them. Hank Hanegraaf was quoted in the *Christian Research Journal* regarding the changes in the WCG:

> This is unprecedented in church history. It's the very kind of thing that those who have given their lives in ministry to the kingdom of the cults hope for. Rather than developing hurdles for these guys to jump over, our job is to facilitate the process, recognizing they had an enormous tactical problem in winning over their own members. They don't want to galvanize people around Garner Ted Armstrong or other splinter groups.[1]

Many cult-watchers were, in effect, demanding total, complete, and immediate repudiation of all the WCG's past incorrect teaching, a public apology, and a denouncement of Herbert Armstrong. One well-known Southern California pastor, who authored numerous books, helped one of his members compose a letter to us in which he suggested that in addition to all of the above, the entire leadership of the church should resign. What these well-meaning Christians needed to understand is that the Holy Spirit reveals to some people the truth in a blinding moment, as with St. Paul. For others, the truth gradually opens to them as the shadow in which they have lived is slowly illuminated by the light of God's Word. Instead of standing beside us; encouraging us; offering friendship, support, and gentle guidance in our effort to follow the lead of the Holy Spirit, many well-intentioned Christian cult-watching groups and Christian leaders stood on the sidelines, judging and taking care not to compromise themselves by involvement in our struggles. These well-meaning Christians unwittingly took on the posture of Pharisees, sitting in judgment and condemning instead of offering a helping hand of fellowship and encouragement. But there were some wonderful exceptions.

Dr. Ruth Tucker was the first person I became aware of who was a friend of the WCG. A visiting professor at Trinity Evangelical Divinity School, Dr. Tucker stood with us, encouraging our turn to evangelicalism. She had contact with my predecessor, David, and his assistant, in the late 1980s. I met and dined with Dr. Tucker several times and appreciated her graciousness and her willingness to defend the WCG, which was not yet orthodox, as it struggled to work through its legacy of non-biblical teachings. Today she is welcomed among the women of the Worldwide Church of God as a guest lecturer and a valued friend.

David Neff, editor of *Christianity Today*, was an early contact as well. I had invited David to visit us in Pasadena during a trip to California—an invitation he accepted. Once such a contact was established, I would arrange a luncheon that included Joe Tkach Jr. (at the time the director of church administration), Mike Feazell (executive assistant to Mr. Tkach Sr.), and Greg Albrecht (editor of *The Plain Truth*). The four of us virtually always met as a team with church and religious leaders. The meeting with David Neff went well. Through our discussion, he was convinced the WCG was on the road to orthodoxy, but he was not ready to give a blanket endorsement. To his credit, he did walk out on a limb to use *Christianity Today* to announce to the Christian world that some encouraging things were happening in the WCG.

David and I maintained loose contact after that meeting as I endeavored to keep him posted on the progress we were making. I knew it was important to convince *Christianity Today,* a well-respected publication, of the reality of the budding reformation occuring in our fellowship. David gave prominent space in the July 15, 1996, edition of *Christianity Today* to an article authored by Dr. Tucker entitled "Worldwide Church of God Sees the Plain Truth." Dr. Tucker's article became *Christianity Today's* official endorsement of the new orthodoxy of the Worldwide Church of God.

Another man who was quick to accept my request for an audience was Hank Hanegraaf, the Bible Answer Man of the Christian Research Institute in Orange County, California. Hank had succeeded the late Dr. Walter Martin as spokesman for the *Bible Answer Man* program, a daily syndicated radio program widely broadcast in the United States. Dr. Martin had authored the well-known book on cults titled *The Kingdom of the Cults.* I remember the anticipation that the four of us felt as we drove from Pasadena to Orange County to visit with Hank. We had no idea what to expect and were ready for the worst because we knew the Bible Answer Man would cut quickly to the heart of the matter and would wield the Bible as the sword of truth, cutting quickly through false doctrine.

We arrived on time at the offices of the Christian Research Institute and were ushered into Hank's modest but tastefully decorated office. With him were members of his staff who remained with us through about four hours of discussion. Our party was comprised of the usual four men. Generally, once contact was made and we were past the introductions, I remained quiet, deferring to Joe Tkach, Mike Feazell, and Greg Albrecht. (The three of them were and still are close friends and spend a great deal of time discussing matters of the church.)

At that time, things in Pasadena were in such a constant state of flux and our theological views were changing so rapidly that I never felt totally informed of "what we believed." The church's position generally became what these three men agreed on and Mr. Tkach Sr. would endorse. Therefore, prudence dictated that I remain silent regarding the theological position of the church. In fact, it was not uncommon that in these meetings I would first hear what the WCG position was or would be on a given issue. I believe this occurred in part because of the rapidity with which things were changing and an unfortunate chronic problem with timely and clear communication. These two factors probably provided the impulse for the active and far-reaching grapevine that ministers and members alike employed to learn the latest from Pasadena. Naturally, much of what was passed along the grapevine or over the Internet was either totally or partially incorrect, but that did not curtail its use.

Hank proved to be a gracious Christian. He asked good questions about our spiritual journey and listened to Joe, Mike, and Greg tell the WCG story. They spoke truthfully, sincerely, and candidly. Sometimes I felt as if they were too candid and self-effacing. After some of these meetings, I would diplomatically attempt to suggest that certain points might better be left unsaid. Nevertheless, Joe, Greg, and Mike always did a splendid job of truthfully and frankly representing the history and reformation of the Worldwide Church of God. I know WCG members would have been pleased to hear how well these men told the church's journey of reformation.

After four hours, Hank surprised us by referring to us as "brothers in Christ" and offering to help our church in any way he could. He offered use of his radio program to tell our story. I advised Joe to decline for the moment because none of us felt the WCG membership was ready to hear the church's leadership interviewed on *The Bible Answer Man*. There were some issues that could not be publicly addressed until they had been released to the ministry and membership. On the way home from our meeting, Joe tuned the car radio to Hank's program. Hank reported on our meeting and publicly endorsed the Worldwide Church of God's reformation. After Mr. Tkach Sr.'s untimely death in September 1995, Joe Tkach Jr. felt it was time to accept Hank's invitation. I agreed, as did the others, so arrangements were made for him and Greg Albrecht to be interviewed. That was the first of several significant radio invitations to come. Hank Hanegraaf has remained a good friend of the Worldwide Church of God and seems to have developed a fondness for Joe and Greg.

As with all our meetings with church leaders and religious writers, we did not seek an endorsement; rather, we desired to explain what was happening in the Worldwide Church of God and answer any questions. After most meetings, the outcome was a positive endorsement of the sincerity of our changes, which was important because it created pressure on the skeptics who were hesitant to accept what we claimed at face value. One such group appeared to be Watchman Fellowship, a well-known cult-watching group located near Dallas, Texas. The Watchman Fellowship had followed the developments in the WCG closely and was perhaps the best informed group on late-breaking changes. To its credit, Watchman Fellowship was accurate and sought to be thoroughly informed through personal contact with me or other WCG ministers. I did not think highly of the Watchman Fellowship because of its abiding skepticism and lack of encouragement. As time progressed, however, I developed a telephone friendship with Phillip Arnn, an executive with the group. Later he said that he and his staff had to come understand the need for a more gracious attitude toward people in cults. It is easy to be negative about cults because of genuine abuses and doctrinal error. However, cultists are people who are in need of a clear understanding of the Gospel of God's grace in offering forgiveness through Jesus Christ. Philip Arnn came to reflect a caring attitude toward us as people. We can love those in cults while at the same time clearly exposing the error of their beliefs.

Rev. George Mather of The Lutheran Church—Missouri Synod played an important role in my life and became a helpful partner to the WCG. I had read Rev. Mather's book, *Dictionary of Cults, Sects, Religions, and the Occult,* which he co-authored with Larry Nichols. As a routine matter, I sent Rev. Mather a letter briefly outlining the significant changes in the WCG since the book had been printed. What they had written was correct, but the article was outdated. I asked that he consider a revision for a future edition. I included my telephone number should he want to contact me. To my great surprise, he called. Many authors or publishers I had written would acknowledge by letter their intent to review the material on the WCG in a future printing, but virtually no one called. Rev. Mather called to confirm what I had written. By the end of the conversation, he was praising God for what was happening in the WCG. He stated that, as far as he knew, such reformation had rare precedent in church history.

Not long after that conversation, Rev. Mather took a call to pastor a Lutheran church near Pasadena. He accepted my invitation and dropped by to talk with the WCG leadership. He presented a letter of encouragement from his church's leadership. He also arranged for us to visit on a regular basis with some Lutheran scholars at Concordia University in Irvine, California. These were helpful exchanges as we discussed in a mutually respectful atmosphere the doctrines of the Worldwide Church of God.

George Mather and I became good friends, as did our wives. We visited privately, which gave me opportunity to discuss theological issues with George. I found him to be open-minded, honest, and non-judgmental in our discussions. George's friendship was important because he was outside the WCG experience and I could trust him to discuss deep spiritual issues. George also arranged a meeting between the leadership of the WCG and The Lutheran Church—Missouri Synod. At that meeting in St. Louis, Missouri, Dr. A. L. Barry, the synod's president, greeted us and welcomed us as brothers in Christ.

Much happened in my personal faith journey from about 1992 to the summer of 1994. It began with a discussion at a Friday morning operational directors' meeting. The subject of declining income had come up, and one man mentioned that some members were tithing on their net income instead of gross income. For years the general ruling of the church had been to tithe on one's gross income. Some international areas, however, had appealed to Mr. Armstrong for tithe relief because government taxation was so high that paying as many as three tithes on gross income in one year presented a severe financial hardship. Armstrong granted tithe relief in a few international areas by allowing the tithe to be calculated on net rather than gross income. In some countries where the social net was well developed, he even permitted the deletion of the third tithe (which was used for widows and the needy). As the years passed, only U.S. members were tithing on gross income. When someone commented that perhaps as many 25 percent of the U.S. membership was tithing on net income, Joseph Tkach Sr. did not seem disturbed. *If tithing is mandated by God, its administration must be the same for everyone,* I thought, but I didn't pursue the matter. After the doctrinal change on the nature of God was announced, I realized that I should begin to reinvestigate my own doctrinal positions. My confidence in what I had been taught was beginning to erode and I needed to begin afresh in searching for the truth of God's Word.

I began my studies with tithing, researching several reference works. It did not take me long to discover that the WCG's "third tithe" practice was not biblically warranted. It was not that the poor and widows were not cared for from tithes, but Armstrong's teaching and administration of the third tithe was not supported by any recognized biblical authority. Armstrong taught that one must pay a full third tithe (an additional 10 percent on top of the regular 10 percent first tithe and the 10 percent second tithe saved for the festivals) during the third and sixth years in a seven-year cycle. This money was used to support widows and the poor. Since coming to Pasadena, I had learned that Mr. Armstrong had used the third tithe to pay ministers' salaries and even cover some travel expenses, which I found disturbing. Once I reached the conclusion that the third tithe was not binding on Christians, I logically had to investigate the second tithe, which we saved to finance our annual festival attendance. It did not take long to find that there was no biblical grounds for this practice either. With the second tithe gone, the question of the festivals themselves came to mind. How would we finance them if there is no biblical mandate to save a "second tithe"?

I was considering this question when I flew to Denver, Colorado, with Joe Tkach Jr. and another church executive to attend a ministerial conference of the Church of God (Seventh

Day). The question of holy day observance arose, and the Church of God (Seventh Day) theologians presented a convincing case for ceasing our observances. I was not shocked at their view because I already knew that this denomination did not observe the Old Testament holy days. What was helpful to me, however, were the biblical texts they presented to demonstrate the liberty of the Christian in regard to these days. Desmond Ford, a former Adventist scholar, was the guest speaker at the conference and graciously spent time with me, answering my questions on a number of subjects, including the observance of holy days. One day during our stay, I was alone with Joe and asked if he believed the holy days were binding on Christians. He answered that they were not, which had become my personal position. I mused that this news would come as an almost heretical statement to the ears of most WCG members. Usually, when one of the church's top leaders shared such views with me, I knew that if his view differed from official WCG position, it would be only a matter of time before the WCG position would change. This impending change did not disturb me because I had become suspicious of past WCG doctrinal teachings on this subject anyway.

After the Denver conference, I was convinced the next logical step was to question the weekly Sabbath, but I was reluctant to do so. That would strike at the bedrock of the WCG, and I was not prepared for that. Desmond Ford had defended boldly the Sabbath observance during our visit with the Church of God (Seventh Day), which made me uncomfortable to tackle the question. Linda encouraged me to pursue the issue. But it was only after a trip to Atlanta several months later and a casual conversation with a WCG minister there that I determined to pursue the matter. While we drove to the Atlanta airport, this minister nonchalantly asked if I had read *Sabbath in Crisis* by Dale Ratzlaff. When I said I had not, he replied that several cases of the book had been sent to Pasadena. This surprised me because I didn't know anything about it, but this was not unusual. Often I was not directly informed of the theological direction church leaders were pursuing. Back in Pasadena, I ordered the book and received the shock of my life.

Ratzlaff had grown up a Seventh-Day Adventist, the son of Adventists, yet he had become a Baptist minister. As I read his book, it was as though he had spent his entire life in WCG pews. He knew all the arguments we used for maintaining the Sabbath observance was a necessity for modern Christians. Later it became clear to me that WCG arguments for the Sabbath actually were Adventist ones that Herbert Armstrong had picked up from his study of Adventist literature. Most WCG members do not know that Armstrong had personally collected and read many works of G. G. Ruppert, an Adventist. These undoubtedly influenced Armstrong's theology. One by one, Ratzlaff knocked down my theological reasons for observing the Saturday Sabbath. It became clear that when Christ said, "Come to Me, all you who are weary and burdened, and I will give you rest" (Matthew 11:28), He meant that He (Jesus) is our rest. The true spiritual rest that is foreshadowed by the weekly, annual, and jubilee Sabbaths is fulfilled in Jesus Christ, who becomes the true Sabbath for Christians. That understanding hit me like a ton of bricks. I shared the book with Linda, who read it quickly and said she was convinced of the correctness of Ratzlaff's biblical presentation.

As we began to consider the consequences of our newfound conviction, I would shudder. I wrote to Desmond Ford under Linda's name and asked a few questions regarding the Sabbath. I used Linda's name for fear that word would reach WCG leadership that I was questioning the church's Sabbath teaching. Dr. Ford sent a gracious response, but left me unconvinced that he was correct. I had no idea that the Worldwide Church of God leadership already was of the persuasion that Sabbath observance was not mandatory for salvation. This was something that Mr. Tkach Sr. and a few others were keeping quiet as they tried to determine when and in what manner to share this information with the membership. Suddenly, I found myself (or so I thought) outside the doctrinal boundaries of my church. Because I was not a pastor of a local congregation, I determined to keep this newfound belief to myself. Linda was clear in her desire to live as she believed. She no longer wanted to be constrained by Sabbath strictures that were not binding on Christians. I cautioned her to pursue a moderate course because I was still employed by the church. She agreed to do so, but quickly changed her Saturday routine around the house. She vacuumed, washed clothes, worked in the yard, and helped neighbors with yard sales—a radical departure, considering she had been a WCG member since childhood. Because my schedule had not changed, my Sabbath practices changed little at first. I did begin to watch television, read secular books, and putter around in the garage. Caution forbade me from obvious yard work lest a church member would observe me "at work." Our concern was not to cause offense with the new liberty we had in Christ, yet we did want to enjoy it.

Fast on the heels of understanding a Christian's view of the Sabbath, I concluded my study of tithing and saw that it was no longer mandatory. At the time, I was paying a hefty sum to the church as a first tithe each month while inflation was eroding my income. I had not received a raise in years, and our costs kept rising, especially as our sons grew and their needs became more expensive to meet. Despite my understanding of the freedom regarding Christian stewardship, I continued to pay the tithe lest I be discovered through a "tithe check" that could be ordered by a WCG executive.

About this time, *The Subtle Power of Spiritual Abuse* by David Johnson and Jeff VanVonderen came into my hands. As I realized that for 30 years I and many WCG members had been victims of spiritual abuse, I cannot describe my emotions. No one set out to abuse us spiritually, but such abuse was commonplace in the WCG fellowship. The authors state:

> Spiritual abuse is the mistreatment of a person who is in need of help, support or greater spiritual empowerment, with the result of weakening, undermining or decreasing that person's spiritual empowerment . . . Spiritual abuse can occur when a leader uses his or her spiritual position to control or dominate another person.[2]

This was startling information because I had experienced exactly such treatment for decades and was still encountering it to a lesser degree under Mr. Tkach Sr.'s administration.

In chapter 5 of *The Subtle Power of Spiritual Abuse*, Johnson and Vanvonderen detail the identifying signs of an abusive system. As I read these signs, I was overwhelmed to grasp that what I had experienced and was experiencing was a known and studied phenomenon. According to the authors, relationships between people in spiritually abusive systems are dictated by some of the following dynamics.

1. *Power-Posturing*: "Power-posturing simply means that leaders spend a lot of time focused on their own authority and reminding others of it, as well." This definitely had been the case with Mr. Armstrong and initially with Joseph Tkach Sr. Armstrong was fond of fuming and asserting that he was "God's apostle," serving directly under Jesus Christ. He would state he had been taught by no man, but had received his teaching from the Living Word. Mr. Tkach made no such claims, but he did like to remind us that he was in charge. Again, to Joseph Tkach Sr.'s credit, he improved greatly in this area and became far more conciliatory as he neared the end of his life.

2. *Performance Preoccupation*: "Obedience and submission are two important words often used . . . Do we come to church to be encouraged about trusting Jesus, or to be pressed to try harder?" For Herbert Armstrong, the mantra was "building godly character." It was our job, "using" the Holy Spirit as a tool, to become more like God so we could "qualify" for the kingdom. Joseph Tkach Sr. began to point us to Jesus and His sacrifice, moving us away from a works-righteousness religion.

3. *Unspoken Rules:* "In abusive spiritual systems, people's lives are controlled from the outside in by rules, spoken and unspoken. Unspoken rules are those that govern unhealthy churches or families but are not said out loud." As an example, "Do not disagree with the church authorities—especially the pastor—or your loyalty will be suspect. ... If you do disagree openly or publicly, you would break the silence—and you would quite likely be punished." This had always been the case in the WCG and only in recent years has the situation improved. In the past, many of us in the ministry felt we had to take "the loyalty oath" before or immediately after uttering any semblance of criticism about the church or its leadership.

4. *Paranoia:* "In the church or family that is spiritually abusive,

there is a sense, spoken or unspoken, that 'others will not understand what we're all about, so let's not let them know—that way they won't be able to ridicule or persecute us.'" Certainly this was how Armstrong operated. The WCG was secretive and careful not to divulge too much about the church to outsiders. We felt they were "blind" and, unless their minds were opened by God, they would not understand. Therefore, they would only use the information against us. Mr. Tkach changed the paranoia by opening the church to the world, thus bringing a more balanced and normal attitude in the membership.

5. *Misplaced Loyalty:* "[A] system where disloyalty to or disagreement with the leadership is construed as the same thing as disobeying God. Questioning leaders is equal to questioning God." Mr. Armstrong used to hammer away on this point, making it clear that he was answerable only to God. Armstrong was fond of using Korah, the Israelite who opposed Moses, as a threatening reminder. To disobey Armstrong was the same as rebelling against God. I believed this and feared to disagree or disobey lest I be found rebellious like Korah. Joseph Tkach Sr. stopped this posturing, taking a more balanced position as the years passed.[3]

There are other dynamics mentioned in the book, but these gave me a reality check, convincing me that Linda and I had been spiritually abused throughout our adult lives. First, I was shocked, then angry. How could I have let myself be duped? I felt as though all the years I had given to the church had been wasted as I learned and promulgated false teachings wrapped in abusive packaging. Had I not been sincere? Had I not taken severe correction, abuse, mistreatment, and unfairness, believing God was humbling and shaping me? Had I not put my dear wife through mental and emotional stress when I accepted the assignments to Europe in the name of serving God? I was angry at Herbert Armstrong and Joseph Tkach Sr. for creating and continuing to sponsor a system that hurt people spiritually and emotionally.

It took several months to work through this inner turmoil. After much prayer and meditation, I decided to look for an exit and leave the whole system behind. Although there were and are many people in the WCG that I deeply love, I had to get out. But getting out would not prove easy. There was the financial reality of owning a house in a real estate market that was severely depressed. By 1994, Linda and I decided to sell the house and work our way out of the WCG. It took six months, but our house finally sold at a substantial loss. We lived inexpensively for the next year, which enabled us to pay off the loss on the house. I was not sure where we would go or what we would do, but I knew we had to go. We did not want to disrupt Dustin's final year in high school, so we put off a decision until after his graduation.

It seemed I had our dilemma worked out. Then I was summoned to a meeting in the summer of 1994 with Joe Tkach Jr. He asked if I would consider pastoring a congregation in Reseda, California. I had been suggesting for some time that we needed to overhaul our entire concept of pastoral care at the local level. I even had submitted an outline of a lecture entitled "The Disciple-Making Pastor," which I had proposed to deliver to our ministers at the U.S. regional conferences. Joe Tkach Jr. and Mike Feazell had agreed this was the direction our pastors should move. (My lecture proposed practical steps to implementing the Protestant Reformation ideal of "the priesthood of all believers.") When it came time to present the paper to a regional conference planning committee, I was greeted by silence. Then one long-time evangelist loudly proclaimed that the church would never go in that direction. He and others felt the current style of centralized control with the pastor responsible for all spiritual duties was proper. Both Joe Tkach Jr. and Mike offered no support at the meeting, so my proposal was rejected. (Interestingly, the concepts I had proposed were publicly endorsed years later by many of those same men who sat silently in that meeting. I suppose there were undercurrents of which I was not aware that convinced the men to delay moving forward at that time.)

The pastor in Reseda was retiring, and Joe saw this as an opportunity to implement some of the new pastoring concepts that we had discussed in private. We had considered starting a new church with pre-screened volunteer members, but we rejected that notion because the field pastors would fault any success by correctly claiming that we had stacked the deck. We also considered starting with the congregation at headquarters but dismissed this idea because Mr. Tkach Sr. was not ready for such a bold step. Thus Reseda seemed to be a wise choice. I felt I had to agree because of my adamant call for change and my previous lobbying for a test site. However, my view of the Sabbath, holy days, and tithing were contrary to the church's official positions. I didn't know what to do. After prayer and counsel with friends, I decided to accept the offer. Hope was rekindled in my heart that this might be the crack in the door for which I had been waiting. Maybe the WCG was willing to consider some bedrock structural changes and I could be a part of the process.

My first Sabbath in the pulpit was right after the Feast of Tabernacles in October 1994. I remember driving 45 minutes west from Pasadena to Reseda, getting out of the car, and asking myself aloud, "What have I done now?" However, I was not unprepared. In August I had begun to meet with the elders of the Reseda church. I had set up an advisory council. I invited the elders and their wives, plus Wanda, a member of my staff at headquarters, to constitute the council. In only a few meetings, we planned the reorganization of the Reseda congregation and the reformatting of the worship service. Shortly after assuming the pastorate, I began to introduce the changes. Predictably, there was mixed reaction to the new emphasis on music and prayer, the shorter messages, and the virtual elimination of lengthy announcements. We were making nice progress with the congregation, which numbered around 225 people, until the Christmas season brought a disturbing surprise for the WCG that rocked it to its foundation. When the dust settled several months later, we had lost 100 people from the Reseda congregation, which was a major blow to my ministry there.

In late December 1994, I was invited to lunch at a restaurant not far from the Pasadena campus. Mike Feazell, Joe Tkach Jr., Greg Albrecht, and myself met to discuss an upcoming trip Mr. Tkach Sr. was going to make to Atlanta. The WCG pastor in Atlanta was preaching a strong grace message, which alarmed many members. His tapes were being widely circulated along the East Coast, even heading overseas to WCG members. People were concluding from his preaching that our legalistic approach to the Sabbath, unclean meats, tithing, etc. was incorrect and that we truly are saved by grace through faith in Jesus Christ. Sides were being formed as members and ministers alike called for Mr. Tkach Sr. to take a position and resolve the dispute. Joe Tkach Jr. said he wasn't sure what his dad was going to say in Atlanta. He then mentioned that he may even announce the Sabbath command was no longer binding on Christians. That shocked me because until that statement, I had no certain knowledge that WCG leaders had arrived at that position, though I had independently reached the same conclusion. Earlier Greg Albrecht had said rather cryptically that there might be movement on the Sabbath, but I thought I could be reading more into his statement than he meant. Despite the surprise, I tried to remain neutral and cautioned against Mr. Tkach Sr. making such a proclamation until the ministry could be prepared. We all agreed that should Joseph Tkach make such an announcement, the membership loss could be substantial. The conversation shifted to other matters.

I left the lunch elated and disturbed. I was elated because I was still on track doctrinally with my church. I was disturbed because of our helplessness to manage this monumental change. These men with whom I had just met were the church's leaders, yet they were powerless to persuade Mr. Tkach Sr. to undertake a planned approach to introduce such dramatic change. Joseph Tkach Sr. did not mind listening to counsel from trusted friends, but he had a mind of his own. When he felt he had to do something, he eventually did it.

On Saturday, December 24, 1994, Pastor General Joseph Tkach Sr. did speak to the congregation in Atlanta, introducing the concept of grace under the New Covenant. Within hours, word spread throughout the world, shocking and disturbing some, elating others. Telephone calls came in to headquarters from all over the world to confirm the news from Atlanta. Joseph Tkach Sr. had indeed announced that Christians are saved by grace through faith in Jesus Christ and that Sabbath-keeping did not determine one's ultimate salvation. This was a clear Gospel message in the tradition of St. Paul and other godly men of the

Word down through the centuries. It was the call of Martin Luther, who decried the works-righteousness of the Roman Catholic Church. Joseph Tkach Sr. lifted up Christ and the message of the cross in Atlanta. In the process, he launched a ground-shaking reformation within the WCG that literally transformed it into a different church than the one founded by Herbert Armstrong. Joseph Tkach Sr. and other church leaders publicly credited this reformation to the Holy Spirit, who worked to open their eyes to the truth of the Gospel and gave them the courage to preach the truth. After that eventful Christmas, WCG members experienced their own "Pentecost event." The Holy Spirit worked mightily to the glory of Christ, transforming a fellowship that had lived and worshiped outside the pale of orthodoxy to one that embraces the historic Christian faith.

Historically, there had been "tension" in the Worldwide Church of God caused by the challenge to the membership to accept the high demands of doctrinal understanding and commandment living. These high demands seemed of little consequence when the leadership taught that the Worldwide Church of God was the "one true church" and God's end-time vessel to witness to a godless world and apostate Christianity. The kingdom of God to be established on earth belonged to us. Christ would grant rulership over cities and nations of the world to us so all people might be taught to reverence God, keep His commandments, and observe His holy days (the weekly Sabbath and the seven annual holy days of ancient Israel). Because the WCG in the past had failed to recognize the Person and work of the Holy Spirit, much less fully grasp the sacrifice of Christ at Calvary, we fell into a pharisaical Christianity. The WCG had taught that the Holy Spirit was God's power that enables the Christian to keep the commandments. Not understanding God's grace ministered through God the Holy Spirit in Word and sacraments, we sought God and eternal life through the exacting crucible of commandment keeping.

Despite understanding that the Holy Spirit was received at the time of repentance, we did not experience the comfort and assurance given by Him to those who believe and put their trust in Jesus because, for us, the Holy Spirit was merely "God's power" and not a Person. God the Holy Spirit comforts believers through the Word and the sacraments of Baptism and the Lord's Supper, reassuring believers that they have been forgiven not because of what they have done, but for Christ's sake and because of what He has done for us. There was precious little comfort in the WCG; only the dauntless task of keeping the commandments not only in the letter, but also in the spirit.

Although members of the Worldwide Church of God strived to live godly lives, in retrospect, we viewed ourselves as slavishly burdened by the Law. Because the Law is a cruel taskmaster, we were deprived of much inner joy. We struggled mightily against sin and tried to qualify for eternal life by commandment keeping, yet we were left empty and without assurance of salvation because God the Spirit was not known nor praised in our midst.

Referring to his Jewish brothers who had not come to the truth in Christ, Paul said:

> But their minds were made dull, for to this day the same veil remains when the old covenant is read. It has not been removed, because only in Christ is it taken away. . . . But whenever anyone turns to the Lord, the veil is taken away. Now the Lord is the Spirit, and where the Spirit of the Lord is, there is freedom. (2 Corinthians 3:14, 16–17)

The veil covering the eyes of the WCG leadership was gradually lifted, beginning with the death of Herbert Armstrong in January 1986. Soon after Mr. Armstrong's death, Joseph Tkach Sr., his appointed successor, explained that the Gospel message was indeed centered on the person and saving work of Jesus, not His end-time return to rule the earth as Armstrong had maintained.

I think the pivotal issue that began to lift the veil was the change in teaching regarding the nature of God. In the August 17, 1993, issue of the church's in-house newspaper, *The Worldwide News*, Pastor General Joseph Tkach Sr. wrote:

> The Bible tells us there is one and only one God, and presents us with the Father, the Son, and the Holy Spirit, all eternal, and all doing things only God can do . . .

> Likewise, the Bible reveals that God is one and only one, yet is also, at the same time, the Father, Son, and Holy Spirit . . . we understand that God is one, and that the Holy Spirit is God, just as the Father is God, and the Son is God.

Understanding the nature of God seems to have been fundamental in bringing down a theology that could not stand the test of objective scriptural investigation.

The next and last major "unveiling" was the understanding of the new covenant given in Christ's blood. Until December 1994, the church saw itself as between the old and new covenants, which contributed to its pharisaical Christian worldview. In grasping the significance of the new covenant, the church was brought to two of the fundamental articles of the Protestant Reformation: *sola fide* and *sola gratia*. Instead of defining a true Christian by lifestyle, the WCG now agrees with the testimony of Scripture and the historic church that a true Christian is one who believes in the sufficiency of the sacrifice of Christ for salvation and becomes the temple for the indwelling of God the Holy Spirit.

After experiencing the shock of Joseph Tkach Sr.'s statement that salvation was by grace through faith alone, the ramifications for the Christian walk of those in the WCG became clear rather quickly. It was perhaps best stated by Joseph Tkach Jr. in the *Christian Research Journal:*

> Gone is our obsession with a legalistic interpretation of the Old Testament, our belief in British Israelism, and our insistence on our fellowship's exclusive relationship with God . . . Gone is our long-held view of God as a "family" of multiple "spirit beings" into which humans may be born, replaced by a biblically accurate view of one God who exists eternally in three Persons, the Father, the Son, and the Holy Spirit. We have embraced and now champion the New Testament's central theme: the life, death, and resurrection of Jesus Christ.[4]

The shadows in which we had lived for decades were dispelled. The veil had been removed as the Holy Spirit led us to clarity in Christ. But this came at a high price. The shock waves that we anticipated during our discussion in that Pasadena restaurant hit with a fury that caught us all off guard. Within a few weeks after Mr. Tkach's Atlanta sermon, some 150 ordained WCG ministers around the world resigned. I walked into Joe Tkach Jr's office several times to find him staring at a large metallic map of North America on which were magnets with the names of ministers. The magnets were situated over the cities that had WCG congregations. He had identified the ministers who had resigned by turning his magnet upside-down. Then he would move across the board, pointing to names that he felt would probably resign. For a while, Joe Tkach Jr.'s office seemed like a war room as he tried to manage the rapid desertion of ministers. He was pushed to the limits of physical endurance, often appearing haggard, but remained calm.

Membership in the WCG eventually shrank by 50 percent or more, which led to a dramatic decline in income. Several splinter groups were formed to perpetuate the errors that had long held the WCG captive and blind to the "plain truth." Families were severely wounded as members sometimes chose between the WCG and one of these many splinter groups. Could such loses have been prevented? Certainly the manner in which the truth was revealed to the membership could have been better addressed. Mr. Tkach Sr. felt pressured to take a stand and may well have believed the losses wouldn't be so dramatic. Many long-time ministers and members decried the direction Mr. Tkach was taking the church and summarily resigned. Many of these people formed the United Church of God. The WCG administration quickly labeled the United Church of God a dissident group, which it was indeed. The administration disfellowshiped every-one who joined its ranks. There were less-than-Christian reactions on both sides as lines were drawn. Regrettably many of the resigning ministers and members did not read the study papers produced after Mr. Tkach's Atlanta sermon. Those who left felt the WCG was abandoning God's Law, especially the Sabbath, by no longer making it compulsory. By the time of the Atlanta sermon, there already was a deepening distrust among the field ministry toward the leadership in Pasadena. Mr. Tkach's explanation

of grace only served to confirm the suspicion that he had rejected the fundamental "revealed" teachings of Herbert Armstrong.
Angry, perplexed, confused, and with righteous indignation, they
left the WCG fellowship in the worst split the church body had
experienced in more than 60 years of existence.

Today the wounds are healing. Pastor General Joseph Tkach
Jr. wrote in his *Pastor General's Report* on November 10, 1995,
"Through the love and mercy of God and the leadership of the
Holy Spirit, we have set our minds and hearts on Jesus Christ and
have come to trust explicitly in Him." The members of the
Worldwide Church of God are experiencing the freedom of Christ
that He won for them at Calvary. Although smaller in number,
WCG members are humbly grateful for the mighty working of
the Holy Spirit among them. They are changing not because of
their Herculean efforts to keep the Law, but because of their submission to and trust in Jesus as Lord and their belief that God the
Holy Spirit sanctifies and leads people into a life of holiness.

The historic reformation within the WCG has not gone
unnoticed by the Christian world. David Neff, editor of
Christianity Today, a 1995 editorial commended the WCG leadership for staying the course despite the high price.

The demands on Joseph W. Tkach Sr. were great. He had
risen from obscurity to become the personally anointed heir of
Herbert Armstrong. He had been moved by the Holy Spirit to
break with the past, admit Armstrong's error, and embrace the
true Gospel of Jesus Christ. His decision, based on the clear teachings of the Bible, and had come at a high personal price. He was
vilified by his peers and seen by many as a sellout to liberal
Protestantism. Some accused him of weakness and of allowing
himself to be manipulated by others. Did he have his weaknesses? Yes, he did, as do all people. Yet he humbly yielded himself to
the urging of the Holy Spirit to lead the WCG out of the shadows
of doctrinal error and into the light of truth.

By August 1995, Mr. Tkach Sr. was complaining about pain
in his side, and he checked into Huntington Hospital in Pasadena
for a thorough examination. The worst fear was confirmed. He
was diagnosed with cancer. Shortly before the Feast of Taber-

nacles, he lay dying in his hospital bed. Joe Tkach Jr. called me early one morning to tell me that his father might pass away and that I should prepare a press release. I asked to come to the hospital where I joined him, other family members, and close friends in his father's room during his last hours. Mr. Tkach Sr. was in a coma, which he never came out of while I was there. His breathing was labored, and after struggling for hours, he died holding his beloved wife's hand. His still and lifeless body lay covered by a blanket patterned after the United States flag—a reminder of his great love for his country and his patriotism. We cried at the passing of a great man who, despite his human inadequacies, had yielded himself to his Lord. Indeed, God had worked a miracle through the life of that man—a church that had been a cult was led into the orthodox Christian faith.

A church was reborn. A historical reformation had occurred. Where the Holy Spirit was once essentially denied, His work was being recognized and praised. After decades in the shadow of Mt. Sinai teaching and living a works-righteousness salvation, the Worldwide Church of God was humbled by the living Lord to admit its error and embrace the light of Calvary. Truly a new day dawned for this group of faithful Christians.

ENDNOTES

1 "The Worldwide Church of God: Resurrected into Orthodoxy," *Christian Research Journal* (Winter 1996): 7. Used with permission.

2 Johnson, David, and Jeff Vanvonderen, *The Subtle Power of Spiritual Abuse* (Minneapolis: Bethany House, 1991), 20. Used with permission.

3 The five dynamics and their "definitions" come from Johnson and Vanvonderen, *Subtle Power,* and are used with permission.

4 Joseph W. Tkach Jr., "Church Reborn," *Christian Research Journal* (Winter 1996): 53. Used with permission.

Chapter 9

Quo Vadis?

The keys of providence swing at the girdle of Christ. Believe it, Christian, nothing occurs here without the permit or the decree of your Savior.—Charles H. Spurgeon

Shortly before Joseph Tkach Sr.'s death in 1995, he appointed his son, Joe Tkach Jr. to succeed him as pastor general. The polity of the WCG is such that the appointment of a new pastor general has to this point been the sole province of the current pastor general. The appointment is not a matter of vote nor a matter of the consensus of the membership or the ministry at large. But the church board must confirm the appointment, which it always does. The appointment of Joe Tkach Jr. was witnessed and agreed on by the church board. When I heard the news that Joe Tkach Jr. had been appointed to the office of pastor general, I hoped this would be the beginning of a new era for the church.

I reiterate what I said earlier, Joseph W. Tkach Sr. was a man of God who stood for Christ and the Gospel at a crucial time in the history of the Worldwide Church of God. He heard the Holy Spirit's call, yielded, and began a reformation unparalleled in modern church history. Mr. Tkach will be remembered and honored for this. Those who remain in the WCG owe him a debt of gratitude for his faith and fortitude. Like any great man, he struggled against his own human frailties. As I worked with him, I saw some of those human foibles to which many others were not privy. These were not moral weaknesses, but ones of character and business acumen. These weaknesses increasingly made life in Pasadena difficult for me. Perhaps one of the most burdensome things was his lack of business expertise, which proved crippling. Mr. Tkach Sr. was a micro-manager. He wanted to know everything and be involved in the most insignificant details, which made it difficult for me to work because I needed breathing room to accomplish my responsibilities. I needed freedom to make decisions and be responsible and accountable for my actions and judgments. With Mr. Tkach, this was difficult because he wanted to know and decide matters himself, rather than delegating authority and responsibility.

For example, one time I sent a memo to a Pasadena executive suggesting the addition of a baptistery to a model church building that was being planned. I stated why I thought public baptism would be a blessing for the witnessing members. A few days later, I received a call from Mr. Tkach's secretary, telling me the boss wanted to see me. Such an invitation was usually a harbinger of unpleasantries. Once I entered the executive suite, the secretary escorted me to Mr. Tkach. He usually sat behind his desk, which was generally piled with books and papers. He seldom rose to greet me when I entered, and this particular meeting proved not to be an exception to the rule. With a brief motion of his hand, Mr. Tkach asked me to be seated in one of several chairs arranged in a semicircle in front of his massive solid wood desk. His television in the background was tuned to CNN or some other all-news network. Mr. Tkach did not waste time with small talk. He immediately raised the issue at hand. "Tom, what's this I hear about you wanting a baptistery in our new church building?"

Totally unprepared for such a question, I paused to gather my thoughts. I wondered how he had heard of this because I had not copied him on the memo. And why should it bother him? He would decide the matter anyway. Later I was told that while sharing my note with Mr. Tkach, the executive to whom I had written put a negative spin on the request, thus raising Mr. Tkach's ire. "Mr. Tkach, it was just an idea that I suggested, knowing that the final plans had not yet been drawn up," I said. I briefly explained my reasoning.

Then Mr. Tkach told me that when I had such ideas, I was to report to him directly because he alone would decide such matters.

Astonished, I replied, "Mr. Tkach, I work directly for your son, Joe, and I report to him." In a tactful way I was trying to make clear to him that his request was violating his own organizational system, but that made no difference.

"You come to me first with any new idea you have, then you can tell Joe," was his answer.

I countered with the fact that I had lots of ideas, many of which may not be worthy of his time. "I find it helpful to discuss my ideas with others first, to see if they have merit before bothering you with them," I said.

Again the words were ignored. "When you have an idea, come to me first. Is that clear?" Mr. Tkach repeated.

I told him it was clear and left his office feeling as though I had just encountered an unreasonable man. I was determined not to follow Mr. Tkach's instructions and to be careful about sharing my future new ideas.

There were many such interplays between Mr. Tkach and me, which created much stress in my life. Many times he contradicted himself, for example, stating publicly that he understood the Christian church to be the universal body of Christ (known as the invisible church or universal church in theology), then in private telling me that he felt the WCG encompassed most of the true Christians on earth. I believe that before he died, Mr. Tkach Sr. finally came to reject his earlier understanding regarding the extent of the true church of Christ. Another example is that he would say the tithing law is not binding on Christians yet preach forcefully that truly committed Christians would give more than a tithe. Several close friends who worked with Mr. Tkach told me they had stopped believing him because of the frequent shifts in his statements. At times I was not sure what he believed because of his tendency to tell one person one thing and another person something else. Administratively, he might give me a directive, then become upset when I began to carry it out. Finally, I resolved to leave the employ of the church and even the WCG itself so I could avoid further contact with Mr. Tkach's administration. Thus I hoped to find a measure of personal peace.

Not everyone reacted to Mr. Tkach as I did, and Mr. Tkach certainly was not an ogre. He had a tender, kind side along with a sincere smile that would melt ice in December. Our personalities simply clashed. We had different ideas about how things should be done, which resulted in frequent misunderstandings and a gradual buildup of stress.

I did not rejoice when Joseph Tkach Sr. died. Nor did I believe, as some heartless souls charged, that he was a poor miserable soul whom God had struck down for his sin of "apostasy from the truth revealed through Mr. Armstrong." He was not only a great man of God, but he was a father, husband, and grandfather too. He dearly loved his family as he did the church to which he had dedicated most of his adult life. His passing brought grief to my heart, as it did to many thousands who knew and loved him.

Mr. Tkach's son, Joe, is different from his father in many ways. In his late 40s, Joe Tkach Jr. exhibits a keen intellect, deep humility, and graciousness. Joe and I are about the same age and have always gotten along well. I was convinced that Joe, as the WCG's new pastor general, would take a strong lead in continuing his father's reformation and do so with a softer touch. Joe has a master's degree in business administration, as well as a doctorate of ministry. He has worked in a local church congregation, is well read, and is about as easy-going, calm, and kind a man as one could ever meet. Once Joe assumed the office, I abandoned my plans to leave the church. I was determined to assist Joe in any way I could. He asked me to continue in church relations, which I was happy to do.

Soon I was arranging meetings for him with well-known Christian leaders. He was making his own contacts as well. Our plan was to build bridges to the larger Christian community, and Joe was, and is, a wonderful bridge builder. Unlike his predecessors, Joe was willing to meet and greet as many Christian leaders as possible. He decided to accept Hank Hanegraaf's invitation to do a radio interview, which went exceptionally well. Hank devoted several programs to the Worldwide Church of God, which were well received by his radio audience and the WCG membership.

I organized a trip to meet with Dr. James Kennedy in Florida. Dr. Kennedy had done several programs on the WCG, interviewing Phillip Arnn of Watchman Fellowship, a cult-watch group headquartered in the Dallas area. After listening to the broadcasts, I suggested to Joe that we call Kennedy and arrange a meeting to give him a firsthand report on our church. Joe, Mike Feazell, Greg Albrecht, and I flew to Ft. Lauderdale. I had seen Dr. Kennedy on television and was not particularly captivated by his television persona. I had followed his ratings closely during the years when I was responsible for buying television airtime for the WCG's *The World Tomorrow*. I was excited to meet such a prominent Christian leader. The evening before our meeting, the four of us drove to a nearby restaurant for a relaxing meal. It lasted several hours as my travel companions began swapping tales of their Imperial School experiences. Imperial School was a K–12 private school operated by the WCG for decades. At one time there were three Imperial campuses—one in Pasadena, one in Bricket Wood (United Kingdom), and one in Big Sandy, Texas. (Today all three campuses are closed.) Imperial School was supposed to pioneer "God's education." In reality, Imperial School provided the church's children with an education heavy on control and discipline—even for the smallest infraction. Public spanking was administered, as were other forms of humiliation. All this was done to teach children to obey the Law. As I heard the tales they shared, I was aghast at the legalism that had reigned supreme. Mike and Joe had gone through Imperial at about the same time, whereas Greg had been four or five years ahead of them. After listening and laughing with them for several hours, I could see these men enjoying a close bond partly forged by common childhood experiences. I could not relate because I had grown up in a Baptist setting and attended a regular public school.

On the morning of our appointment, we drove the short distance from our hotel to Dr. Kennedy's church facility in Ft. Lauderdale. Mike, who had had a migraine the day before, was feeling a bit queasy. I suggested he rest in the car and join us in the meeting when he felt better, but he pulled himself together to make it through the gathering. Dr. Kennedy's complex includes office, worship, and school facilities. We were greeted by his secretary, who disappeared and quickly reappeared with Dr. Kennedy. It is always somewhat thrilling to meet someone whom you have known only through television. Dr. Kennedy welcomed us and invited us into his office. He sat behind his desk, the four us arranged in front of him. "Well, gentlemen, what can I do for you?" he asked.

I recall Joe stating that we wanted to meet him and tell our story. It was a simple, truthful, and disarming introduction. Joe went on to tell the marvelous story of God's gracious work in our fellowship. Dr. Kennedy listened and interjected comments as Joe, then Mike, and then Greg explained the history of the WCG reformation.

As we neared the end of the discussion, Dr. Kennedy asked if he might pose a question. We agreed. "When you die, what reason will you give God that He should grant you entrance into heaven?" he asked.

As a decades-long WCG member, I had been taught to think that heaven is a false Protestant notion of fluffy clouds, harps, and pearly gates. In the last few years, it had become clear to the WCG leadership and to me that heaven is not a place at all, but the state of being with the Lord. Therefore, none of us had any difficulty answering. The response we gave in our own words was that we would answer the Lord that our entrance into heaven must be granted on the basis of the merits of Christ in whom we placed our faith.

I was the last of the four that Dr. Kennedy pointed his finger at with that question. After my response, he clapped his hands with joy and said he truly believed that we were Christians. Why? Because we had encapsuled in our answers the core of the Gospel, the central call of the great reformer Martin Luther, *sola gratia* and *sola fide*. We confessed that we are saved by grace alone through faith alone, in Christ alone, not by our good works. This belief in salvation by grace through faith is now the central doctrinal platform of the new Worldwide Church of God. This understanding alone is responsible for the tremendous reformation in WCG ranks. Many Christians start their journey with this understanding but somewhere along the road lapse into legalism and works-righteousness, burdening their lives with unnecessary guilt and anxiety. They misunderstand the relationship between justification and sanctification, believing that their works become part of what it means to be declared righteous before God. Another reason for such a lapse is that we are legalists by nature. St. Paul writes in Romans 2 that the Law is written on the heart. It is only through the Gospel that legalism's fierce grip is broken, and it is grace that sustains us from legalism's tendency to constantly take over.

Dr. Kennedy was reminded of a pressing appointment, looked at his watch, and wondered aloud if he had time to interview the pastor general of the Worldwide Church of God immediately. After considering it briefly and checking with his programmer, it became clear such an interview would not work on the spur of the moment. However, he asked Joe to schedule time for a telephone interview in the coming weeks. Joe agreed. On the way to our car, I suggested to Joe that he should return to Florida for a live interview, which he did several months later.

The ball was rolling now, and doors were opening for us to be received and welcomed. The radio interviews and positive coverage we received in the Christian press made Christian leaders less apprehensive about meeting with us. Hank Hanegraaf's *Christian Research Journal* had written about the Spirit-led changes in WCG under the title "The Worldwide Church of God: Resurrected into Orthodoxy" (Winter 1996), praising WCG leadership for yielding to the lead of the Holy Spirit.

Dr. John Holland, president of the Four Square Gospel Denomination, introduced WCG Pastor General Joseph Tkach Jr. to some 3,500 Four Square pastors and missionaries at the May 1996 International Convention in Pasadena, California. He said he wanted to be the first denomination to publicly welcome the WCG into the broader Christian fellowship. Other wonderful contacts developed in the first 18 months of this public relations initiative. For any Christian leader to dismiss the WCG as a cult by this time revealed a failure to keep abreast of the news or to maintain contact with the Christian press.

Despite the wonderful press the WCG received around the world, its membership continued to slip, as did its income. An organization that had once boasted an annual income of nearly $180 million began to struggle to pay its bills on a revenue stream of less than $40 million. Of that amount, some $4 million had to be spent to maintain the grounds in Pasadena. Painful cuts were made and more employees found themselves jobless. In 1996, we were legally constrained under the WARN Act to issue a public statement and notify all employees of pending mass layoffs. Some believed that the church leadership was callous and dispassionate about laying-off long-time employees, but this was not the case. It was with great sadness that Joe Tkach Jr. had to do what his father could not bring himself to do—lay-off hundreds of dedicated workers. But income was dwindling and we could not allow the church to go under financially. Those who were laid-off or volunteered to leave were treated generously, including a week's salary for each year of employment, job counseling, and the use of office space, telephone, and office equipment in the pursuit of new employment. WCG critics had a field day, taunting us and proclaiming that God was cursing us for denying the Sabbath. Such an accusation was as ridiculous as it is unscriptural. The income dropped because many members determined to walk down other paths than the one WCG leadership was taking. They unwittingly chose to stay in the shadows of Mt. Sinai with the burden of the Law than to acknowledge the clear light of God's grace at Calvary. Thus, our joy at the reforms became mixed with anxiety regarding the ever-present possibility of job losses.

Shortly after the death of Mr. Tkach Sr., Mike Feazell was named director of church administration. Soon Mike asked if I would become the pastor of the Pasadena congregation. This was the highest honor that could be afforded a pastor, yet not one to which many men aspired. Up to this point, the real pastor of the Pasadena headquarters' church had been either Mr. Armstrong or Mr. Tkach Sr. They were seemingly omnipresent, and with the church administration, they had determined the direction of the campus congregations. (At the zenith of the WCG, there were four English-speaking and one Spanish-speaking congregations at the headquarters. Together they totaled more than 3,000 members, a number that has since declined drastically.) I was aware of the leadership to which the Pasadena church has become accustomed and I did not want to be put in such an unpleasant position. Mike persisted. He said he wanted to combine the remaining English-speaking congregations into one and suggested that I look after the Spanish congregation as well. He wanted me to introduce the same changes in Pasadena that I had made in the small congregation that I was currently pastoring.

"Why me?" I asked.

Mike replied that others had been considered, but I was the only one who could do the job.

"What does Joe think?" I asked.

"He doesn't care who does it," Mike replied.

That response certainly popped my bubble. It made me wonder about the level of support I could count on from Joe. I said I would think about the offer and let Mike know in a few days.

This proved to be a real predicament. I had no interest in taking the job. The worry of interference from my superiors concerned me. There was no way I could establish a credible ministry that would endure if I were forced to struggle with my superiors over issues of pastoral oversight. I sought counsel from friends, and they felt I should take the job. They said it was an opportunity to have a positive impact on the entire church. One friend said, "This is a great deal for the church, but not for you. Nevertheless, for the sake of the church, you should do it."

During my years in Pasadena, I had wondered what purpose God was preparing me to fulfill. Surely there was a special calling for me. At first, I thought it was to support my college friend

David and ease his travel and workload. There were the hours we spent talking as he struggled through his turf wars with the administration. Then I felt my calling was to lend a confidential ear, my friendship, and my encouragement. But after David lost the media responsibilities, we drifted apart. Eventually he left the WCG completely.

His departure returned me to my original question—why was I in Pasadena? When the decision was made to create evangelism support services and I was appointed to move the church into local congregational outreach, I thought this was my calling. Within a short time, we were experiencing wonderful and notable success. Then, while being praised and encouraged to resign at the same meeting, I wondered again, "Why did You bring me here, Lord?"

Now I had the call to lead the way in establishing a model for worship and for pastoral management. Mike had said it was time Pasadena took the lead instead of trailing in the area of worship. Surely this was the Lord's answer to my questions about why I was in Pasadena. After days of prayer and deliberation, I accepted the job—with some conditions. I was in Mike's office, directly across from Joe's in the executive suite. Joe joined us as I outlined my conditions. "First, if I am to be named the pastor of the headquarter's congregation, then I must be the pastor not only in name, but also in deed. Historically the pastor general has been the de facto pastor of the congregation. If either of you want to be the pastor, that is fine, but then I am not interested in the job. I do not want to be the associate pastor."

They both agreed.

"That means I determine who speaks and how often I speak. Of course, I would work closely with you, Mike, but I should have that authority," I clarified.

Again, Mike agreed and Joe said, "I've got no problem with that."

Then I named the few men that I felt should preach in the Pasadena church. It was a short list of names that could be counted on the fingers of one hand. They agreed.

"Further, I want to make the Pasadena congregation a local congregation and not some special headquarter's congregation. To do this, you must resist the temptation to interfere."

Once again, they agreed, Mike stated this was exactly what he wanted. I added that I could not pastor the Spanish-speaking church. The task should be given to a Spanish-speaking minister. They agreed again.

These stipulations on the table, the only remaining question was what to do with the current pastor and when. We decided to make the change in pastors right before the Feast of Tabernacles and reassign the current pastor. They had agreed to everything I wanted. I was happy because things apparently had fallen into place. Finally, Pasadena had a chance to become a normal congregation, free from the administrative monstrosities of the past. With the Lord's blessing, I knew I could change the cold, somewhat aloof, and increasingly jaded mind-set of the congregation. Yet at the same time there was a nagging doubt that my superiors would not stick to their commitments. The WCG administration had a steady and persistent record of being unreliable when it came to keeping commitments. The intention was always sincere and honorable, but it often faltered when it came time to deliver on the promises. Since the death of Herbert Armstrong, there had been numerous occasions in which announcements were made regarding intentions but nothing materialized, which contributed to the general lack of trust among the ministry and membership.

A few years before accepting the position as pastor of the Pasadena congregation, I had looked for an outlet to relieve my stress. An old childhood wish came to mind—karate. I determined that exercise of a different nature with a non-church crowd might do me good. After abortive attempts at some karate dojos, I walked down Green Street from the church administrative building to find a karate studio within two blocks of my front door. It was run by Larry Tatum, a man my own age. Larry looks like a tough customer, and he is. He has been teaching karate for nearly 30 years and has had ample opportunity to use it in his own defense. He invited me into his office. We spent a good while discussing the art and the possibility of training with him. I returned several times for additional conversations before deciding to give it a try.

Of significance in this story is the friendship that developed between Larry and me. He turned out to be a devout Christian of Presbyterian background. He loved to talk about the Lord and the Bible whenever we were together. Larry possessed a remarkable depth of spiritual understanding, as well as a deep reverence and humility toward the Lord and His Word. I often reflected on how strange it was for this tough-looking man to be so motivated by the love of Christ to encourage and help those who came to him. Over the years Larry has helped and strengthened many, including me. Many times he would remind me of my particular calling to minister and teach, telling me never to abandon it. In the most difficult days, I could count on Larry to lend a willing ear and give salient advice drawn from his three decades in the discipline of the martial arts. It is amazing where the Lord puts his servants to witness and serve. Larry gave me the surprise of my life on a hot July night in 1996 as a group of us tested for our black belts. After the test we lined up in a rigid karate attention stance while Larry walked down the line, pausing in front of each student to relay to the high-spirited audience some insight about the person. Stopping in front of me, Larry said, "And this is Tom Lapacka who is a minister. He is my pastor." You could have knocked me over with a feather! That complement announced unabashedly to the entire crowd made me realize that in our many talks together, I had contributed to his spiritual life.

Just before the Feast of Tabernacles in 1995, I assumed the pulpit in Pasadena, beginning a series of sermons aimed at building a spiritual foundation on the Gospel of grace. The grace of God through Jesus Christ was a message that the members had not heard with any degree of clarity, as I was told by many members after beginning the series. One problem had been that someone different spoke each week. There was no planning regarding the direction of the messages and each preacher chose his own topic. Generally the subjects addressed were the "safe ground" of "Christian living" sermons. By the time I began preaching, the announced changes in doctrinal direction were taking their toll on attendance, which fell from an average of 1,000 each week to a little under 700. But I stayed the course, determined to lift up Christ crucified and God's forgiveness through Him. Some members, no doubt, saw this as liberal theology because I was not stressing good works.

Many people in the Pasadena congregation helped me introduce new ministries that nourished with the Gospel, something that had been lacking in their spiritual diet. Mike Feazell's wife, Vicki, launched a successful children's ministry, making use of some under-utilized campus facilities to provide a permanent place for our little ones to learn about Christ each week. With the help of my associate pastor's wife, a women's ministry was launched. However, there was some initial startup misunderstandings with the associate pastor's wife. She took her concerns to Joe Tkach's wife, Tammy. Tammy related the story to Joe, and the next thing, I knew Joe called me at home to ask what was happening. I explained the matter to his satisfaction and added as tactfully as I could, "Joe, I find it amazing that the Pastor General of the WCG must involve himself in such a small local church matter." That was my reminder that Joe had agreed not to interfere in the administration of the local church. Joe quickly picked up on my message, and explained that he did not want to be involved, but had been dragged in to the situation.

Shortly after this incident, I was at a regional pastors' conference having lunch with ministers and their wives. Tammy, Joe's wife, asked me how I felt about women reading Scripture during services. I told her I had no problem with it, but first we needed to undergo a doctrinal study on the entire subject of the Christian woman's role in church leadership. After such a study, our theology would drive our practice, not the other way around. I said that Joe and others would have to decide matters of theology. Tammy said she understood, but expressed impatience for things to move along more rapidly.

I believed the matter of women reading Scripture during worship services was settled for the moment—at least my part in the discussion. Within a couple months, however, Joe brought the subject up, telling me that other congregations already were allowing women to read Scripture and lead worship. I told him the same thing I had told his wife. He said he had raised the subject because Tammy had mentioned it. Feeling mounting pressure on the subject, I asked Tammy to drop by my office to discuss the matter. Again I explained that I felt it was of paramount importance that the WCG first complete and publish a theological study that clarified the woman's role in the worship service. Again Tammy said she saw my point, yet she expressed frustration that nothing had been forthcoming. I thought the issue was resolved, but not long afterward, Joe made a lighthearted comment about the fact that I would not permit women to read Scripture during services. I caught Joe alone and repeated the sentiments I had expressed to Tammy. I assured him that I was not stonewalling, but I felt some theological statement should be issued first. Joe assured me that he knew I was not blocking him. I felt tremendous pressure during these discussions, yet I believed my view to be rational, reasonable, and in the best interest of the church at large.

Aside from this issue, Joe allowed me to do my job as the pastor, which I appreciated. My immediate boss, Mike, also initially did not interfere with the local administration of the congregation. He would make periodic suggestions, which I was glad to consider. Where possible, I implemented them when I felt the timing to be right. Many members had trouble accepting my dramatic changes to the worship service format. The old format was as familiar as an old shoe, and changing it meant another hurdle. Once the new format had been firmly established, I didn't want to make any significant changes for a while. This thinking grew from members' frequent pleas to reduce the frequency of change.

Mike hired Dan, a gifted man from a pastorate on the East Coast, to help him in Pasadena with church administration. Dan would free Mike so he could help Joe, especially in the area of writing and editing. Mike had done much of the writing that went out under Mr. Tkach Sr.'s name. In late spring 1996, I was walking in a hallway in the administration building talking with Randal, who was director of international church administration.

I had known Randal a long time, and we often discussed the European congregations when we had time to linger. On that particular day, I had asked about the state of affairs in the German-speaking area and specifically about the situation in Switzerland. Over the years, I had maintained loose contact with a few European members. News kept reaching us that the membership was unsettled and generally unhappy with their church pastors. They complained of lack of leadership and no direction, which was the same cry I had heard for years in the United States regarding our own church administration. I could see that Randal was in a bind regarding the German-speaking churches. He had few good options, so I casually mentioned that I would consider becoming involved—but I would not move overseas. I felt the problems needed to be and could be solved by the members themselves. Randal responded positively to my offer and suggested we discuss it at greater length in a couple days. I was excited about the possibility of helping my friends in Europe, yet I had a clear personal boundary about relocating or taking on any permanent responsibility.

Over the next couple days, Randal and I met in his office as friends, discussing the current dilemma in the German-speaking area of the WCG. Weak, ineffectual leadership, as well as poor doctrinal teaching, had set the churches on a directionless drift. After a while, we agreed that I would visit as soon as possible and work with the churches. First, I would assess the situation, then I would offer suggestions for a remedy. I was to call John, the regional director in London, to secure his blessing and coordinate my efforts.

I called John in London. He was delighted to hear that I was coming. Mike gave permission for me to be away for a couple weeks in August, which coincided with a meeting the German church leadership was planning in the Swiss Alps near Bern. Soon I was winging my way back to Germany. On the plane I had time to consider the significance of this newest venture. The German-speaking members knew and trusted me. I spoke their language, knew their culture, and had lived with them for years. They would give me a positive hearing and would, most likely, follow my suggestions—at least one time. I felt the visit had to be successful, otherwise the church may well drift into total disarray. My messages were prepared, but I was nervous because I did not know how things would end.

In the village of Juan in Canton Bern, Switzerland, the moment of truth arrived. I stepped in front of the assembled body of the leadership who had come to Switzerland for the five-day conference. I knew most of them, but there were some new faces from central and northern Germany. In my private dinner discussions before flying to Switzerland, it had become clear that most of what I had prepared to give them was not needed. I had heard so much talk of despair, division, and dissatisfaction that it became clear we needed to return to some basic Christianity. After asking the Lord to give me the necessary skills to speak clearly and with inspiration, I started my presentation. Out came the German. While first there, I had some difficulty with the language, but as the days passed, I became more fluent so by the end of the first day, members were saying I spoke as though I had never left the country. For that I praise God, who has helped me like this many times during my ministerial career.

I spoke on the subject of prayer, then broke the group into small circles to pray. Over the course of the next four or five days, we did this often. I asked them to pray for one another and for their pastors. The chill in the air gave way to warm embraces, and joy radiated from their faces. We spoke of values and planning, and I secured from them a commitment to work together for a stable church. The European director from London, John, joined us on the last day and remarked, "Something has happened here. I see it in their faces. I've not seen such a look of joy in a long time." That was the work of the Holy Spirit, moving us to repentance and unity. By the end of the conference, everyone was committed to start afresh and work together. I wrote a full report with suggested practical steps for John to follow when giving direction to the German-speaking churches.

After finishing in Switzerland, I flew to London to meet John at Heathrow for dinner. We spent about three hours going over each step of the plan. He was delighted and thanked me profusely for coming to the church's aid at a time of great need. I felt honored and privileged to help.

While in Germany, I received word that Mike had changed the speaking schedule and made format changes in the worship service at the Pasadena church. This troubled me because it was contrary to our agreement. Back home, I went to his office and told him I disagreed with his actions and stated that, in my opinion, he had overstepped his reach. This was a bold move on my part, but I felt principle demanded it. I gambled that Mike would see my point, apologize, and withdraw. Mike calmly listened to my comments and after further clarification, said he saw my point of view.

When I had taken the job as pastor of the Pasadena congregation, it was with the understanding that my tenure would last until the campus was sold. After that I would relocate with the headquarters' church and continue pastoring at the new location. However, before my trip to Germany, Mike had indicated that he wanted to move the date for installing a new pastor forward. This did not trouble me. I believed that once the new course was set, another man could keep things going, allowing me to devote my energies to church relations, especially internal relations, which I believed was a weak area that needed immediate attention.

Shortly after that meeting with Mike, he mentioned making the pastoral change in January. "The campus may not sell until next spring, and that's a long time," he said. By then I had come to the conclusion that I was blocking Mike's desires for more change in the Pasadena congregation. He wanted a greater hand in determining music and speakers. It was apparent that he wanted to be involved with the direction of the Pasadena church, which I did not agree with for two reasons. First, administrative moves were to be my responsibility. We had agreed on this from the beginning. Second, I disagreed with some of his concepts.

I knew it was useless to oppose Mike because no one else would support me and Mike generally got his way. Joe left such things up to Mike and remained distant. Besides, I recalled that Joe had agreed to my appointment as pastor in Pasadena, but he would have been just as pleased with someone else. Rather than fight for the pulpit, I decided to step aside because that seemed to be the leadership's desire. I offered Mike the option to move the pulpit change date to November 1, 1996. He agreed immediately, which confirmed my suspicions that he wanted me out.

Meanwhile, I busied myself writing a 1997 strategic plan for church relations, envisioning a significant role in improving internal relations. Everyone in the administration agreed that this area was in a sad state. When I reviewed the first draft with Mike, he told me that he and Dan, his new assistant, would take care of internal relations and I should focus on external relations. I believed this was a mistake because Mike's gifts and strengths seemed to lie in areas other than public relations. Nevertheless, the boss had spoken, so I rewrote the plan, confining my attention to external matters. I even consulted a friend, a professor at the University of Southern California's school of business, while putting together a professional presentation.

Once done, I experienced difficulty getting Joe and Mike together for a presentation. Our schedules never seemed to coincide for such a meeting. An uneasy feeling washed over me that they were avoiding me. I tried to shake it off, but the more I thought about it, the more I suspected that the wind had shifted and I was on my way out. My time in Pasadena was coming to an end, and I knew it.

The church's income reports from the treasurer's office produced only a steady stream of bad news. Layoffs were a routine part of life, and I knew I would have to lay-off some of my staff. Thankfully, the press did not follow up on earlier stories of the financial malaise of the church. I did not want to talk to the *LA Times* or *Pasadena Star News*. The truth about our situation did not make for a great story about the church. Besides, the secular press usually tends to be cynical about religion. We were concerned that if the press discovered how bad things really were, they would take the opportunity to lace an article about the WCG with enough barbs to cast a shadow over our future. Bad news tends to feed on itself, creating more bad news, so I was relieved that the press finally was leaving us alone.

Talk about terminating full-time ministers in the field to meet the demands of an ever-shrinking budget became commonplace around the executive offices. The mood was gloomy. I often prayed that God would lead us, directing our steps in doing His will. My hopes of a long and distinguished career with the WCG were beginning to fade. There was the dream of finishing a master's degree in pastoral studies and maybe even going to Ambassador University to teach. That goal seemed fairly remote. It was looking more like I would either be let go or reassigned to the field ministry.

Normally I would have considered a church assignment, but I was becoming more certain of my personal direction. Several things were of great concern. First, there was the perilous financial condition of the WCG. Second, there was what I considered a not-so-subtle shift in our worship tradition. We were steadily leaning toward a charismatic approach to worship. Joe, Mike, and Dan had spent a lot time promoting and defending the raising of hands in worship. Not that this is wrong, but the emphasis seemed to be that raising our hands would make us more expressive in worship. Numerous members said they felt pressured to "get with the program" of raising hands in worship, but they did not feel comfortable. Joe's wife, Tammy, had asked my opinion about this matter one day. I responded that I saw nothing wrong with raising hands in worship, if one felt so moved. Our leadership, however, did not seem to be leaving this up to choice but were urging members to do so in worship. I said I felt more like kneeling in the presence of God than waving my hands. WCG leadership had become friendly with the charismatic Four Square Gospel leadership in Los Angeles, no doubt this contact had some influence.

The WCG worship services traditionally had been non-emotional and more cognitive because they were lecture intensive. In my last years in Pasadena, many people wanted a change in the worship style to make it more conducive to worship. That was why I became pastor of the headquarter's church and what I successfully accomplished. However, some in the WCG leadership wanted to push beyond the blended service format that was developed and add even more expressiveness. I was concerned the leadership was moving faster than the membership might be willing or able to handle. Additionally, the WCG tradition was to be extremists, moving from the right ditch to the left. I was concerned that moving too far too fast from a "Word"-centered worship style to a "spirit"-centered worship style might cause another backlash that the WCG could ill afford. It was clear that my foot-dragging in the area of more charismatic worship had limited my usefulness in Pasadena. I feared that a transfer to a full-time field position would set me up for future termination. It seemed my options were becoming fewer.

I had maintained contact with Bobby, my business friend in Texas. I spoke with him about the possibility of returning to Lubbock to work with him. We discussed terms and timetables on several occasions. Although we could not come to an agreement, we continued our talks. One morning I walked into the office and noticed a staff member in a sad mood. This person relayed the concern she had heard expressed by a top executive about the church's declining financial situation. I tried to cheer her up, then went to my office and sat in front of my computer. Suddenly, I experienced an urgent feeling I had never felt before that seemed to tell me it was time to go—now. I called Bobby. We talked, came to a broad agreement, and I said I would get back to him within a week. Then I visited another friend who was close to the daily pulse of the church. I told him I was considering leaving the full-time ministry of the church and considering requesting status as a bi-vocational pastor, which meant I would have two jobs—one a secular endeavor, the other pastoral. This arrangement had been rare in the WCG. He agreed I should present my proposal quickly because it would surely be approved. A couple of years earlier during a similar conversation, he had encouraged me to stay and help the church. Now, he said it was a good time to go. I had learned to respect this man's candor and his integrity. What we talked about privately had always remained confidential, which was a rare thing in Pasadena. I thanked him for his advice and left to pray about the matter and work on details.

Within a couple days, I had worked out the particulars and again discussed them with my friend. He felt my plan sounded reasonable. I made an appointment to present my proposal to Mike. He was joined by his assistant, Dan. Without mincing words, I said, "Mike, I have been thinking that in light of the difficult financial situation the church finds itself in that I should go bi-vocational."

This was not exactly the direction the WCG administration was encouraging its full-time pastors to pursue, but Mike was receptive. "This comes as a relief because we were not looking forward to meeting with you. The job in church relations would no longer need a full-time man. We thought of offering you a position as a regional pastor," Mike said.

Under normal conditions such an offer would have been attractive. With the church in a financial tailspin and in light of my lack of confidence in WCG leadership to turn things around, however, I thanked Mike and said that I would rather pursue a bi-vocational path. I suggested a gradual reduction of salary over the course of one year, which would allow me time to build my income from secular work. He was happy and did not seek to deter me. I agreed to give him my final decision within one week. I called Texas again and concluded my negotiations with Bobby. We agreed I would move to Texas in November.

In September 1996, I returned to Mike's office and told him I had chosen to move to Texas to become a bi-vocational WCG pastor. We determined I would relinquish the Pasadena pastorate to Curtis on the first weekend in November. At the time, Curtis was the pastor of the Los Angeles WCG congregation and a regional pastor. Mike used the word *termination* several times in our conversation, which alarmed me. I reminded him that we had discussed a bi-vocational arrangement and that I did not want to terminate my employment with WCG. He agreed, but the word *termination* came up again as I talked to one of his assistants in church administration who was assigned to arrange the details of my transfer to Lubbock, Texas. I reminded the man that I was not terminating; rather, I was becoming a bi-vocational pastor. After my years in Pasadena, I had become sensitive to word choice. The use of *termination* sent the message to me that it was only a matter of time before I would indeed be terminated. I didn't want to be terminated at that time. Such an action would imply my work had been unsatisfactory, which by my superiors' testimony had not been the case. In fact, they praised my work.

The Feast of Tabernacles was almost upon us, and Linda and I were scheduled to visit Italy and Germany to speak to the German members. The entire trip was to last a month, giving us time to visit several congregations and spend time with the ministers. I had given a written proposal to Mike regarding my change of employment status and was informed that it had to be submitted to the church board for approval because the bi-vocational arrangement represented a policy innovation. That was fine because I knew all the men on the board and felt confident they would vote in favor of Mike's recommendation. On the day of our departure for Germany, the board approved my bi-vocational status and followed it with a written agreement that spelled out the terms of my employment status with the WCG for one year, at which time the matter would be discussed anew. While away in Europe, Mike again involved himself directly in some of the affairs of the Pasadena congregation. The time had definitely arrived for me to disengage myself from further leadership of the congregation.

Upon our return from Europe, Linda and I flew to Lubbock, Texas, and bought a house. On November 11, we officially left Pasadena, driving a Ryder truck with our car in tow. I had chosen not to speak anymore in the Pasadena congregation. I was so stressed and upset that support for my ministry had been withdrawn that I feared I would betray my frustration and unnecessarily upset or offend the members, who, of course, were innocent bystanders. As far as they were concerned, everything was progressing in an orderly fashion and everybody was happy. One long-time employee did state at a going-away party that "We appreciate what you have done for us and are sorry that you are leaving. They think we don't know what is going on around here, but we know what has happened to you." I was a taken aback by his forthrightness, but I remained calm and neutral as I thanked him for his support and changed the topic.

By the end of December, Linda and I had started a new life in Texas. Gone were the tremendous pressures we endured in Pasadena. We felt better physically and welcomed the opportunity to pause and consider what kind of future we would like to have. What direction to take was a question I pondered daily. I had not satisfactorily answered the meaning of my experiences in Pasadena. Maybe in years to come the Lord would show me the purpose of those 10 years of my life. I have arrived at some answers, though. At a very early age, I dedicated myself to the Lord and committed my life to serving Him. Unfortunately, my own insecurities, as well as a lack of sound spiritual guidance, caused me to be predisposed to embrace the heretical message of Herbert W. Armstrong. This led me into the shadows of spiritual ignorance, yoking me for decades to a rigorous system of legalism with its salvation by works doctrine. I praise God the Holy Spirit, who opened my eyes to the errors I had believed and lived. I am also indebted to those in the WCG leadership who forsook the shadows and now walk in the true light of the Gospel of grace. There is no turning back for me or for the Worldwide Church of God—we both have stepped into the full light of the Gospel, leaving the shadows behind forever.

Was the WCG experiencing a necessary part of God's plan so I might come to the light? Some in the WCG believe God put us through this experience so we would be ready to receive the truth. I strongly disagree with such sentiment because that implies our Lord led us into error so He could reveal the truth to us. The Spirit leads into truth, not error. No, we must come to grips with reality. We were deceived, in many cases willingly, because we desired to be special through the esoteric "truths" that Herbert Armstrong preached. The Worldwide Church of God was a cult—of that there is no doubt. Whether theologically or psychologically, the WCG fit the classic definition of a cult. It is painful and embarrassing to admit, but it is a fact. The present reality is that the WCG is no longer a cult. The WCG has publicly and privately repented of its error and now embraces evangelical Christianity.

I continue in my search of the Scriptures for a clearer understanding of God's will. My studies continue as I read widely the theological works of other authors. I am a deeply committed Christian who desires to know and do the will of our Lord. There is nothing more important to me. The question arises regarding my return to the full-time ministry. Most likely I will in the future, but now I need time to think, pray, and study, seeking the Lord's will in my life.

I am thankful to Pastor General Joe Tkach Jr., Mike Feazell, and the church board for the generous transition arrangement that they approved, which provided Linda and me the opportunity to catch our breaths before making big decisions about our future.

So, *quo vadis*, Worldwide Church of God? Will it collapse or continue to exist? That is a question I cannot answer. There is no question that it could disappear. I believe the WCG is at a crossroads. Its future will be secured or imperiled based on the decisions of its leaders in Pasadena. It is hard to say with absolute certainty the contours that the WCG ultimately will take. Its leadership has a history of changing direction quickly, so the administrative direction of today could be quite different tomorrow. I can say with confidence that those in top leadership positions are godly men with a love for Christ and a sincere desire to do the right thing. They are committed to following God's will as they understand it and leading the membership to a closer walk with Christ. They are also good stewards.

Despite serious challenges that still face the WCG administration, I am encouraged by what I know to be their deep personal commitment to walk with Christ. I pray that the leadership will continue to pursue the mind of our Lord as they search the Scriptures and remain open to dialogue with Christians across a broad spectrum of doctrinal understandings, especially those with traditional orthodox roots. Ultimately the future of the Worldwide Church of God is in the hands of our Lord. He will determine if the church is to survive and what role it will play in bringing future glory to His name. The WCG already has brought glory to the name of Christ because it has yielded to His call to repent and to walk out of the shadows and into His light. The WCG is living proof of the power of Christ through the Holy Spirit to convert an entire heretical organization. To Him be glory now and forever.

As for me I, too, have left behind forever the shadows of deception and rejoice in my daily walk in the glory and light of Calvary's cross. As St. Paul wrote in Romans 1:16: "I am not ashamed of the gospel, because it is the power of God for the salvation of everyone who believes." That same Gospel I heard as a small boy in the Venerable Street Baptist Church had again confronted me and converted me to a follower of Christ. Walking with Jesus as the center of my daily life and realizing how much He has done for me, I consider those who still struggle in the shadows of error, often compounded by a burdensome legalism. The shadows not only cloud one's vision theologically, but impact one psychologically. I have met many former WCG members who struggle with what has happened to them. I also know some in the WCG today have not come to grips fully with their past. Instead, they try to escape the pain of personal confrontation through denial or self-delusion.

It is imperative that as Christians, standing in the grace of God through Christ, we become whole spiritually and psychologically. I am convinced only Christ can give that wholeness. He heals us through the reassuring words of forgiveness heard in the Gospel. I offer the following thoughts to those past or present members of the Worldwide Church of God, as well as all Christians who have suffered under the yoke of legalism posing as Christianity.

CONFESSION

Healing began for Linda and me when we confessed to God and each other that we had "swallowed the bait." We had been duped into believing a false gospel, which really was no Gospel at all. There is no "good news" in a system of legalism that binds, controls, depersonalizes, and condemns. When we confessed, we acknowledged our responsibility—our personal accountability—for forsaking the truth to embrace a lie. Did Herbert Armstrong carry blame? Absolutely! But no one held a gun to our heads. We jumped on the cult bandwagon with zeal and conviction, ignoring the warning signs that occasionally flashed before us. It is almost like making that difficult introduction at an AA meeting: "Hi, our names are Tom and Linda. We were cult members. We embraced heresy. We denied the historic Christian faith." That is painful! That is awful. But that was the truth. In confession, there is absolution through the Word of Christ. In Him all sins are forgiven, including ours. That gives us great comfort, joy, and assurance for the future. There are those in the WCG today, as well as the scores of thousands who have left the WCG, who cannot bring themselves to make that confession. But confession brings healing.

I Need to Be Helped

So many former WCG members have given up on the church. The experience under Armstrong was so deeply wounding and personally devastating that they lost hope that the Christian church can help. Linda and I had to deal with such depressing thoughts. In particular, Linda was on the verge of forswearing any further connection with the church. Yet I knew the truth was out there. Jesus is the truth, the life, and the way. He promised to lead His apostles on whom the Church rests into the truth. That truth was delivered once and for all in the first century. Although men have misread it, obscured it, and even denied it, the truth has survived to be with us today.

I needed help to have the truth of God's love for us in Christ explained—in detail. It was to the orthodox Christian church that I turned, that church whose doctrines have stood the test of time and the repeated assaults of heretics. It was humbling to start over after admitting that I really didn't know. But Linda and I found help to be instructed in the historic Christian faith.

Beyond instruction in the Scriptures, some may need professional help to deal with deep-seated latent anger. I was angry too. Angry at Armstrong, Tkach, the WCG, and myself. With the Lord's help, Linda and I worked through our anger. We voiced it, vented, then moved on. For us to continue in anger served no purpose. The past is behind us, and there is nothing that can bring back those lost years or undo the mistakes we made. We confessed, repented, and now forgiven, we move on.

PERSONAL IDENTITY

I have talked to a few former WCG people who mirrored Linda's and my feelings. In Armstrong's WCG, we lost our personal identity. Who were we? We were servants of God called to hold up Herbert Armstrong's arms as he did "the Work." Like little cogs in a great machine, we turned and worked, giving and sacrificing all for the cause. In the process we lost ourselves. Because she grew up in the WCG, Linda particularly has struggled with coming to know who she is, what she believes, and what she wants. In the past answers to such questions were given to her to accept unconditionally. Now we answer them ourselves. For some it is a confusing and painful experience because for the first time ever—or for the first time after years of being controlled by others—they begin to think for themselves.

The ultimate answer to our identity lies in Christ. St. Paul uses the term "in Christ" when he refers to the spiritual and mystical union of the believer with Christ, which occurs through Baptism (Romans 6). It is in Christ that Linda and I now see ourselves. We are His. He loves us individually and personally. He died for me personally. He lives for me personally. Through Baptism, I am united with Christ, and by the regenerating power of God the Holy Spirit working in me, I live in Christ and He lives in me. My identity is no longer tied to an organization, a group of people, or anything. I am found, forgiven, and identified in Christ.

I Need the Church

The church is, according the Apostle's Creed, "the communion of saints." It is the invisible body of Christ composed of all those past and present who believe and trust in Jesus Christ as Redeemer and Lord. This "communion of saints" gathers for worship to hear the Word of God, the message of salvation given to us in the Gospel. We gather to receive through the Gospel both in Word and in its visible exposition—the sacraments of Baptism and the Lord's Supper—the promised grace of forgiveness. The message of Scripture is clear. Believers in Christ are not Lone Rangers, each living apart from other believers, but a communion of saints that meets together to be fed and strengthened by God's Word. For me and Linda, it became clear that we had to find a Christian church body where we could fellowship, where we could serve, and that could teach us. I encourage and plead with those who have left the WCG, any other such fellowship, or the Christian church to begin worshiping with God's people again in a legitimate Christian church.

Which church should you attend? Each must make his or her own choice. My guiding principle was to find a church that is Christ-centered and grace-centered. No more esoteric novelties. No more rules for Christian living. No more elitism. I looked for message—first and last. Size of parking lot, youth programs, worship format, even friendliness of the people played no primary role in selecting a church. The big question was, "What do you believe and teach?" The message had to be that we are saved by grace alone, through faith alone, in Christ alone, which I have since discovered was the same call of the great Reformers of the 16th century. The church we were to join had to understand the importance of the sacraments as the means of grace the Lord uses to forgive, regenerate, and sustain us in faith.

Doctrine is extremely important because doctrine expounds the truth of Scripture and forms our thinking. Thus, it shapes our spiritual walk. Erroneous doctrine is like poison to the system. You get some and you can still live and function, but not at optimal levels. To those who claim doctrine is unimportant, I say doctrine is critical to understanding who God is, what He has done for us, and how we may now live. Truth as expounded in clear doctrine enlightens, refreshes, and rejoices in granting assurance and comfort for each day of our lives.

Charles Spurgeon, the great British preacher of the 19th century, once said, "The keys of providence swing at the girdle of Christ. Believe it, Christian, nothing occurs here without the permit or the decree of your Savior." Has my life experience in the Worldwide Church of God been in vain? Although the 30 years in that organization represent the most personally trying and difficult time of my life, I believe the Lord never left that little boy who trusted in Him as he learned from his granddad and the Christians at Venerable Street Baptist in Richmond, Virginia. The grace of God in Christ was on me all those years, and in the process of time, Jesus again knocked at the door of my heart and the words of Malachi have been fulfilled in my life and Linda's:

But for you who revere My name, the sun of righteousness
will rise with healing in its wings. (Malachi 4:2)

May the peace of our Lord keep us in His light now and forever.

Epilogue

A Christian will find it cheaper to pardon than to resent. Forgiveness saves the expense of anger, the cost of hatred, the waste of spirits.—Hannah More

Several years have passed since I penned the final words of *Out of the Shadows*. My life has changed for the better, but there are deep scars of the soul that probably will be erased only when the Lord raises me to eternal life with Him. Meanwhile, I have forgiven those whom I have needed to forgive, as difficult as that has been. The alternative is unthinkable. I know friends who have not forgiven those who have caused suffering, and as a result, they suffer anguish of soul, bitterness, resentment, and even hatred. What a waste, and it only forestalls the healing that Christ offers to those who will forgive even as they have received His forgiveness.

What has transpired in my life? The central question for me during those tumultuous years in the early- and mid-1990s was, Who will teach me? Who knows the real truth as believed and taught by the early church? Where can I hear the Gospel of forgiveness in Christ, which assures me of God's saving work through His Son? Who will remind me repeatedly of the centrality of grace—God's unmerited favor to us through the work of His Son? After years under the bondage of the Law with both feet planted firmly on Mt. Sinai, I never wanted to return to such slavery. Now that Christ had led me out of the shadows into the light of His truth, which had been preserved in the orthodox faith for 2,000 years, I shudder at the prospect of being lured back.

My search for a new church began in the early 1990s. While living in Lancaster, California, about 60 miles north of Pasadena, I began cautiously to explore other churches, looking for a new home, a place to rest in Christ and to be taught. My first excursion was to a Seventh-Day Adventist church, the denomination out of which the Worldwide Church of God had sprung. One service, though pleasant enough, convinced me that it was not the place for me. Why? The Sabbath issue. The Adventists still place high value on keeping the weekly Saturday Sabbath as part of Christ's expectation of a committed Christian. This was exactly the position I had determined to leave. Then the Baptist church tugged at my heart. In times of stress and uncertainty, it is not uncommon to return to the familiar. Yet one visit to a local Baptist church helped me to see that my spiritual pilgrimage was taking me in another direction.

What was I searching for? I determined the church I eventually would join would have clear theology that had stood the test of time. It would have to espouse a theology that is Christ-centered and rooted in the teachings of the early church as encapsulated in the great ecumenical creeds. With that as the criteria, the choices began to narrow to Lutheran, Catholic, or Presbyterian. And it was the Lutherans who had helped me the most to examine my own theological positions. No one had tried to "convert" me to Lutheranism; instead, new friends such as Rev. George Mather and Dr. Charles Manske were patient and kind in challenging my views while encouraging me to look deeply into Scripture and the historical position of the church on major issues such as the nature of God and Christ, salvation, the means of grace, etc. It wasn't long before I found myself drawn to the historical Lutheran view on these questions.

Meanwhile, Linda suffered the pain of disillusionment to the point of despair. The hurts, sacrifices, and personal losses had taken a huge toll on her spiritual life. She was not looking for another church. In fact, by the time we moved to Lubbock, Texas, in the fall of 1996, Linda desperately needed time to heal. I was the part-time pastor of the small WCG church in Lubbock, and Linda dutifully attended church each week to support me, but her heart was no longer in it. Our oldest son, Rhett, was in the Coast Guard and stationed in Galveston. He displayed no interest in church. I had told him several years earlier of the many errors taught by the WCG, which had been hammered into his head. It was difficult to process that these "truths" were, in fact, error. Although he said nothing, I know Rhett must have struggled with the thought that his parents had put him through the paces of a legalistic religion for nothing. I have apologized to both of my sons for the error, and I believe all is forgiven between us. For Dustin, our youngest son, our admission of errors in the WCG was not as traumatic. He had spent his last three years of high school in a small Baptist school, so his regular daily instruction included the truth about Christ and His work on our behalf. By the time we returned to Texas, Dustin was a freshman at West Texas A & M in Canyon, Texas.

The personal questions I wrestled with after our move to Lubbock were: Would I join the Lutheran church? Would I continue in a business career as the newly appointed sales manager for Bobby's Marquis Supply Co. or return to full-time ministry? For a while I did not know where the road would take me. Bobby and the business had changed—as had I. We were both older (it had been 16 years since our previous work relationship). To return to the same job after so many years and so many experiences was both comforting and depressing. It was comforting because I knew several employees from my previous tenure with the company, and I was familiar with the environment. It was depressing because I thought I had come full circle and had reached "the end of the line." Business was good, Bobby was still a great boss, and other wonderful people at Marquis welcomed me and made my stay successful. Although sales figures were turning upward, I could not shake the conviction that the Lord had something else in store for me. I wasn't sure what it was, but within a couple months, I knew things would change in my life.

Near the end of December 1996, I was speaking with Rev. Mather on the telephone and I told him that I had decided to join the Lutheran church. He arranged for me to do so. Now that I had taken this step, what would Linda say? I walked into the living room to announce my decision to my dear wife. After nearly 30 years together, she still surprises me. I expected her to say, "That's great, but I'm not interested." Instead, Linda said she would study for herself to see what Lutheranism was all about! And she did. Thanks to a helpful Lutheran pastor in Lubbock, Linda was given clear and concise study helps that acquainted her with the Lutheran faith. Within a short time she, too, had joined The Lutheran Church—Missouri Synod.

After joining the LCMS, I still had to deal with my work with the local WCG congregation. My solution was to keep my teaching within the confines of the WCG theology while using every opportunity to deepen members' understanding of the Christian faith. I never encouraged a soul to leave the WCG for another Christian church; instead, I sought to strengthen their faith and leave it to the Lord to lead them where He willed.

Shortly after becoming a member of the LCMS, I decided to devote my working life to serving the Lord in His church. Could I have stayed with Bobby and been pleasing to the Lord? Absolutely. Yet there was this tug at my heart that pulled me back into ministry. I decided to become a Lutheran pastor, which I found was not the easiest goal to accomplish. The Lutheran Church—Missouri Synod has high academic and professional standards for its pastors. Virtually all are seminary graduates with a master of divinity degree. I felt unqualified and ill-equipped for the challenge, but I was prepared to do what it would take to reach the goal. I desired to preach to others the same liberating Gospel in all its fullness so they, too, could find the peace I had been given.

Not knowing where to begin, I called Rev. Mather to ask him what to do. He referred me to his district president, who was helpful in starting the process. I filled out forms, sought letters of recommendation, and wrote personal testimonies. I contacted the LCMS seminary in Ft. Wayne, Indiana, and Professor Lockwood proved helpful in navigating the process. I was enrolled in DELTO (Distance Education Leading to Ordination), a correspondence program under the supervision of a local LCMS pastor. Every two weeks, this pastor reviewed with me the material I had studied. The studies took months and were arduous if for no other reason than because I was often dead tired after work, yet had to absorb vast amounts of historical information and deep theology.

By spring 1997, talk of a vicarage had begun (a vicarage is like an internship during which parish pastors mentor seminarians and shape them for a life of service to Christ and His Church). One Sunday evening, I called Rev. Mather for a chat and learned that Dr. Chuck Manske was visiting with him. Rev. Mather asked if I would like to speak to Dr. Manske, and I readily agreed. Chuck asked how I was doing and what I was doing. I brought him up to speed on the changes in my life. I also said I would like to do my vicarage in Southern California so I could pursue a master's degree in Reformation theology, which was offered at Concordia University in Irvine, California.

Chuck volunteered to do what he could to help the process and was as good as his word. Not long after our conversation, I received word from Rev. Loren Kramer, the president of the Pacific Southwest District of the LCMS. He offered the possibility of completing my vicarage requirement in a mission church in Castaic, California, about 40 miles north of Los Angeles. I expressed my interest, but I knew there would be a hurdle in convincing Linda that a return to Southern California would be in our best interests. Needless to say, Linda was somewhat exasperated when she heard that not only did I want to return to full-time ministry, but I wanted to return to the area we had just left. Again Linda proved herself a woman of faith and an incredible support as we launched into another bold, new venture in response to what I felt to be God's clear call on my life.

Now I faced another unpleasant task—telling Bobby that I was repeating my actions of 17 years ago and leaving him to return to church work. This was particularly difficult because Bobby had been extremely supportive, business was good, and he had recently given me a raise. After a particularly successful sales call one evening, Bobby and I stopped at his home in southwest Lubbock to pick up my car. I asked to come inside for a moment to discuss a matter, so we sat in the kitchen. "Bobby, I have enjoyed working for you and appreciate you for giving me the job," I began. "However, I feel the Lord is leading me back into ministry, and I must leave you."

A cool customer, Bobby looked at me and asked, "Is there something I did? I really don't want you to go."

"No, Bobby, " I replied. "It's nothing to do with you. Sales is just not where my heart is. I need to follow what I believe my call is."

"Okay, Tom. I respect that," Bobby replied, and that was it. Two weeks later, I stepped away from sales and moved to serve as vicar at Prince of Peace, the small Lutheran mission congregation in Castaic, California.

For the most part, I was "on my own." The Lutheran pastor at a neighboring congregation was my supervisor, but he quickly surmised I needed little direct supervision and simply maintained regular contact with me. I found the other LCMS pastors in my immediate area to be warm, welcoming, and supportive. The congregation of some 30 souls also gave me incredible support. Often I mused that it had only been a short time since I had pastored a congregation of 1,700 members. But it didn't bother me. What was important was preaching and teaching the Gospel of grace— whether it was to one person or to hundreds.

The church's location meant I could visit again with Pastor George Mather, who sheperded a Lutheran congregation in nearby Sherman Oaks, California. In the course of our many conversations, George raised the question of my baptism. Was it indeed valid? I had been baptized by immersion with the use of the trinitarian formula, but the WCG denied the Trinity at the same time. This was a perplexing and deeply personal question. George and I drove to Concordia University at Irvine to confer with a theology professor. Together we concluded that by virtue of my childhood confession of faith in Christ as my Savior, there was no question regarding my salvation. However, my baptism was most likely invalid. There was no pressure from anyone to consider rebaptism, but it became the obvious conclusion in my mind. First, however, I had to work through the obvious shock to my peace of mind as I contemplated that the step I had taken years earlier had been a misstep. I concluded there were several reasons why I needed to be baptized:

1. I desired to be in complete compliance with the instructions of my Lord.

2. I wanted to be baptized by a legitimate church that not only used the trinitarian formula in Baptism, but also faithfully taught the orthodox doctrine of the Trinity.

3. As a future Lutheran pastor, I did not want to give any member reason to doubt my pastoral office by questioning the legitimacy of my baptism.

4. Finally, I felt a personal need to publicly make the final and complete break with Armstrongism.

I shared my thoughts with Linda not in an effort to convince her to follow suit, but to state my personal position. To my surprise, Linda said, "If you get rebaptized, so will I." So I called George and requested a private baptismal ceremony in the sanctuary of Sherman Oaks Lutheran Church. He agreed, and on the appointed day Linda and I stood before Pastor George at the church's altar with Sharon, his wife, as witness. Together, Linda and I received the gift of God's forgiveness through the Word of promise and the waters of Baptism.

The feeling that afternoon standing before the altar of Christ was tremendous. Finally the long journey was over. We had left the shadows behind, fully embracing the light of Christ's promises of grace and forgiveness given in His Word and conveyed by His church. Where there had been only uncertainty, now there was complete assurance. Where there had been fear of never quite measuring up, now there was confidence that Christ had measured up for me.

I started my vicarage in November 1997. In January 1998 I was required to appear before a panel of theologians and pastors at Concordia University Irvine to undergo an oral examination of my theology. This was the last great hill to climb before I could be ordained as an LCMS pastor. As far as I knew, it was a pass or fail examination. What should I study? I wasn't certain, but Pastor Mather encouraged me to have a good grasp on Luther's *Small Catechism*, which gives a succinct overview of the Christian faith. I studied long and hard, and George quizzed me in preparation for the examination. On the big day, George, who had been asked to sit on the panel, drove to Irvine with me. Dr. Manske was another familiar face among the examiners. I had been told to expect about 45 minutes of questioning.

The panel was chaired by Dr. Eugene Bunkowske, a kindly theologian, who had arrived from Concordia Theological Seminary in Ft. Wayne, Indiana (one of two seminaries in the LCMS). He called the meeting to order, a prayer was offered, and the questioning began. The 45 minutes stretched into an hour and a half as I was peppered with questions from all sides of the room. As suddenly as it began, it was over. Dr. Bunkowske asked me to leave the room so the panel could deliberate. As I stepped into the foyer, my heart sank and my lips moved in prayer, "Dear Lord, I gave it my best shot. I don't know what else I could do. The rest is in Your hands." I thought I had failed miserably, and I awaited the executioner's sentence.

Within 15 minutes, I was called back into the room by Dr. Bunkowske. He warmly greeted me with, "You did well. Welcome to the ministry of The Lutheran Church—Missouri Synod." What a relief! My self-imposed storm clouds dissipated in an instant as I realized the Lord had seen me through the examination and indeed had prepared me for this new ministry.

The nine months as vicar flew by, which meant the congregation could now call me as its pastor, which it did. But this call raised yet another question. Should I be reordained, or was the ordination of the WCG sufficient? I discussed the question with Rev. Kramer, at the time president of the LCMS district in which I served. We reached the mutual agreement that being reordained would place my ministry above reproach. In November 1998, I knelt before the altar in Bethlehem Lutheran Church in Santa Clarita, California, as Rev. Mather, along with several other LCMS pastors, conducted the rite of ordination and installation. Even a few dear friends from the WCG came to witness this momentous event in my life.

The mission congregation of Prince of Peace grew slowly but surely. It increased not by leaps and bounds, but steadily as new people arrived—some new members were Lutherans who had moved into the area; others were individuals from Catholic or other Protestant backgrounds. Castaic is situated in a rapidly growing area that attracted young families with children. Within three short years, the 33 members had swollen to more than 140 with an average church attendance of 73, up markedly from only 25 at the start of my work at Prince of Peace. Granted, these were not large numbers, but it was encouraging to see the faith of so many people being strengthened by the Word of God in Christ.

What I thought would be a lifetime calling as a pastor was suddenly interrupted by a call from the national church body to work in St. Louis, Missouri, as the executive director of Communications and Public Affairs. It was not an easy deliberation. Prince of Peace was growing and had an exciting future, but I knew the church's headquarters had a real need for someone with my experience and gifts. After much prayer and consultation with friends, I decided the Lord had yet another challenge ahead for me.

What a marvelous and curious way God works in our lives! I found myself once again in an executive position at a denominational headquarters. What is the Lord doing in my life? I can only muse. Yet my heart's desire is the same as that of the little boy in Virginia: I desire to serve my Lord in His church in whatever way He will use me. May my life and walk with Jesus of Nazareth bring hope and encouragement to others who heed the Master's call.

To Him be all the glory. Amen.